RISK AND BUSINESS CYCLES

How does monetary policy affect the real economy?

Risk and Business Cycles develops an integrated framework for assessing the roles of both monetary and real shocks in the business cycle. The author uses modern treatments of risk, finance and expectations to develop an innovative and challenging critique of the Austrian school of economics. Drawing upon contemporary methods of empirical and econometric research, the work examines how changes in risk, real interest rates and finance constraints alter the likelihood of intertemporal plan coordination. The author presents a synthesis of the older 'Austrian' perspective on business cycles with contemporary theories of financial risk and real business cycles to construct a unified framework. A case is put forward for the revival of an important role for monetary causes in business cycle theory, which challenges the current trend towards favoring purely real theories.

Presenting a challenging critique of the Austrian school, this volume will be of interest to all those interested in business cycles, as well as Austrian economics.

Tyler Cowen is Professor of Economics at George Mason University.

FOUNDATIONS OF THE MARKET ECONOMY
Edited by Mario J. Rizzo, *New York University* and
Lawrence H. White, *University of Georgia*

A central theme of this series is the importance of understanding and assessing the market economy from a perspective broader than the static economics of perfect competition and Pareto optimality. Such a perspective sees markets as causal processes generated by the preferences, expectations and beliefs of economic agents. The creative acts of entrepreneurship that uncover new information about preferences, prices and technology are central to these processes with respect to their ability to promote the discovery and use of knowledge in society.

The market economy consists of a set of institutions that facilitate voluntary cooperation and exchange among individuals. These institutions include the legal and ethical framework as well as more narrowly 'economic' patterns of social interaction. Thus the law, legal institutions and cultural or ethical norms, as well as ordinary business practices and monetary phenomena, fall within the analytical domain of the economist.

RISK AND BUSINESS CYCLES

New and Old Austrian Perspectives

Tyler Cowen

London and New York

First published 1997
by Routledge
11 New Fetter Lane, London EC4P 4EE

Simultaneously published in the USA and Canada
by Routledge
29 West 35th Street, New York, NY 10001

© 1997 Tyler Cowen

Typeset in Garamond by Intype London Ltd
Printed and bound in Great Britain by
MPG Books Ltd, Bodmin, Cornwall

British Library Cataloguing in Publication Data
A catalogue record for this book is available from the British Library

Library of Congress Cataloging in Publication Data
Cowen, Tyler.
Risk and Business Cycles: New and Old Austrian Perspectives/Tyler Cowen.
p. cm. (Foundations of the modern economy)
Includes bibliographical references and index.
1. Business cycles. 2. Risk. 3. Austrian school of economists. I. Title. II. Series.
HB3711.C684 1997
338.5′42—dc21   97–13794

ISBN 0–415–16919–4

CONTENTS

v

LIST OF FIGURES AND TABLES

ACKNOWLEDGEMENTS

I have received useful comments from many individuals, including Fischer Black, Meyer Burstein, Kevin Grier, Robin Grier, Randall Holcombe, Steve Horwitz, Randall Kroszner, Axel Leijontiufvud, Marc Poitras, Mario Rizzo, George Selgin, Jim Strain, Alex Tabarrok, Lawrence White, Katarina Zajc, an anonymous referee, and seminar participants at New York University, George Mason University, and the Southern Economic Association. My thanks also to Alan Jarvis and Alison Kirk in their roles as editors at Routledge.

1

INTRODUCTION

THE PROBLEM

Entrepreneurs seek to match their production to market demands. To the extent that chosen outputs satisfy market demands and earn profits, the plans of consumers and producers are coordinated. How this coordination ever comes about, and why it might sometimes fail to occur, remain central questions for macroeconomics. In this book I shall focus on the coordination of investment and product purchase plans over time.

More specifically, I will examine whether intertemporal coordination provides a useful organizing theme for business cycle research. This investigation pursues the research program of the 'Austrian' school of economics (e.g., Menger, Mises, Hayek), using modern treatments of risk, finance, and expectations, and drawing upon contemporary methods of empirical and econometric research. I examine how changes in risk, real interest rates, and finance constraints alter the likelihood of intertemporal plan coordination. I will attempt to synthesize modern real business cycle theory, the work of David Lilien and Fischer Black on sectoral shifts, and the older Austrian analyses of monetary and capital theory, with the purpose of constructing an investment-based approach to business cycles in its most plausible form.

The questions I address include the following:

1 What risk–return trade-offs do entrepreneurs face in evaluating alternative investments, and how might these trade-offs account for some features of business cycles? Chapter 2 examines this initial question in purely real terms, focusing on intertemporal coordination.
2 Can changes in the nominal money supply create real sectoral shifts? Chapter 3 considers whether real and monetary theories of business cycles can be unified in terms of a general theory of sectoral shifts towards and away from riskier investments.
3 What are the policy implications of intertemporal coordination theories of the business cycle? Chapter 3 considers commodity standards, fixed

money growth rules, interest rate smoothing, nominal GNP rules, and other policy options, including fixed and floating exchange rates.

4 Does the traditional Austrian theory of the trade cycle satisfactorily unify real and monetary business cycle theories? Chapter 4 argues that the traditional Austrian approach fails to establish its central contention – the link between positive rates of nominal money growth and excessive capital-intensity.

5 How might an investment-based approach to business cycles avoid some of the problems with the traditional Austrian approach? Chapters 2 and 3 can be read as replacing the traditional Austrian emphasis on capital-intensity with an emphasis on risk. I explicitly contrast the 'old' and 'new' Austrian approaches in Chapter 4.

6 Does the evidence support risk-based, investment-based, and Austrian theories of the business cycle? Does the evidence support the case for real effects of monetary policy, operating through an investment channel? Chapter 5 surveys the empirical work that has been done on these issues.

I will present the business cycle theory outlined in this book as a complement to neo-Keynesian and real business cycle approaches, rather than as a substitute or a direct competitor. The neo-Keynesians focus on why markets may not clear, or why markets may respond to shocks imperfectly. The neo-Keynesians, however, have devoted less attention to specifying how shocks might be propagated through an investment mechanism, or how much initial vulnerability to shocks economic agents will accept. Alternatively, real business cycle theory examines how shocks are propagated through time and through different sectors, but most versions of the theory (with some notable exceptions, discussed later) do not give a central place to investment. Real business cycle theorists typically speak of positive and negative 'productivity' shocks. Using a broad interpretation of the concept of shocks, I examine changes in an economy's capital structure as a particular case of real business cycle theory.

I will focus on sectoral shifts across investments of different kinds. In the simplest scenario, entrepreneurs must choose between risky investments and less risky allocations of resources towards consumption. More generally, entrepreneurs face a trade-off between risk and expected return on investments, as emphasized by modern finance theory and the business cycle theory of Black (1995). Business cycles arise when subsequent expenditure patterns do not validate investors' initial choices of particular time profiles of inputs and outputs. The disappointment of entrepreneurial plans will give rise to a negative real shock. Economic busts arise when risky, information-sensitive investments are not validated by the subsequent course of events.

The time-consuming nature of production implies that entrepreneurs must make resource commitments based on forecasts of market conditions for the relatively distant future. Black (1995) speaks of the difficulty of matching tastes and technology, given the 'roundabout' or time-consuming nature of production; related themes have been stressed by the Austrians. Although information on the time element in production is difficult to find, the data do provide a rough idea of the relevant magnitudes for time to build. Mayer (1958, p. 364) surveyed 276 companies building new industrial plant in the United States. He found that the average time from the decision to invest until the completion of the investment is up to thirty months. Bizer and Sichel (1991, p. 28) calculated the average durability of capital in various industries to be between eighteen and thirty years.[1]

Table 1.1 Average durability of capital

Industry	Average capital longevity (years)
Food	24.6
Textiles	30.8
Paper	22.7
Chemicals	22.9
Rubber and plastic	18.9
Stone, clay, and glass	22.9
Primary metals	28.1
Fabricated metals	26.3
Non-electrical machinery	27.3
Electrical machinery	24.0
Transportation	26.0

Source: Bizer and Sichel (1991)

I characterize risky investments as long-term, costly to reverse, high-yielding, and having returns highly sensitive to the arrival of future information. For purposes of contrast, I characterize safe investments as more liquid, lower yielding, and less sensitive to the arrival of new information. Consumption typically represents a safe means of resource allocation; the returns are received immediately and do not involve reinvestment. Sectoral shifts across less risky and more risky investments provide the crux of the business cycle mechanisms I will examine in Chapters 2 and 3.

The prices of capital investments depend upon both real interest rates and risk, and changes in these variables therefore will influence economic cyclicality. For reasons discussed in Chapters 2 and 3, declines in real interest rates will tend to increase aggregate macroeconomic risk and cyclicality. Increases in expected volatility will have the opposite effects – they will penalize risky, information-sensitive investments with special force. The induced move to lower-yielding investments will imply an economic

---

[1] See Table 1.1 for a list of the industries and exact figures for durability of capital. On the time needed to complete investments, see also Nickell (1978, p. 289).

downturn. As we will see in Chapter 2, the asymmetric effects of raising and lowering risk imply that economic busts arrive suddenly and unpredictably as discrete events, rather than as mere fluctuations in the rate of economic growth. Business cycles and changes in the growth rate are theoretically unified phenomena but they are not identical, as some modern real business cycle theories suggest (e.g., Long and Plosser 1983).

Both real and monetary factors may influence real interest rates and risk. Changes in government spending, budget deficits, oil prices, the forecasting abilities of entrepreneurs, and monetary policy all may affect risk and real interest rates, and thus may affect economic cyclicality. Without wishing to pre-judge the empirical issue of whether monetary or real shocks are more important, I will devote special attention to whether changes in monetary policy can create the real sectoral shifts behind a business cycle.

I consider how changes in monetary policy might affect the coordination of saving and investment plans. Monetary economics and monetary approaches to business cycles have fallen into general disfavor, given the current popularity of real business cycle theories. Yet the earlier neo-classical tradition bridged both monetary and real theories of cyclical activity. In these models, monetary factors have real effects by creating sectoral shifts through their influence on capital markets.

In the monetary scenarios I will consider the central bank can stimulate an economy in the short run. Monetary policy, by lowering real interest rates or relaxing finance constraints, can induce entrepreneurs to accept more risk, thereby making the economy more or less cyclical. In other words, monetary expansions can create sectoral shifts in favor of long-term, high-yielding, riskier investments. In the short run, before the relevant uncertainty is resolved, these investments do bring higher expected returns; the economy will appear wealthier. In the long run, however, the additional risk sometimes turns into systematic economic busts; long-term investments are highly sensitive to expectational error. Monetary policy sometimes brings lasting booms, and sometimes brings a boom/bust cycle – the final outcome is never certain in advance. This approach attempts to account for the stylized facts that first, monetary policy often is potent in the short run; second, monetary policy has unpredictable long-run effects; and third, monetary policy cannot improve economic welfare on average.

Instead of producing an inflationary surprise, central banks sometimes increase monetary volatility. In this case entrepreneurs will respond by shifting from riskier to less risky investments. The economy will experience an immediate downturn, and possibly also a high rate of price inflation. If the level and volatility of nominal money growth are positively related we will observe stagflation. These real effects of monetary policy work through capital markets, rather than through non-rational expectations or sticky wages and prices.

The positive theory of monetary cycles presented in Chapter 3 is *not* a monetary misperceptions theory as commonly defined. Cycles can be induced by real forces as much as by monetary forces, as discussed in Chapter 2. More fundamentally, I do not assume that individuals are tricked by the current money supply. Monetary misperceptions theories have fallen out of favor precisely because it is difficult to generate plausibly large costs from ignorance of the current money supply. In the scenarios I consider, monetary policy has real effects either through lowering real interest rates or, in the ancillary case of imperfect financial markets, through easing finance constraints.

The theories I consider attempt to match not only the empirical data but also some common economic intuitions. Both Wall Street and policymakers demonstrate an almost obsessive concern with capital markets and interest rates. Market participants place great emphasis on the successful prediction of interest rates, and see movements in interest rates as having great import for the economy. Yet capital markets and interest rates play a minor role in most current business cycle theories. Examining sectoral shifts across investments of differing risks attempts to remedy this discrepancy between theory and observation.

Concern with sectoral shifts across different kinds of capital goods is by no means new. The influence of real and monetary factors on the coordination of saving and investment plans dominated macroeconomic research for the first forty years of this century. Wicksell, Hawtrey, Mises, Hayek, Marget, Robertson, Kaldor, Myrdal, Lindahl, Keynes, and Hicks, among many others, all saw the integration of monetary and capital theory as central for business cycle theory and growth theory. Keynes's *General Theory* was the final significant contribution to this tradition, although ironically, Keynes's own influence discouraged the further pursuit of capital theory as a research topic. Yet for all its disparaging remarks about capital theory, the *General Theory* was obsessed with the topic of capital and its relation to money.

The earlier neo-classical economists failed to satisfactorily integrate monetary theory, capital theory, and the theory of finance. Hayek provided implicit models in his *Prices and Production* (1935) and other trade cycle writings, but he recognized the incompleteness of his treatment. In response he planned a two-volume set on capital theory. The first volume, *Pure Theory of Capital*, appeared in 1941, but dealt only with capital theory in a barter setting. The second volume, which was to deal with capital theory in a monetary economy, was abandoned when Hayek turned his attention to political philosophy. Arthur Marget had similar plans to produce a treatise on money and capital theory, to be called *Money and Production*, but this project also failed to come to fruition. Unfortunately, these earlier economists did not know contemporary microeconomics and possessed no more than a rudimentary understanding of financial theory, and for this reason their planned works proved intractable. I view modern financial theory as the proper substitute for the books which Hayek and Marget never wrote; Austrian capital theory and its offshoots focused too much upon the abstract properties of capital and not enough on its payoff streams in different world-states – a concept we now interpret as risk.[2]

Today's macroeconomists are well versed in the theory of risk and finance but, with some prominent exceptions, they have tended to ignore capital theory. For the most part, intertemporal coordination has remained an underground topic, relegated to non-mainstream economists, such as the Austrians and the Post-Keynesians. Intertemporal coordination is a trivial issue in the representative agent models favored by many rational expectations theorists. Overlapping generations models often have no durable capital at all. The neo-Keynesians study coordination failures, but to date have focused on wage, price, and interest rate rigidities, rather than on disappointed expectations and failures of plan coordination. Lilien (1982) gave impetus to the modern literature on sectoral shifts and plan discoordination, but he did not focus on capital and investment.

Capital theory has received some attention in contemporary mainstream macroeconomics, most notably from Kydland and Prescott (1982) in their seminal article 'Time to Build and Aggregate Economic Fluctuations.' Greenwald and Stiglitz, in a variety of writings on credit rationing, have reintroduced capital markets into macroeconomics. Fischer Black's recent *Exploring General Equilibrium* (1995) has emphasized 'roundabout production' as a fundamental source of taste–technology mismatches, thus emphasizing the role of capital in sectoral shocks. Black also stressed the trade-off between risk and return in entrepreneurial investment choice. All of these ideas play prominent roles in this book.

The sectoral shift literature and the earlier Austrian tradition stand apart on a variety of issues, most notably on monetary theory. Sectoral shift theories tend to emphasize real factors; Black (1995) goes so far as to dismiss monetary theories of business cycles altogether. The Austrians, in contrast, emphasized how monetary policy can change the relative demand for capital goods of differing kinds. Chapter 3 examines what assumptions are necessary for monetary policy to create real sectoral shocks.

SOME ASSUMPTIONS

Unless otherwise stated, constant returns and perfect competition hold in both the real sector and the financial intermediation sector. All prices and wages are perfectly flexible, unless otherwise stated. All investors maximize expected risk-adjusted pecuniary returns.

---

[2] When I heard Hayek lecture in 1984, he announced that he still had plans to complete the second volume. He died in 1992 with no further sign of the work.

I define capital goods as the inputs used for marketplace production. I refer to capital and investments in a broad sense. Purchases of durable consumer goods, development of human capital, and the cultivation of land all qualify as capital investments.

Incorrect investments in capital goods can entail high costs. Once an automobile factory has been built, for instance, converting that factory to different uses may be either impossible or prohibitively costly. Disassembling the factory and transporting those capital goods elsewhere also involves a considerable loss of value. For these reasons entrepreneurs must forecast economic conditions with a reasonable degree of accuracy if they are to earn profits and serve consumer welfare. Entrepreneurs who incorrectly forecast economic conditions often fail to earn even the risk-free rate of return on their investments.

Adjustment costs, by definition, result from reallocating factors of production to alternate uses. Misallocation costs result from keeping resources in non-ideal employments. Misallocation costs arise when resources could produce more value elsewhere but the potential adjustment costs discourage a shift. The private costs of investment errors consist of adjustment costs and misallocation costs exclusively. When adjustment costs and misallocation costs are sufficiently high that entrepreneurs earn less than the risk-free (or minimum-risk) rate of return, I refer to that investment as a malinvestment.

I define money as a generally accepted medium of exchange. Individuals who wish to engage in indirect exchange will hold a common asset – money – to reduce their transactions costs. Loans, in particular, will occur through the medium of money rather than through bartering real commodities. In Chapter 2 I assume an economy in which money does not matter. The other chapters, however, deal with a monetary economy with a single dominant medium of exchange. Whether currency and reserves bear interest, whether traders post prices in terms of the money asset, or whether the money is paper or backed by a commodity, will not affect the basic analysis (see Chapter 3 for a discussion of these matters).

In the short run and medium run, risk and return are correlated in the manner suggested by standard finance theory. In the *very* long run, investment risks and returns may be negatively rather than positively correlated, perhaps due to increasing returns to scale, asset complementarities, or the benefits of specialization. Today's world brings higher returns than the world of the caveman, and probably also involves smaller risks. Most individuals now survive past their thirty-fifth birthday, for instance, due to their relative freedom from predators and parasites. Since the time of the caveman, the successive accumulation of risky, high-return investments may have *lowered* long-run risk for everyone at the societal level. We (and our ancestors) have undertaken more risks than the caveman, with an aggregate result of lower risk.

Given this point, the choice of relevant time horizon provides a potential divider for cyclical theory and growth theory. Cyclical theory applies to the short run where risk and return are positively correlated, both for individual investors and for the economy as a whole. Growth theory applies to a longer run where risk may fall as returns rise, perhaps due to an aggregation effect over time. I restrict this investigation to cyclical theory, and therefore I assume that risks and returns are positively correlated, both for individual investors and for the economy as a whole.

Expectations

With the exception of Chapter 4, which examines the arguments of the Austrian school, I assume that individuals maximize expected utility and have rational expectations. The rational expectations assumption serves as a tool of analytical organization rather than as a descriptive assumption about the real world. Rational expectations models help us trace which economic results can be generated without assuming systematic forecasting errors and which cannot. Whenever we wish to specify a coordination problem, rational expectations theory requires us to justify, or at least outline, the underlying informational asymmetries. I view the rational expectations assumptions as a useful form of discipline. Rational expectations does not rule out significant marketplace errors, but it does require us to specify the source of these errors in some explicit informational asymmetry.

I define rational expectations as follows: Individual economic forecasts are efficient and unbiased; subjective probability distributions for an economic variable correspond to the true distribution. As a result, individual forecasting errors are serially uncorrelated over time.

The above definition leaves out two features that are contained in some treatments, or perhaps caricatures, of rational expectations. First, the above definition of rational expectations does not imply small forecast errors. The variance of actual outcomes, relative to forecasts, may be significant. Uncertainty, or the scope of potential error, increases to the extent that the relevant probability distribution becomes more volatile. Individuals know the 'true model' of the economy in general terms but they cannot predict perfectly particular variables, and perhaps they cannot even come close.

Second, I do not assume that all individuals share common information about all economic variables. The assumption of homogeneous information shows up in representative agent models, which reduce the economy to a single agent and a single forecast. The chapters which follow violate the homogeneous information assumption by postulating at least two informational asymmetries. Entrepreneurs do not have perfect knowledge of demanders' future spending and saving patterns, and entrepreneurs do not always have perfect knowledge of future monetary policy, even if the monetary authority can predict its own behavior. In both cases entrepreneurial forecasts will sometimes diverge from true realized variables, although entrepreneurial forecasts nonetheless satisfy rational expectations for the entire distribution of possible outcomes. In the scenarios I consider, all individuals know the true distributions for economic variables, and some individuals (but not all) also know the exact outcomes for particular variables.[3]

Strict, homogeneous information interpretations of rational expectations neglect specialized human capital, diversity of circumstance, and the usefulness of the price system in transmitting decentralized information. Under strictly homogeneous information, the very justification for a market economy becomes open to question (Frydman and Phelps 1983). By assumption, individuals already have common knowledge of the information that the market is supposed to generate. The assumption of homogeneous information, consistently applied to all economic variables, would pave the way for effective central planning as advocated by Oskar Lange.

Rejecting homogeneous information rational expectations does not represent a strong break from previous practice. Even Lucas's original 'islands' model (1972) does not use homogeneous information rational expectations in its strictest form. Individuals on one island do not have information about what is happening on the other island. More importantly, individuals do not have perfect information about the actions of the policymaker (i.e., the money supply). The policymaker has a model predicting the behavior of private sector individuals, but private sector individuals do not have a model predicting the behavior of the policymaker. If individuals know as much about the policymaker as the policymaker knows about them, monetary misperceptions will not result. Individuals would use a model of the monetary authority to determine what money supply the policymaker has chosen. Homogeneous information applies to the islands model only by excluding the policymaker from the set of relevant individuals, and redefining the policymaker as a universally unknown 'state of nature.'

---

[3] On different versions of rational expectations, and on informational homogeneity and heterogeneity, see Frydman and Phelps (1983), Carter and Maddock (1984), Pesaran (1987), and Redman (1992). For criticisms of the idea that individuals can estimate probability distributions, or that economic processes can be described by such distributions, see Knight (1971), and O'Driscoll and Rizzo (1985). We can accept these criticisms and still adhere to the idea that errors are serially uncorrelated. Even if the idea of a population mean is not well defined, individual forecasts may, on average, still hit the mean of the observed sample.

NEW AND OLD AUSTRIAN PERSPECTIVES

The Austrian school of economists – Mises, Hayek, Rothbard, Garrison, and others – has attempted to integrate both money and capital into a general theory of business cycles. These writers have emphasized the real effects of inflation-engineered increases in loanable funds supply. The Austrians follow a long and distinguished tradition in monetary theory starting with Henry Thornton, running through Ricardo, Thomas Joplin, J. S. Mill, other nineteenth-century classical economists (see Hayek 1939), and culminating in Knut Wicksell and the Stockholm School of economics.

In the basic Austrian model, monetary inflation induces an initial economic boom. By assumption, the new money enters through the banking system, thereby causing real interest rates to fall. The lower real interest rates in turn cause long-term investment to expand. The boom later turns into a bust as the new investments prove to be malinvestments. Therein lies the original Austrian proposition – the claim that banking system inflation will increase long-term investment to an unsustainable level.

In this book I will consider two statements of investment-based business cycle theory. The first view, which I call the traditional Austrian theory, is defined as follows:

1 The traditional Austrian theory: positive rates of nominal money growth induce unsustainable increases in long-term investment.[4]
2 The risk-based theory: increases in the money supply, or other sectoral shifts, may make an economy riskier. When the economy shifts towards additional long-term investment, sometimes a sustainable boom will result, and other times a boom/bust cycle will result. Entrepreneurs will not err on average, but policy may make the economy riskier and thus more cyclical.

The second statement, which I present in Chapters 2 and 3, constitutes my attempt to revise the Austrian theory. This risk-based approach, as I present it, follows from grafting rational expectations and modern finance theory onto the original Austrian theory.

Both the traditional Austrian and risk-based theories postulate a relationship between positive nominal money growth and real interest rates. As will be discussed in Chapter 3, increases in the rate of nominal money growth will cause real interest rates to fall, at least under plausible conditions. The divergence in opinion comes after this point. The traditional

---

[4] The seminal statements of the traditional Austrian claim can be found in the writings of Mises, Hayek, Rothbard, and Garrison, as cited in the bibliography. Chapter 4 offers more specific citations.

Austrian theory claims that expansionary monetary policy will induce capital-intensity to expand *too much*, a proposition which I have labeled The Austrian Claim. The traditional Austrian view rejects the rational expectations assumption and argues that monetary policy will induce systematic entrepreneurial errors. Entrepreneurs will increase long-term investment to unsustainable levels.

The risk-based theory suggests an alternate perspective on The Austrian Claim and the traditional Austrian theory. Inflation may lead to more errors, but it will lead to errors of various kinds, not of a single systematic kind. Inflation may increase aggregate risk, but it will not induce systematic malinvestment in long-term production processes. Following a burst of loanable funds inflation, long-term investment *should* increase to some degree. For at least one period, maybe more, potential investors enjoy a lower real interest rate. The injection of liquid funds into the loanable funds market produces a potentially sustainable sectoral shift in favor of capital goods, at least if that shift is sufficiently small. Whether the *actual* shift will be too large or too small cannot be determined *a priori*. Rather than overcommitting business cycle theory by postulating a particular kind of mistake, I attempt to rebuild the traditional Austrian theory with an emphasis on the general likelihood of future mistakes.

Contrary to most Austrian school writers, I do not treat the new patterns of resource allocation induced by inflation as *prima facie* 'distortions,' 'resource misallocations,' or 'malinvestments.' These conclusions must be demonstrated rather than assumed. Chapter 3, which argues that all monetary policy changes can be 'decomposed' into changes in fiscal policy, helps illuminate why monetary changes do not necessarily represent distortions. Monetary shocks operate through individual portfolios to change the initial distribution of wealth and liquidity. Real resources shift only to the extent that private spending patterns have changed. Resources *should* shift to some degree to reflect the new market demands. Entrepreneurs may over-react to the new pattern of demands, they may forecast the new pattern of demands incorrectly, or they may overestimate the permanence of the new pattern of demands, but each of these outcomes needs to be generated by an explicit analysis of the forecasting problem and the risk-return trade-offs behind investment decisions.

The plan of the book proceeds as follows. Chapter 2 outlines the basics of a risk-based business cycle theory in real terms, and Chapter 3 considers some monetary scenarios and extensions. These two chapters focus on changes in the level of economic risk, and ask whether an approach based on the risks of alternative investment prospects can provide a coherent and intuitively appealing understanding of the business cycle. Chapter 3 also considers some topics and extensions, including credit rationing, policy implications, and the international transmission of cycles. Chapter 4 provides a critique of the traditional Austrian theory, and compares the traditional and risk-based approaches explicitly. Establishing an inflationary bias towards systematic capital-intensity will prove to be an Achilles heel for the Austrian claim. Chapter 5 examines some empirical evidence relevant to both approaches, and evaluates the applicability of the theories to the real world.

2

A RISK-BASED THEORY IN REAL TERMS

WHY A CENTRAL ROLE FOR RISK?

Business cycle theories can be divided into two groups: theories where entrepreneurial errors drive the cycle, and theories where errors play a secondary or negligible role. The traditional Austrian theory of the business cycle falls into the former category, whereas most varieties of real business cycle theory fall into the latter category. The Austrian view postulates that entrepreneurs make systematic mistakes (in response to monetary policy), and the real business cycle mechanism does not rely on individual mistakes at all. Risk-based theories, as considered in the next two chapters, provide a middle ground or halfway house between these two views.

A business cycle theory based on risk is the logical outcome of a focus on entrepreneurial errors. Once we take all possible signal extraction problems into account, the economic theorist cannot easily pinpoint the net direction of signal extraction errors. Economic theories of learning and expectations simply are not advanced enough to produce such definitive results (see Chapter 5 for more on related points). Furthermore, the very nature of an error suggests a factor which the economist cannot easily model or comprehend. We should not deny the concept of error outright but, rather, economists should make strong claims about errors only at a very general level, rather than at a very particular level.

Most monetary misperceptions theories, such as Lucas's islands model (1972) or traditional Austrian business cycle theory, attempt to make definite claims about the nature of forecasting errors. For Lucas, unexpected inflation leads to excess labor supply in present periods, and for the Austrian inflation induces excessive long-term investment. In my perspective inflation may distort resource allocation, but it does so in a variety of ways, and in ways which are hard to predict or foresee in advance. Rather than trying to isolate particular distortive effects, and argue their relative potency, an alternative version of monetary business cycle theory considers the impact of inflation, and other exogenous shocks, on economic riskiness. Inflation generates greater economic cyclicality only when it leads to higher

13

levels of risk. The concept of risk provides a general base for business cycle theory, without requiring highly specific assumptions about the content of signal extraction errors.

By building business cycle theory on risk, I am attempting to synthesize modern finance theory and earlier Austrian writings in capital theory, two fields which have developed as separate and independent fields of investigation. The Austrians argue that declines in the real interest rate will increase the capital-intensity of an economy and may lead to an unsustainable structure of production. Variations in capital-intensity play a central role in the progress of the business cycle. I hold no objection to the Austrian concept of capital-intensity, but changing the focus to risk links the theory more directly to the payoff patterns of investments. After a real interest rate decline, or some other positive inducement to invest, investors accept a wider spread of possible outcomes and the economy becomes riskier, at least under some assumptions outlined further below. The increase in risk implies greater economic cyclicality and a greater likelihood of either a sustained boom or a subsequent economic downturn.

The concept of risk helps resolve outstanding problems in real business cycle theories. Real business cycle theories, such as Long and Plosser (1983), postulate positive and negative technology shocks as the driving forces behind business cycles. The size of such technology shocks, however, must be very large to account for observed swings in output. Furthermore, it is not obvious which technological regression accounts for the Great Depression, or which technological advance accounts for the boom of the 1980s. These criticisms of real business cycle theory are well known, and have prevented that approach from persuading the skeptics.

Smaller shocks can drive large output fluctuations only if we consider propagation mechanisms which allow small *ex ante* shocks to translate into large positive or negative outcomes *ex post*. In other words, we should consider shocks which change the level of risk in an economy, or which induce entrepreneurs to change the level of risk. Such shocks can be relatively small in expected value terms, since they involve the potential for either positive or negative outcomes, but they may nonetheless produce highly levered effects on economic cyclicality. Once the risk is resolved, the *ex post* result may be much greater in size than the *ex ante* impetus. To use an analogy from the context of the individual, a small change in the price of a ticket to Las Vegas may have a large impact on family income, once the vacation is over.

Emphasizing changes in the level of risk also helps resolve the problems of asymmetry and comovement that plague investment-based business cycle mechanisms, including the traditional Austrian theory. In the original Austrian theory the move from short-term investments to long-term investments brings an economic boom, whereas the contrary switch brings an economic downturn. In investment-based theories more generally, investment increases are associated with booms and investment declines are associated with busts. Why? Investment increases take away resources from the immediate production of consumer goods, and therefore might instead be associated with falling real wages and perceptions of economic decline, at least in a large number of sectors (Tullock 1988). In reality, however, business cycles consist of concerted upward and downward swings in economic activity; most economic sectors rise and fall together.

Rationalizing business cycle comovement within investment-based theories requires that long-term investments have higher expected yields. If an economic boom is identified with a move to higher-yielding investments (i.e., riskier investments), then perhaps the boom can bring a general expansion, at least in the short run, even when sectoral shifts are under way.

Risk remains a 'ghost' variable in neo-Keynesian theories, despite playing a significant underlying role in the argument. Assume, for the moment, that we accept the possibility of efficiency wage or menu cost inefficiencies. When these rigidities or market failures become binding, at least some individuals (e.g., laborers, customers, suppliers) will suffer sub-par returns. Yet suppliers and demanders must have entered these sectors with the knowledge that sub-par outcomes were possible (neo-Keynesian models typically assume rational expectations). The possibility of sub-par outcomes thus must be counterbalanced by a corresponding upside potential. Neo-Keynesian theories focus on the mechanics of the negative outcomes, without discussing how entrepreneurs, laborers, and customers choose or determine the initial vulnerability of the economy to negative shocks. Placing risk at the center of business cycle theory puts neo-Keynesian theories in a context consistent with real business cycle theory. When a negative real shock comes along markets may fail to clear, but supranormal returns will be earned when neo-Keynesian traps fail to bind; in that case a boom results.

The analytical emphasis on risk implies that economic downturns are voluntary, at least in *ex ante* terms, even though they are regretted *ex post*. Entrepreneurs accept initial investment risks with a knowledge of the potential downside. With some exceptions (e.g., pollution control technologies), government regulations and mandates do not force individuals to undertake particular real investments on a large scale. Government, through monetary policy, fiscal policy, or other means, may increase the difficulty of entrepreneurial forecasting, but individual entrepreneurs still accept risk with the unreliable nature of government in mind. In this regard all business downturns indicate a market failure, even if the government causes the relevant negative shock, or is responsible for the volatility of the policy environment.

The remainder of this chapter outlines how risk might produce some more specific scenarios for business cycles, focusing on real scenarios. The second section of the chapter outlines and explains the basic framework and assumptions. The third section focuses on which factors may set off an investment boom, and also discusses the interest elasticity of investment, a common issue for many investment-based theories. The fourth section analyzes what generates the comovement of the boom, another classic problem for investment-based theories of the business cycle. The fifth section focuses on the downturn, paying particular attention to why entrepreneurial errors might come in clusters, rather than canceling each other out in the aggregate. The sixth section considers increases in the volatility of the economic environment, and how volatility increases can set off immediate downturns without a preceding boom. Section six also examines whether business cycles and changes in the rate of growth are essentially similar phenomena, as suggested by some versions of real business cycle theory.

FRAMEWORK AND ASSUMPTIONS

The business cycle theory of this chapter and the next focuses on the risks of specialized investment. Entrepreneurs invest in accordance with expectations of forthcoming savings and consumption demands, but the economy's capital structure will not always be in equilibrium with the purchase plans of demanders. *Ex ante*, all capital structures can be interpreted as equilibria, if we account for risk, expectations, and the costs of information-processing. *Ex post*, capital structure disequilibrium arises to the extent that chosen projects turn out to be unprofitable, contrary to expectations. Investors will earn less than the risk-free rate of return and consumers may not be able to purchase their goods and services at prices they had expected. Business cycles arise when entrepreneurs accept risks but encounter systematic disappointments of their plans.

The focus on investment risk defines the context for the business cycle theory of this chapter. Real business cycle theories focus on the risk or volatility introduced by technology shocks. Traditional Austrian theories identify the risks created by distortionary monetary policies by the central bank. Neo-Keynesian theories, although they view risk in implicit terms, concentrate their attention on the risk of non-clearing markets. In contrast to these theories, I focus on the risks that investments will not match consumer demands, and thus will decline in value. Technology shocks, monetary policy, and non-market-clearing prices all may constitute particular causes of supply/demand mismatches, and in this sense a risk-based theory does not contradict the other options listed. None the less I focus on the initial willingness of entrepreneurs to accept vulnerable positions with regard to shocks in general, rather than on a single kind of shock.

The basic analytical apparatus of this chapter is drawn from financial theory. Each supplier faces a choice between investments of varying risk and return, consistent with modern finance theory. High *ex ante* risk will imply high *ex ante* expected return, and vice versa. The well-known risk–return trade-off can be represented in Figure 2.1.

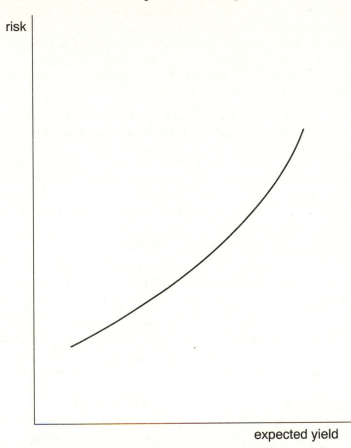

Figure 2.1 The trade-off between risk and expected yield

Translating Figure 2.1 into a macroeconomic theory will require addressing several questions, including the following: What determines the slope of the risk–return curve? What factors induce investors to move along the curve? And how do the decisions of individual investors interact on an aggregate or macroeconomic level? To proceed along this path, I will next outline six basic assumptions that I will use to put structure on the risk–return trade-off represented in Figure 2.1.

The six assumptions are:

1 Investment involves greater risk than consumption.
2 A decline in the real interest rate will increase investment and will increase risk for each investor.

3 Increases in investment risk for each entrepreneur translate into increases in aggregate risk.
4 Riskier projects, at least those which are implemented in an equilibrium, will yield higher expected pecuniary returns.
5 Entrepreneurs have greater certainty about investment returns in earlier periods than in later periods.
6 An exogenous increase in the real economic risk of investments will induce a contraction of investment.

Of these six assumptions or propositions, the first four define the basic or essential mechanisms of the theory. I accept assumptions five and six as working hypotheses which flesh out the scope and details of the theory but are inessential to the basic mechanisms. Also significant is what I do not assume. Consistent with a rational expectations approach, I do not assume that changes in real interest rates trick investors, or that investors systematically choose incorrect investments in response to monetary shocks or changes in real interest rates.

Let us now consider each assumption in turn.

1 Investment involves greater risk than consumption

Typically, we are more certain about the value of our consumption decisions than about the value of our investments. If we choose to buy a dinner, for instance, we are sometimes disappointed or surprised, but on average buying the dinner is less risky than investing in a new capital project. Increasing investment at the expense of consumption therefore raises economic risk.

We may interpret this proposition in either of two ways. First, the assumption may be interpreted as an empirical regularity which holds true in most cases but not as a matter of theory. Second, the proposition can be interpreted as true *a priori* if we define risk in terms of measurable macroeconomic variables rather than in terms of utility. The risk of immediate consumption – the quality of the purchased dinner – is utility risk alone, rather than risk in terms of measurable GNP. GNP will be the same, regardless of how good the dinner was, and for this reason the utility risk of consumption decisions does not account for fluctuation in measurable macroeconomic aggregates. Macroeconomics seeks to explain fluctuations in measured national income, rather than fluctuations in utility. For this reason, investment is necessarily riskier than consumption in terms of measurable macroeconomic variables.

2 A decline in the real interest rate will increase investment and will increase risk for each investor

If we accept that investment is riskier than consumption, the second assumption follows from a standard substitution effect. The real interest rate decline will encourage investment, which implies a riskier set of portfolio holdings. Note that the concept of a real interest rate decline is a general one, and may include relaxation of finance constraints, as well as declines in observed market rates. When an individual cannot borrow, he or she faces an effective real interest rate which is prohibitively high or infinite; the subsequent ability to borrow implies a fall in real rates.

In addition to the substitution effect on investment, real interest rate declines will bring wealth and portfolio effects as well. Following standard practices of economic theory, I assume the substitution effect predominates, at least on average. Incorporation of income effects, however, would not alter the basic result, at least not under traditional assumptions about utility functions. Typically, risk aversion declines with wealth. A decline in the real interest rate, by increasing the value of investment portfolios, will increase risk-taking through income and portfolio effects as well.

Although I speak of allocations between consumption and investment, the same business cycle mechanisms apply when entrepreneurs switch from less risky investments to more risky investments. The change in risk drives the basic results, whether the forgone alternatives are labeled 'consumption' or 'less risky investment.' We can imagine entrepreneurs deciding between more risky commitments and less risky commitments; they can use their capital to maintain an existing and relatively safe line of production, or they can allocate that capital to a new and risky venture. The economy offers a 'term structure' of differential returns on projects of varying risks. The riskier long-term projects will offer higher expected pecuniary returns, and the safer short-term projects will offer lower expected pecuniary returns.[1]

3 Increases in investment risk for each entrepreneur translate into increases in aggregate risk

Following a decline in the real interest rate, the increase in risk holds in the aggregate as well as in the partial equilibrium settings traditionally studied by finance theory. Each entrepreneur chooses a project which is riskier than the project that would otherwise have been chosen. If each

---

[1] The term structure for risk in the real economy ought, on average, to be steeper than the term structure on financial assets; a 30-year investment in real plant is typically much riskier than the purchase of a 30-year Treasury Bond. Earlier writings in Austrian capital theory do not always remark on the greater riskiness and lesser liquidity of longer-term investments. Hayek (1975, p. 401) is one exception.

entrepreneur has a riskier position after the new investment, so does the economy as a whole.

I assume that adding a sequence of risky projects does not lead to a riskless total package. Increases in individual risk will translate into increases in aggregate risk, unless the new investments create as many new countercyclical assets (e.g., gold mines) as cyclical assets. In this unusual case, each individual might take on more risk but the economy as a whole would not be riskier or more volatile. Under the normal case, however, the riskiness of the economy will rise with the riskiness of its component parts.

This result does *not* violate the Law of Large Numbers. In many cases the issue of large numbers does not even apply to sectoral shocks. Economies do not possess large numbers of truly independent sectors. Long and Plosser (1983), for instance, usefully portray the American economy in terms of six sectors (agriculture, mining, construction, manufacturing, transportation and trade, and services and miscellaneous); those six sectors are strongly dependent upon each other. If independent negative shocks hit four or five of those six sectors, a systematic downturn may result.

To the extent that economic sectors are dependent, the likelihood of co-movement through purely stochastic shocks increases. A small but definite preponderance of positive or negative shocks across various sectors can spread and induce comovement across the economy as a whole. Projects typically are not independent in their risks but, rather, increased risk for one project adds to the risk of other projects. This result follows from the theory of capital complementarity and the importance of economic coordination (Lachmann 1978). Entrepreneurs, when making production decisions today, attempt to estimate the production decisions of other entrepreneurs in the future. The suppliers of railroad tracks, for instance, will attempt to forecast the plans of the suppliers of locomotives. To the extent that the locomotive supplier faces risk, so does the supplier of railroad tracks. To some extent, the risks borne by some entrepreneurs will be imposed on other entrepreneurs as well.[2]

Even when the number of sectors is large and sectors are economically independent, the Law of Large Numbers does not rule out business cycles caused by risk. A large number of economically independent sectors may rely on common forecasting procedures, or they may seek to forecast common events. In these cases errors can be correlated across sectors, even though the bad fortunes of one sector do not directly cause the bad fortunes of another sector.

Given the rational expectations assumption, all entrepreneurs expect population means for the variables they are trying to forecast. To the extent

---

[2] On the difference between partial and general equilibrium perspectives on risk, see Gehr (1979).

entrepreneurs try to forecast common variables, *ex post* deviations of these variables from their population means will cause all entrepreneurs to be wrong at once. Contrary to some intuitions, rational expectations theories have no particular difficulty accounting for clusters of entrepreneurial errors. To the extent we derive errors from a rational expectations framework, we build in commonality of error at the ground level. All rational expectations individuals with uncertainty expect the same population mean; common errors arise when the real world does not deliver that mean. The assumption of homogeneous expectations is not intended as descriptively true, but it does reflect the broadly common expectations about the future held by many individuals. To the extent that future events deviate from the band in which real world expectations are bunched, common errors will be made in common directions.[3]

Finally, and most fundamentally, many invocations of the Law of Large Numbers confuse multiplication of risk with subdivision of risk; the latter lowers aggregate risk but the former does not. If the unfavorable resolution of risk can cause cycles in particular economic sectors, it can cause cycles in a multiple of those sectors; i.e., an economy. The package is not safer than the single risk. The Law of Large Numbers does not claim that flipping a coin fifty times involves less aggregate risk than flipping a coin once (Samuelson 1954). If an individual finds a coin flip bet too risky with one trial, that same coin flip bet will be even riskier with fifty trials. The unconvinced should consider each of the fifty trials, and ask each time if they would be willing to forgo the final flip, if they find a single flip too risky. Backwards induction then applies.

We *can* make the following comparison: an economy composed of fifty small, independent shocks (i.e., subdivision of the risk) is safer than an economy whose fate depends upon a single shock. That is why we do not have a business cycle every week. It does not follow, however, that an economy (i.e., a bundle or multiple of sectors) is safer than a single sector; in fact, the bundle is necessarily riskier. Multiplying a single shock fifty times over does not decrease risk for the resulting aggregate. If we believe that risk resolution can account for sectoral cycles, risk resolution may account for aggregate cycles as well.

4 Riskier projects, at least those which are implemented in an equilibrium, will yield higher expected pecuniary returns

Risk is positively correlated with expected pecuniary return, at least for those projects undertaken in equilibrium. Again, I assume this effect holds

---

[3] In fact, non-rational expectations (non-RE) theories often have greater difficulty in generating comovement. To the extent we derive entrepreneurial errors from non-rational expectations, commonality of error becomes problematic; not all non-RE individuals will err in the same way or at the same time. The resulting heterogeneity of error may work against comovement and dampen cyclical tendencies.

both in the individual case and in the aggregate. When each entrepreneur decides to take more risk and seek higher expected returns, the economy moves into a similar position. The higher expected return to one project does not cancel out the higher expected return to any other project.[4]

The combination of assumption 2 and assumption 4 implies that a decline in the real interest rate brings a higher average rate of return on investment. Marginal rates of return on investment still will fall, even if risk and average returns increase overall. Following the interest rate decline, the new marginal investment project will have a lower (risk-adjusted) rate of return than the previous marginal investment project. Nonetheless, aggregate risk and returns increase for two reasons. The new investment project still brings higher risk, and higher returns, than the consumption allocation that otherwise would have been made. Furthermore, the real interest rate decline brings inframarginal shifts in the composition of investment, which also increase total risk and returns. After these shifts are complete, average gross rates of return have risen, but risk-adjusted marginal rates of return remain in equilibrium with the new (and lower) real interest rate.

Investment risk involves both a systematic component and an idiosyncratic or unsystematic component. Systematic risk exists to the extent information-sensitive investments covary with the market portfolio. These investments yield relatively poor returns when entrepreneurial forecasts prove incorrect, and relatively high returns when forecasts prove correct. Under the assumption of rational expectations, as discussed in Chapter 1, entrepreneurs hold common expectations and make common forecasts (although some individuals may know the true variable with certainty). To the extent common events influence the profitability of various projects, the downside for information-sensitive investments shows up as systematic risk.

Some recent articles in the finance literature have questioned whether systematic risk and expected returns are correlated as the capital asset pricing model suggests (e.g., Fama and French 1992; Roll and Ross 1994). The arguments of this book do not require that the capital asset pricing model has predictive power for the cross-sectional returns of different stocks. I focus on a far blunter comparison between risk and return. If entrepreneurs are to invest in risky and ambitious ventures, rather than holding T-Bills or spending more on consumption, they must expect relatively high returns from their real productive investments.

Unsystematic risk, or variance, also may influence the behavior of some entrepreneurs. Information-sensitive investments will have greater unsystematic risk from their relatively high variance of returns. Entrepreneurs

---

[4] On aggregate risk, see Gehr (1979). Standard finance theory typically assumes that the remainder of the market portfolio is given and thus does not treat an aggregate effect between risk and returns. French *et al.* (1987), using stock returns data, provide evidence for the aggregate effect as stated.

will care about this variance if they cannot perfectly diversify their holdings. Some firms are privately owned, in other cases compensation schemes for managers and the need for delegated monitoring also induce imperfect diversification, or individuals may hold much of their wealth in the form of non-diversifiable human capital.

5 Entrepreneurs have greater certainty about investment returns in earlier periods than in later periods

I refer to the concept of *information-sensitivity* to characterize risky investments. The value of risky investments is dependent upon future revelations of information about the world, and therefore is information-sensitive.

Entrepreneurs are more likely to correctly forecast consumer demands and costs for the near future, and are less likely to correctly forecast demands and costs for the far future. More generally, individuals find it harder to predict the more distant future, which is more information-sensitive. Investors can build (irreversible) hula hoop factories and immediately prosper from a current fad, but returns over time will be very risky. Hula hoops may either become an established institution or may fall out of favor completely. Undertaking risky investments may bring an immediate boom, but also creates long-run commitments which are costly to reverse. The value of the original information which motivated the investment will decay over time. Long-term commitments, even when profitable, become increasingly precarious over time.[5]

Of all the assumptions listed, informational decay is the least essential to the basic mechanics of the theory. Informational decay, however, will be used to help generate comovement along the upward and downward swings of the cycle.

Informational decay does not contradict the stylized facts that many businesses go bankrupt in the first year, or that the longer a business survives, the longer it is likely to survive. As time passes, the risk of *successful* investments may decrease, rather than increase. (Investors learn that individuals have a steady demand for Coca-Cola, for instance.) Yet overall investment risk still increases with the passage of time; assumption 5 refers to the risk across both subsequent survivors and failures. We do not always 'see' risk increasing over time because the bad outcomes tend

---

[5] Contrary to assumption, in some cases entrepreneurs may have better information about long-run variable values than short-run values for some economic processes. Henry Ford, for instance, may have realized that the demand for automobiles would be very strong in thirty years' time, even if he could not forecast the demand very well for the forthcoming year. Similarly, entrepreneurs might know that everyone will be on the Internet after ten years, even if they cannot forecast the demand for next year with much accuracy. I treat these cases as the exception rather than the rule. Reversing the temporal increase in risk, however, requires only a partial modification of the basic business cycle scenario, as will be discussed further.

to be terminated. Instead of perceiving an ongoing increase in risk over time, we see the errors being truncated, or we see good projects, which may not appear risky *ex post*.

6 An exogenous increase in the real economic risk of investments will induce a contraction of investment

An exogenous increase in aggregate volatility increases the demand for relatively safe assets. In a simple capital asset pricing model with a quadratic utility function, for instance, an increase in systematic market risk will increase the demand for the safe or minimum-Beta asset. More generally, this comparative statics effect follows from the positive relationship between risk and expected return. An increase in the risk of an asset (or class of assets) brings a higher expected return only by inducing investors to move out of that risky asset, thereby inducing a fall in its price.

The specified effects of aggregate risk increases do not follow *a priori*. Under some assumptions, increased aggregate risk actually can increase the demand for the high-yielding, risky asset. Investors who seek a threshold level of return, for instance, may increase their demand for the risky asset in response to the aggregate risk increase; this effect will work through the third derivative of the utility function. Holding more of the risky asset may increase that investor's chance of reaching the specified threshold level. I assume away portfolio effects operating through the third derivative; in any case, their incorporation would not modify the essentials of the subsequent theory.[6]

INDUCED INCREASES IN RISK

Risk-based business cycle theories offer two basic scenarios, depending on whether there is an initial increase in risk-taking or an initial decrease. Under the first scenario, a variety of real factors (discussed immediately below) encourage or induce an expansion of risky, long-term investment. This increase in risk, at least in the short run, is accompanied by an increase in expected returns. If we look at wealth without adjusting for risk, the economy appears better off, and a short-term boom occurs. In the medium to long run, the boom will persist when the risky investments pay off, and the boom will lead to a crash when the risky investments do not succeed. In the context of Figure 2.2, this scenario can be represented by a rightward shift of the loanable funds supply curve. The lower interest rate induces

---

[6] On portfolio effects through third derivatives, see Kimball (1990). The case where increased aggregate risk increases the demand for the risky asset is discussed further. On the effects of risk on the demand for risky investments more generally, Craine (1989) provides the most general treatment of the subject.

greater investment, which increases risk and implies a move to projects with expected higher yields.

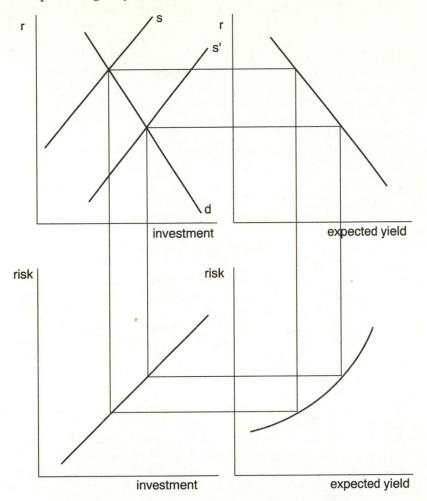

Figure 2.2 Comparative statics of a loanable funds supply shift

The initial increase in risky investment may stem from a variety of factors, most of which are examples of an outward expansion of individual opportunity sets. I will consider five different expansionary causes. First, sudden preference shifts may induce entrepreneurs to accept more risk; changes in Keynesian 'animal spirits' may account for some of the variation in investment and risk.

Second, supply-side factors in the loanable funds market, such as savings increases or monetary policy, may induce the real rate of interest to fall (the operation of monetary policy is considered more fully in the next chapter). The additional quantity of loanable funds lowers the price of borrowing and changes present value calculations, thereby encouraging risky, long-term investment, in accord with assumption 2 above. This scenario has been the center of focus of the traditional Austrian theory. McCulloch (1981) presents a related account, in purely real terms, of why entrepreneurs might extend long-term investment activity. In his approach, the maturity transformation of financial intermediaries ('misintermediation,' in his view) brings about an increase in long-term investment. Aftalion (1927) also considers extensions of long-term investment based primarily on real factors.[7]

Third, the easing of finance constraints may stimulate investment. If lenders ration credit, exogenous changes may improve the efficiency of the loan market. Borrowers' collateral may increase in value, monitoring technologies may increase in efficacy, moral hazard problems may decrease, or lenders may discover more innovative contracts and covenants, to name a few possible reasons for shifts in lending policy.

Fourth, the resolution of uncertainty may encourage investment. When investment commitments are costly to reverse, entrepreneurs may prefer to wait and exercise option value, sampling more information in lieu of making a definite commitment (Dixit and Pindyck 1994). The greater the volatility of the economic environment, the greater the returns to waiting. Once volatility decreases, or the relevant uncertainty has been resolved, entrepreneurs may proceed with their investment plans. To the extent the relevant uncertainty is economy-wide (e.g., the price of oil, the budget deficit, etc.), resolution of the uncertainty may induce relatively large swings in aggregate investment.

Uncertainty resolution holds particular importance for relatively long-term investments. The longer the investment is in place, the greater the scope and chance for subsequent changes in the data, and the more precarious the implied long-term commitment (Baldwin and Meyer 1979).

Fifth, positive shocks to retained earnings will encourage investment. Businesses may either be initially credit constrained, or they may simply prefer to fund investment out of retained earnings, to avoid external oversight or control (Myers and Majluf 1984; Myers 1984). The positive shock to retained earnings must itself come from some other cause, such as a positive technology shock or a Keynesian-style demand shock. This

---

[7] In some models of irreversible investment, decreases (increases) in the real interest rate can cause investment to fall (rise) in the short run. A lower real interest rate decreases the cost of waiting and sampling more information. Although investment may decline in the short run, expected long-run investment will still rise, due to the substitution effect (Ingersoll and Ross 1992). Even if entrepreneurs exercise option value – waiting to sample more information – at some point further investment will be forthcoming. Entrepreneurs cannot earn high returns by exercising option value forever.

scenario therefore borrows from other business cycle theories to explain the source of the original shock, but nonetheless presents an investment-based propagation mechanism of how that shock increases economic risk and cyclicality.

Combinations of these shocks will induce increases in investment, risk, and economic cyclicality. For the purposes of this discussion, it does not matter which particular causes induce the investment increase. In all of these cases the price of risky investments falls and entrepreneurs accept more risk voluntarily. Entrepreneurs will shift from previous low-risk projects to new, higher risk projects with greater expected returns. The expected rate of growth, the degree of aggregate risk, and the likelihood of both booms and busts, will all increase. The economy will become more cyclical.

The above business cycle mechanism involves three main problems, which I will discuss in turn. The theory may not be consistent with observed measurements of the interest elasticity of investment, the theory may not be able to account for the comovement of the boom, and the theory may not be able to explain why entrepreneurial errors come in clusters during the business cycle downturn.

The 'elasticities of substitution' criticism

Some critics have argued that measured microeconomic elasticities of substitution do not suffice to generate large-scale cyclical movements, whether the variable be labor supply or the interest elasticity of investment. Lucas (1981), for instance, rejects the (traditional) Austrian theory of the business cycle on these grounds. He argues that the Austrian theory requires an implausibly large interest elasticity of investment to generate observed fluctuations in investment activity. Aggregate investment fluctuates considerably over the cycle, but microeconomic estimates of the interest elasticity of aggregate investment are relatively small.

The interest elasticity of investment presents a potential vulnerability for investment-based cyclical theories. If declines in real interest rates have only weak effects on economic activity, the resulting sectoral shocks will be too small to cause business cycles. Chapter 5 will examine some issues concerning empirical magnitudes, but several theoretical considerations imply that low measured interest elasticities of aggregate investment need not discriminate against investment-based business cycle mechanisms.

Most generally, changes in real interest rates are not the only potential influence on investment, as discussed above. Lucas correctly criticizes over-reliance on real interest rate mechanisms, but we need not reject investment-based theories as a result. Changes in expectations, shocks to retained earnings, relaxation of finance constraints, and uncertainty resolution all may play critical roles in the cycle.

Even the scenarios which rely on the real interest mechanism do not require that interest elasticity accounts for all of the change in investment over the cycle. The shocks discussed above initiate only the first round of investment fluctuations in the model. To the extent these investments succeed or appear profitable, subsequent changes in incomes and expectations will induce further investment. It is not necessary that all, or even most, observed fluctuations in investment can be traced to the initial shock. The initial investment shock sets off the boom of the cycle, but subsequent investment fluctuations may be caused by the internal dynamics of the boom itself, such as income and expectational effects.

Investment-based cyclical scenarios also involve changes in the composition of investment, rather than changes in the aggregate; these effects will not necessarily show up in measurements of aggregate elasticities. Lower real interest rates, for instance, may induce entrepreneurs to shift from safer short-term investments to riskier long-term investments, giving rise to greater risk and greater cyclicality. Small interest rate changes may induce large shifts in the composition of investment even when the measured interest elasticity for aggregate investment is zero. The subsequent moves in aggregate investment, as observed across the cycle, may follow from income effects, resulting from whether the chosen composition of investment succeeds or fails.

Another criticism of investment-based theories, based on irreversible investment models, rejects the significance of real interest rate effects for a different reason. Pindyck and Solimano (1993, p. 1), for instance, argue that the irreversible nature of investment decisions causes investors to require an expected profit hurdle rate of three or four times the cost of capital; in the absence of high expected profits, investors will prefer to wait and sample more information. With such high hurdle rates for capital investment, changes in borrowing rates appear to have insignificant effects.

The costliness of reversing investment does not rule out or even necessarily diminish the scope for real interest rate effects. When entrepreneurs decide they are ready to commit resources, the real interest rate still can influence whether they commit their resources to investment or consumption. Irreversible investment models typically show only that the real interest rate may have a small influence on the timing of resource commitments, not on the type of commitment (investment vs. consumption) that is made, once entrepreneurs make a commitment. The models compare investment and waiting to invest, rather than considering a tripartite choice among investment, consumption, and waiting.

Presentations of irreversible investment theory do not distinguish between the kind of resource commitment and its timing with sufficient clarity. Many irreversible investment models define the investment decision as identical to the resource commitment decision, which gives rise to misleading conclusions about the interest elasticity of investment. Since

28

investment is the only postulated alternative to waiting, the decision to invest is identical with a decision to stop waiting. If the real interest rate does not much affect the value of waiting, the real interest rate will appear to have little influence over investment as well.

When a tripartite option is considered, the decision to stop waiting means that entrepreneurs face a further choice between consumption and investment. This latter choice, not considered in most irreversible investment models, implies that investment may be elastic with regard to the real interest rate. Consumption, like investment, also constitutes an irreversible resource commitment. Even when the utility value of consumption is certain, the opportunity cost of consumption (e.g., the potential returns on forgone investment) is not certain. Consumption thus involves an irreversible commitment of resources under conditions of uncertainty. When investors decide to stop waiting and to act, the real interest rate will influence which *kind* of irreversible commitment they choose – investment or consumption. Traditional investment theory focuses on the question of which kind of resource commitment will be made, consumption or investment; irreversible investment theory focuses on whether a resource commitment will be made at all. The potential insignificance of the real interest rate for the latter decision does not imply insignificance of the real interest rate for the former decision.

Just as irreversible investment models, properly interpreted, leave room for the real interest rate to influence the choice between consumption and investment, so may the real interest rate influence the kind of irreversible investment that is undertaken. When entrepreneurs are waiting and sampling additional information about macroeconomic events, at some point they will reach the relevant threshold of knowledge, and the returns to waiting will decline. Relative prices, such as real interest rates, still will play their traditional role in influencing the kind of investment commitment which is made.

What generates the comovement of the boom?

Advocates of Austrian business cycle theory did not explicitly address the issue of comovement; furthermore, the basic Austrian cycle theory appears to contradict comovement. In Hayek's *Prices and Production*, and in other early Austrian writings, long-term investments expand when short-term investments contract, and vice versa. Hayek, in his other writings on capital theory, argued explicitly that investment goods and consumer goods were substitute outputs. Yet business cycles consist of large waves of expansion or contraction across many economic sectors, not just resource shifts or transfers across sectors. Investment-based theories of the business cycle therefore experience difficulties in explaining the increases in the output of consumer goods that we observe over the course of the boom. Cooper and Ejarque (1994) make a similar point, although they focus on modern versions of investment-based business cycle mechanisms rather than the Austrian view.

Positive comovement poses a dilemma for theories of the business cycle expansion which start with the assumption of full employment. Comovement requires that all, or nearly all sectors of the economy expand at once, as we usually find in the data. Such a general expansion requires a relaxation of real resource constraints; real business cycle theory advocates sometimes cite this point in support of approaches based on aggregate productivity shocks. If we start with a full employment assumption, the production possibilities frontier must expand to generate positive comovement.

Positive comovement across the boom may be derived from a variety of mechanisms. Extant explanations of positive comovement include the desire to smooth consumption gains and losses across sectors (Long and Plosser 1983), increasing returns and strategic complementarities, and the effects of high demand on profits and output when production involves fixed costs (Murphy *et al.* 1989). Investment-based business cycle theories could be modified to include such factors, if explaining comovement were the primary purpose at hand.

Some potential explanations of comovement arise from the investment mechanism itself. Shifts towards risky, information-sensitive investments tend to create economic booms, at least initially. Those risky investments involve relatively high average returns. Even if a high percentage of these investments later are revealed to be malinvestments, expected pecuniary wealth has risen in the early periods, following initial implementation of those projects. The increase in expected wealth will increase demands for all normal goods. The move to higher-yielding projects will give the economy the supply capacity to meet many of these increased demands. Both demands and supplies may rise in conjunction. A fully employed equilibrium economy can advance across all, or nearly all sectors, by accepting a greater degree of risk and thus higher expected returns.

Debates in the 1930s and 1940s concerned whether unemployed resources could be mobilized to maintain simultaneous expansion in consumer and capital goods industries. Hayek argued that expansions in one sector must come at the expense of the other sector. *Contra* Hayek, the Keynesians assumed the existence of unemployed resources and promoted the 'accelerator' view. In this account, increases in the demands for consumption goods cause complementary increases in the demand for investment goods. Examining the risk–return trade-off for investments creates a position of middle ground on this debate. Full employment of resources is a matter of degree rather than a matter of kind. Even when resources are 'fully employed' twenty-four hours a day, entrepreneurs can increase returns by shifting to riskier, higher-yielding projects.

The move to risky, high-yielding investments can account partially for the mild pro-cyclical productivity found in the data. Although changes in employment account for most of the observed variation in output, productivity none the less tends to rise in booms and fall in downturns. Modern real business cycle theories typically account for such productivity changes in terms of positive and negative shocks to the production function. Yet critics (e.g., de Long 1990; Stiglitz 1992) have pointed out that most booms are not preceded by observable technological advancements, and most busts are not preceded by observable technological regressions. Furthermore, technological regression resists definition when society can store information cheaply; effective technologies cannot easily be forgotten or lost.

Pro-cyclical productivity may come from changes in entrepreneurial willingness to invest and take risks, rather than from changes in the prevailing state of technological knowledge. Capitalist economies always possess potential innovations that have not yet been implemented. The potential innovations, despite their higher expected physical productivity, require a higher tolerance for risk or a lower discount rate for their implementation in the form of concrete projects. Productivity rises when entrepreneurs can be induced to implement these innovations.

The risk–return trade-off is not the only mechanism for linking investment increases and positive comovement. The positive shocks to investment, discussed above, involve increases in the expected marginal product of capital. Capital owners will feel wealthier, and will devote their capital inputs to higher-yielding projects and will work their capital more intensively. To the extent capital and labor are complements, increases in the supply of capital will bring corresponding increases in the supply of labor.

Hercowitz (1986) uses the real business cycle theory technique of simulation to address whether shocks to the marginal product of capital can generate sufficient comovement to account for the data. Using standard procedures, Hercowitz builds an 'artificial economy,' calibrated with estimates of real world supply and demand functions, and introduces shocks into that economy. Hercowitz's calibration places central importance on the time to build phenomenon. Production of outputs requires initial investment of inputs plus the passage of time; he measures the representative period of production as ranging from fourteen to sixteen months. When production takes time, declines in the real interest rate increase the productivity of capital. Higher rates of capital productivity lead to higher rates of investment, capital utilization, and labor demand. Hercowitz generates employment effects from the assumption that capital services and labor services are complements. Lower real interest rates therefore have expansionary effects, not only on aggregate demand, but also on aggregate supply. Consumption, investment, labor supply, and production all comove conversely with the real interest rate.

31

The model simulated by Hercowitz reproduces many essential features of business cycles. In addition to generating comovement, the simulations generate relatively large fluctuations in output. When the real interest rate is defined in terms of the producer price index, a 1 percentage point increase in the real interest rate, for instance, induces output to fall by 0.53 of a percent, and labor input by 0.28 of a percent. When the real interest rate is defined in terms of the consumer price index, the effects increase. A 1 percentage point increase in the real interest rate causes output to decrease by 0.91 percent, and causes labor input to decrease by 0.39 percent.[8]

Informational decay over time also may support comovement and the initial boom. The previous point about returns and risk emphasized high *expected* returns in early periods of the cycle; this point emphasizes high *realized* returns in early periods of the cycle. We can enjoy a temporary boom, for instance, to the extent that entrepreneurs invest on the basis of current fads. The informational presuppositions behind those investments remain fresh in the short run. Realized returns may be especially high in early periods, even though the long-run risks are extreme, given the volatile nature of tastes and fads.[9]

Some investments even may increase the quantity of consumer goods in the short run. A new factory, for instance, might not take long to build (the project still may qualify as a risky, long-term investment because of the durability of the factory). When the new consumer goods arrive on the

---

[8] Hercowitz calibrates his model by drawing on the Canadian economy; he claims that Canada provides the clearest case of an advanced economy with exogenous real interest rate shocks. Once the artificial Canadian economy has been constructed, the real interest rate shocks are taken from American data; he assumes that Canada and America must share the same real interest rate, as determined predominantly in America. Models with real interest rate effects, but without time to build, have yielded different results. In the treatment of Merrick (1984), capital serves as a depreciable, non-renewable stock. Increases in the real interest rate, which are taken as pro-cyclical, cause capital utilization rates to increase. The labor demand schedule therefore shifts out, creating positive employment effects. Merrick tries to generate positive employment effects through the cycle by generating a shift in labor demand, thereby avoiding sole reliance on movements along the labor supply function. Merrick himself notes, however, that if new investment were included in the model, such investment would be counter-cyclical, contrary to observed fact (Merrick 1984, p. 29). Hercowitz (1986, p. 129) compares his approach with Merrick's and emphasizes the importance of the time to build factor in distinguishing the two models.

[9] Note how the cyclical story may vary if investors hold better information about the distant future than about the near future; that is, if we reverse assumption 5 about informational decay. The increase of cyclicality, and the potential for a downturn, would come in the short run rather than after some period of informational decay. A boom or bust would arrive very quickly. After the initial bust or boom ended, the economy would then settle into a relatively healthy high expected return state, at least on average. The relatively sound long-run entrepreneurial predictions would all come to fruition in these later periods, once the economy recovers from the short-run volatility caused by entrepreneurial inability to predict the very near future. The other factors discussed above, however, may still work to enforce traditional comovement, even if informational decay does not.

market quickly, real purchasing power over goods and services will have risen. Comovement is easy to generate in this case.

Positive comovement becomes more difficult to the extent that the new consumer goods do not arrive until the distant future; that is, when the factory takes a long time to build. After the marginal product of capital has risen, the value of capital assets will have risen and individuals will feel wealthier. Given that wealth has increased and future output will be higher, individuals can draw some resources away from previous investments and towards consumption. Both consumption and investment may rise simultaneously, in the aggregate, even though some investments decline or are interrupted. The readjustment of some investment resources towards consumption will, however, induce adjustment costs, which will militate against comovement to some degree.

Finally, much of the positive comovement observed in the actual data springs from the presence of initially unemployed resources. As the business cycle enters its upward phase, previously unemployed capital and labor resources face higher demand for their services. If these factors can be mobilized and brought to employment, through whatever mechanism, we have accounted for much of the observed positive comovement with a relatively theory-neutral construct. Investment-based business cycle theories can use this explanation of positive comovement just as Keynesian and non-market-clearing theories do.

While the basic exposition in this chapter assumes full employment, a richer, more complex treatment could relax this assumption. Even if we choose to stick with the full employment assumption, real world data on comovement typically come from a world with unemployed resources. Full employment assumptions are useful for the theorist, but we should not expect a theory based on a full employment assumption to mimic perfectly the time series behavior of a world with unemployed resources.

Behavior of wages and money supply

The increase in investment which drives the cycle should increase the marginal product of labor, which implies pro-cyclical real wages. Empirically measured real wages are slightly pro-cyclical, remaining largely flat over the course of the cycle.[10]

Tullock (1988, p. 77), in his critique of Austrian business cycle theory and investment-based theories more generally, asked whether real wages can rise when investment increases during the boom. Increases in investment are typically identified with a boom, yet entrepreneurs are producing

---

[10] Black (1995), however, emphasizes that real wages, if we include human capital acquisition, may in fact be strongly pro-cyclical. Incorporating this factor would create no difficulties for the considerations examined below.

more goods for the relatively distant future. We might expect the increase in investment to pull resources away from the immediate production of consumer goods and cause real wages to fall. Similarly, the so-called bust might appear to improve immediate living standards, as resources are shifted away from long-term investment and back into consumer goods production. Those predictions contradict the data and violate our usual intuitions about 'booms' and 'busts.' In spite of Tullock's critique, wages may be pro-cyclical to the extent that the theory can generate positive comovement. The wage puzzle does not present a separate difficulty for investment-based theories, if we can account for comovement, as discussed above.

If we introduce money into the theory as a purely passive force, the monetary aggregates also will be pro-cyclical, as we observe in the data. The broader monetary aggregates are endogenous and will rise with output in booms and contract with output in busts, as analyzed by King and Plosser (1984). Inside money is both an output of banks and an input into the production of other goods. When economic activity rises, both the demand for and the supply of inside money will rise as well.

The price level may be either pro- or countercyclical, depending on the strength of comovement across sectors. Prices will be countercyclical to the extent that the output of consumer goods rises in the boom, and to the extent that money supply increases are small. Prices will be pro-cyclical to the extent that money supply increases are large, and to the extent that increases in investment pull resources away from the production of consumer goods.

The bust and the cluster of errors?

Sustainable booms arise when entrepreneurs correctly choose the proper investments in accord with the subsequent real data. High-risk, information-sensitive investments offer especially high pay-offs if they turn out to be based on correct forecasts. Entrepreneurial interpretations of the initial information do not decay in value but, rather, turn out to have been prescient. For instance, entrepreneurs may have guessed correctly that current demand-side 'fads' will prove permanent. Early returns will have been high, due to project risk, but returns over time will prove even higher as initial forecasts are validated by the data.

When entrepreneurs systematically choose the wrong projects, the initial boom turns into a business downturn. The freshness of the initial information behind risky long-term investment decisions provides initially high returns. Yet returns eventually dwindle as the value of initial information decays over time. The demand for 'moon rocks,' for instance, turned out to be a fad, rather than a permanent shift in demand. The passage of time will reveal expectational errors, causing the value of long-term investments to decline. The economy subsequently bears the downside of high-risk, information-sensitive investments. The problem is not overinvestment *per se*, but rather that entrepreneurs have chosen the wrong kinds of investment, or malinvestments.

Most simply, negative comovement arises from the resolution of investment project risk. The *ex post* realization of returns does not always generate negative comovement (economies do not always have cycles), but it will sometimes generate a systematic downturn, just as it will sometimes generate a sustainable boom. As discussed above, the Law of Large Numbers does not militate against systematic negative comovement. The number of relevant sectors may be small, entrepreneurs may be forecasting common variables and facing common risks, the risks of different sectors may interact, and the Law of Large Numbers holds for subdivision of a risky prospect, not the multiplication of a risky prospect. All of these sources of negative comovement have been discussed in greater detail above.

Economic declines are spread not only across sectors but also across time. A typical business cycle downturn in the United States, for instance, lasts for one to three years.

Adjustment and misallocation costs help account for the persistent productivity decline experienced during a business downturn. Entrepreneurial errors draw resources away from their most productive uses. Entrepreneurs lock some resources into inferior uses, and in other cases search to find the best employments for resources. In both cases productivity will fall even if the available state of knowledge has not regressed. The irreversibility of long-term investments causes many of these entrepreneurial mistakes to continue through time. When confronted with a loss of economic value, some entrepreneurs will prefer to bear misallocation costs rather than to incur one-time large adjustment costs. These misallocations thus persist through time for the remaining life of the investment, and output and efficiency may remain relatively low for many periods, even if the initial mistake was made much earlier. Representative agent real business cycle constructs, which rule out coordination failures, do not have recourse to these sources of productivity decline.[11]

The 'time to build' model of Kydland and Prescott (1982) provides a related source of persistence. The time needed to complete a capital project is long relative to the average length of a business cycle (see Table 1.1 for some figures). Along these lines, Austrian capital theory has traditionally stressed the time-consuming nature of production. If negative shocks induce entrepreneurs to limit their investments today, outputs of

---

[11] Wood (1984), in his illuminating discussion of the traditional Austrian theory, claims misallocation costs are likely to exceed adjustment costs. He argues that profit maximization usually implies finishing long-term projects, even when such projects are unprofitable when all sunk and fixed costs are taken into account.

intermediate and final goods will remain low for subsequent periods, even after investment resumes. Christiano and Todd (1996) extend analyses of this kind by incorporating a 'time to plan' as well.[12]

The durability of capital, in addition to its time period of production, also supports persistence. If investments last several years, investments based on forecast errors will lower growth rates over the entire life span of the relevant capital goods. The time dimension of capital includes not only the time it takes to complete the project, but also the time until the final outputs are consumed.

Persistence also may arise from the desire to smooth consumption losses through time (Long and Plosser 1983). If entrepreneurs suffer a forthcoming loss in consumption value, they will reallocate resources to make up for this deficiency. Consumption smoothing dictates that some long-term projects will be redirected to make up for the forthcoming output deficiency. Output declines in the present or near future will be translated into partial output declines for subsequent periods as well, given the utility-maximizing response of consumers.

Finally, persistence may arise from the autocorrelation of shocks through time (Kydland and Prescott 1982). The probability distribution for the relevant negative shocks may not consist of a series of totally independent observations. Rather, extremely negative shocks, far from the population mean for a given variable, sometimes will come bunched together in time. Entrepreneurs with rational expectations will not always correctly estimate the forthcoming degree of autocorrelation in shocks, although entrepreneurs will correctly forecast the expected degree of autocorrelation on average. When the extent of shock autocorrelation is especially high and above the population mean, periods of resource malinvestment will tend to come bunched together in time.

VOLATILITY AND IMMEDIATE BUSINESS CYCLE CONTRACTIONS

The second real scenario in the risk-based approach involves an exogenous decrease in the attractiveness of risky investments. The five factors which lead to investment booms, discussed earlier in this chapter, can be reversed to produce immediate investment contractions. The list of contractionary causes therefore includes lower risk tolerance, higher time preferences and real interest rates, tighter finance constraints, negative shocks to retained earnings, and increases in uncertainty or economic volatility. Combinations

---

[12] Rouwenhorst (1991) criticizes Kydland and Prescott on the grounds that they rely on autocorrelated shocks for most of their persistence; he does not, however, dispute that time to build, in principle, can generate persistence.

of these factors will induce entrepreneurs to move away from risky invest-ment commitments, as specified by assumption 6 above.[13]

When individuals perceive a higher net cost for risky investments, the economy experiences an investment contraction rather than an investment boom. As a matter of logic, any investment-based business cycle theory which starts with a boom implies a sister scenario where investment contracts without an initial boom. As a matter of empirical fact, downturns are not always preceded by supra-normal booms.

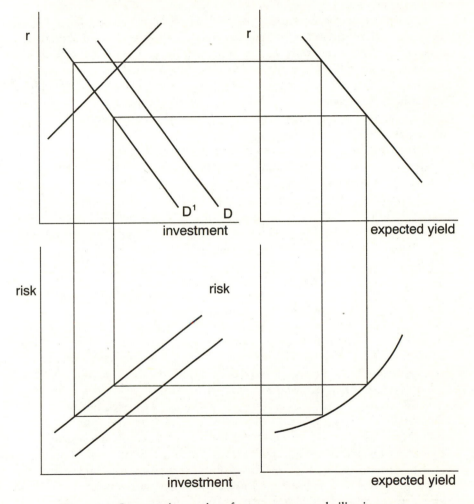

Figure 2.3 Comparative statics of an exogenous volatility increase

---

[13] Note that if exogenous increases in risk increased the demand for investment goods, *contra* assumption 6, we could simply reverse the initial shock to set this version of the cycle in motion.

The arrival of such economic downturns consists of two distinct phenomena. The economy moves from higher-yielding investments to lower-yielding investments, and some previous investments are revealed to have been malinvestments. Entrepreneurs undertook previous investments with expectations that did not come to fruition. Once the relevant change in perceived risk arrives, the economy is revealed to be overinvested in risky endeavors, bringing misallocation and adjustment costs. The economy suffers a form of stagflation, with no boom, an initial downturn, and a lower rate of economic growth (Mascaro and Meltzer 1983).

The details of the downturn proceed as analyzed above. In terms of Figure 2.3, the process can be represented by an initial upward shift of the risk–return locus. This shift, in turn, operates through portfolio effects and eventually causes the demand for loanable funds schedule to move down to the left. Greater risk increases the expected yield required to induce investment. Investment and expected yield will decline, leading to an economic downturn. The final degree of cyclicality may be either higher or lower, as discussed above.

Exogenous increases in volatility may cause an economy to experience both a lower rate of growth and a greater degree of cyclicality. The lower rate of growth comes from the move to lower-yielding investments, from the contraction of investment opportunities brought by the risk increase, and from the adjustment costs of altering investments. Aggregate risk and cyclicality may either rise or fall. On one hand, a given project will involve more risk than before. To the extent that substitution towards safer projects is limited, aggregate risk will tend to rise. On the other hand, entrepreneurs will counteract the overall increase in portfolio riskiness by shifting towards projects or resource allocations which are safer than the allocations they had chosen previously. Aggregate riskiness may decline.

If aggregate risk increases, business cycles will be more frequent and more extreme when they arrive. Entrepreneurs may end up with a riskier overall portfolio of projects, even if they engage in some switching to less risky projects. Many projects have become more risky, and the switch to relatively less risky projects still may leave more risk than before the negative shock arrived. If aggregate risk decreases, however, business cycles will become less frequent. A decrease in aggregate risk implies entrepreneurs have switched to an especially safe package of projects, making future booms and busts less likely. In this case the resulting decline in the rate of growth is likely to be especially severe. The switching effect (to safer, lower-yielding investments) must outweigh the increase in riskiness effect (the increased risk for a given class of investments).

To the extent the switching effect towards safer investments is strong, the difference between returns on risky and non-risky investments will increase. The resulting differential implies especially high relative returns, should entrepreneurs ever wish to take on more risk again. Entrepreneurs have shied away from long-term investments, giving those investments especially high returns if entrepreneurs can forecast the future with accuracy. An entrepreneur with perfect knowledge could well earn greater profits, even though (uncertain) entrepreneurs as a whole earn lower returns and bear more risk.

These results mirror common intuitions about economic volatility. Higher levels of volatility induce undesirable economic results. Output declines and economic cyclicality may even rise. Overall, entrepreneurs face less favorable risk–return trade-offs. Those individuals who can foresee the future in especially risky times, however, may profit extraordinarily, just as gold buyers did in the 1970s.

The analysis of exogenous volatility shocks mirrors Keynesian theory and suggests a link between Austrian and Keynesian approaches to business cycles. The increase in economic volatility, discussed directly above, plays a role analogous to Keynes's increase in liquidity preference. Some Keynesian scenarios also postulate a move from higher-yielding to lower-yielding investments (Cowen and Kroszner 1994b). Alternatively, pessimistic 'animal spirits' might imply that perceived risk has increased, whether or not actual risk has increased. In either case entrepreneurs will shift from high-yielding investments to lower-yielding investments; Keynes designated the latter investments, probably in overly restrictive fashion, as holdings of liquid money. In any case the decline in investment brings an economic contraction.

The framework of this chapter implies that the scenarios of Keynes and Hayek can be interpreted as two special cases of a more general theory of intertemporal coordination. Keynes focused on the case where entrepreneurs had initially over-invested in risky high-yielding endeavors and must later contract their commitments. A real shock to either consumption or expectations induces this contraction; initial market price signals had not signaled these subsequent changes or given entrepreneurs sufficient knowledge of the need for a subsequent contraction. When the initial commitments were made, entrepreneurs had underestimated the subsequent level of economic volatility or they had over-estimated their ability to deal with changes in the economic data.

Hayek, in contrast, focused on the case where government monetary policy induces an increase in capital-intensive investments (risky investments, in my modification of the Austrian approach). These initial commitments must later be reversed, again leading to a contraction. *Ex post* demands turn out to differ from the *ex ante* demands that had been signaled by monetary policy. Rather than postulating that the market sends inadequate signals about future demands, as Keynes did, Hayek argued the government sometimes sends false signals (see Chapter 4). In the scenarios of both Keynes and Hayek, however, the downturn is brought on by the move away from risky, capital-intensive, high-yielding investments (my terminology, not theirs), and towards safer, lower-yielding investments.

Monetary sources of real economic volatility

Although this chapter focuses on real cycles, increases in the volatility of the real economic environment may come from monetary shocks as well. We can imagine the appointment of a new, irresponsible head of the central bank, a detrimental change in fiscal policy, or unfavorable electoral results, to name a few examples of volatility-increasing shocks. By assumption, the increase in money supply volatility does not operate in counter-cyclical fashion, and is not used to offset real shocks to loanable funds supply. Volatile loanable funds supply, induced by volatile inflation, increases uncertainty about future real interest rates, future investments, future prices, and future quantities. By assumption, individuals can read the current money supply, but they cannot predict future money supplies with perfect accuracy. Increased monetary volatility thus leads to a contraction of high-risk, high-return investments, as postulated by assumption 6.

Volatile inflation may increase real interest rate volatility through at least three mechanisms. First, volatility in the supply of loanable funds will induce real interest rate volatility through the mechanisms discussed in Chapter 3, on how money affects real variables. Second, entrepreneurs find the forthcoming rate of price inflation more difficult to forecast when monetary policy is volatile. True, *ex post* realized borrowing rates will become more volatile through the increased unreliability of the Fisher effect.[14] Third, nominal interest rate volatility implies real interest rate volatility when not all individuals face the same price level. A 5 percent rate of money growth may push up prices 5 percent on average, but most individuals will experience differing rates of price inflation for their consumption basket (Michael 1979; Patel and Zeckhauser 1990). Some individuals will face more than 5 percent price inflation and others will face less than 5 percent price inflation. Even if the nominal rate of interest rises 5 percent (i.e., a normal full Fisher effect), inflation will change the real interest rates that most individuals face. Some individuals will face higher real rates, and others will face lower real rates, even if the average real rate remains constant.

The volatility of loanable funds supply and real interest rates implies a corresponding volatility of relative prices for risky, long-term investment goods. Increases in loanable funds supply tend to raise the relative price of long-term capital goods. Similarly, decreases in loanable funds supply

---

[14] Inflation volatility also might lead to a volatile and changing risk premium on borrowing and lending rates. *Changes* in the expected scope of volatility, however, are needed for this result. Volatility itself produces only a constant risk premium.

lower the relative price of long-term capital goods. Loanable funds supply volatility spreads to the structure of relative prices in the economy, and entrepreneurs find it more difficult to forecast the relative profitability of differing investments.

The volatility of real interest rates and relative prices induces a corresponding volatility in quantities. To the extent future prices are volatile and uncertain, the quantities of goods supplied will be uncertain as well. If entrepreneurs cannot accurately guess the future price of cement, for instance, the future quantity of cement production will be uncertain as well. Some entrepreneurs will regard cement as either a relevant complement or relevant substitute for their own activities; these entrepreneurs will face greater uncertainty about future quantities.

Inflation volatility also tends to induce real economic volatility through mechanisms distinct from the loanable funds market. Under nominally based tax systems inflation has real effects on measured business profits, marginal rates of income and capital gains taxation, and the real value of any nominally based deductibility expense. Inflation also produces well-known 'shoe leather' costs through its tax on currency holdings. The higher the rate of inflation, the lower the quantity of real balances held, and the greater the shoe leather costs incurred. In economies with nominal rigidities, whether these rigidities be sticky prices or nominally based regulations (e.g., the minimum wage), the absolute level of prices affects real variables. Although the theories of this book focus on the loanable funds market, these factors none the less operate in the real world and create further links between volatile inflation and economic uncertainty.

The real volatility created by monetary volatility will induce entrepreneurs to increase their demands for relatively safe assets, such as money and short-term government debt, and to decrease their demands for riskier, higher-yielding assets. Gertler and Grinols (1982) and Mascaro and Meltzer (1983) focus on this effect in their studies of monetary volatility. The economy will move to a lower growth equilibrium, for reasons outlined in the previous chapter. Long-run cyclicality may either increase or decrease, again for the reasons outlined previously. On one hand, entrepreneurs move to a safer mix of projects; on the other hand, the world is more volatile in real terms.

Market participants might use interest rate futures, CPI futures, loan commitments, or trading in the term structure of interest rates to protect themselves against inflation uncertainty. Perfect hedges against future inflation rates do not, however, render inflation volatility irrelevant. Inflation not only creates price risk but also creates real economic risk, as emphasized in the discussion immediately above. Inflation brings sectoral shocks and affects how real economic resources *ought* to be allocated. Changes in real interest rates, for instance, do not represent exogenous price shocks but instead reflect real intertemporal shifts in quantities and expenditure patterns. Hedges and insurance can redistribute the pecuniary risks but they cannot eliminate the real resource costs of incorrect resource allocation decisions. If a given investment should not be made, the real social costs of that malinvestment must be borne, regardless of whether the investor holds a hedged position. For this reason, the scenario for monetary volatility does not require a concomitant assumption that individuals refuse to realize gains from trade in the market for inflation insurance.

Some commentators (e.g., Wood 1984) have suggested that the existence of interest rate futures may invalidate Austrian-type explanations of business cycles. Wood's point assumes that investors face price risk alone through interest rate movements; that is, investors need only control the interest rate they pay without worrying about other real effects of monetary volatility. When risk involves real resource misallocation, however, rather than just price risk from interest rates, investment-based theories remain intact. In fact, hedges may even increase the number of poor investments by lowering their private costs. The institution of a hedging market, by allowing for a more efficient allocation of risk, will increase entrepreneurs' risk tolerance and thus may increase economic cyclicality.

Are business cycles and changes in growth rates essentially the same?

Accepting more risk creates the possibility of a boom/bust cycle and accepting less risk moves the economy to a lower output equilibrium and a lower rate of growth. These two possibilities suggest an asymmetric quality to business cycles. Investing too conservatively involves forgoing superior returns, but does not necessarily bring a cyclical pattern of boom and bust. Entrepreneurs are forgoing higher potential returns, and the economy moves to a lower rate of growth than would otherwise have been possible. Entrepreneurs, had they not erred, could have accepted more risk and more return to their advantage and to the advantage of consumers.

Accepting too much risk, in contrast, brings a greater likelihood of a cyclical pattern. Even if the risky investments turn out to have been mistakes, those investments may still bring positive comovement in the early stages of the cycle, as discussed above. Output, returns, and wealth will first rise and will then later fall.

Business cycle downturns and secular changes in the rate of growth – although derived from a unified investment choice problem – will appear to spring from different causes. Downturns are precipitated by the arrival of new information – information which disappoints the expectations behind the earlier choices of risky, high expected growth projects. The downturn, which comes as a surprise, arrives sharply and without prior warning. The bust starts with the revelation of new information about previous entrepreneurial plans. In contrast, rates of growth may change more slowly, more gradually, and without sharp punctuations or surprises. Growth rates will change as investors alter their preferred mixes between risky high-yielding projects and safe lower-yielding projects.

Investment-based business cycle mechanisms will involve a fundamental asymmetry between busts and changes in the growth rate. At least one class of investments involves potentially high irreversibility costs, by assumption. Not all resource commitments, however, can involve such costs; traders can always decline to commit their resources. Holding T-Bills, or engaging in immediate consumption, for instance, involves only small risks in terms of realized outcomes (as opposed to opportunity costs). Entrepreneurs therefore face a choice between safe, slow growth outcomes and riskier, higher expected growth gambles. Relatively bad outcomes may arise from either the deliberate choice of safe, slow growth projects – a lower rate of growth – or from the disappointment of expectations about risky projects – a business downturn.

The costs of business downturns will be correlated inversely with their frequency. The more costly a series of mistakes, the less likely that those mistakes will be made in the first place. Cost asymmetry helps account for the nature of business cycles as occasional, very costly events. To the extent that downturns are especially costly, the initial causes of downturns – such as excessive risk and excessive investment – are less likely to occur. High potential costs for downturns will push entrepreneurs towards safer projects.

Efficient pricing of risks and returns will imply a correlation between sizes of booms and sizes of busts. The greater the additional expected return to long-term information-sensitive investment, the greater the real wealth created by booms. Yet the greater the rewards of potential booms, the less likely that entrepreneurs will play it safe when choosing term-length *ex ante*. The less likely that entrepreneurs will play it safe, the more likely and the more costly downturns will be. When the economy is highly volatile in the upward direction, it also tends to be highly volatile in the downward direction. For similar reasons, decreases in the risk differential for more risky and less risky resource commitments smooth out the business cycle and increase its frequency. Shifts from more risky to less risky investments will involve smaller expected return differentials; the difference between the best outcomes and the worst outcomes will decline.

3

A RISK-BASED THEORY IN MONETARY TERMS

TWO BASIC MONETARY SCENARIOS

This chapter takes the cyclical mechanisms of the previous chapter and fleshes out the details of how they apply to a monetary economy and monetary policy. The real analysis of Chapter 2 can be translated directly into two basic monetary scenarios for business cycles. In the first scenario, increases in the rate of base money growth lower real interest rates, setting off a boom and a subsequent increase in economic cyclicality. In the second scenario, an increase in monetary uncertainty or volatility induces an economic contraction without any prior boom. The courses of these scenarios already have been presented; this chapter expands upon these scenarios and relates them to the relevant issues in monetary theory and policy.

I will consider whether these two scenarios are consistent with the stylized facts about money and business cycles and then I will examine how the monetary models operate when banks ration credit and loan markets do not clear; in that case monetary policy has real effects through finance constraints rather than real interest rates. How the monetary scenarios vary across institutional regimes, including money supply rules, nominal interest rate smoothing, nominal GNP targeting, commodity monies, and New Monetary Economics systems is discussed as well as the transmission of monetary cycles from one currency area to another. The concluding section considers some foundational issues and examines how and why monetary policy affects real variables and real interest rates at all.

This chapter keeps all of the assumptions outlined in Chapter 2, while focusing on the real effects for monetary policy. As in Chapter 2, I do not assume that investors are fooled by the money supply, or that investors do not understand the effects of monetary inflation.

WHAT STYLIZED FACTS DOES THIS CHAPTER SEEK TO EXPLAIN?

The scenarios discussed here are geared towards accounting for several stylized facts about monetary policy and economic cycles. A realistic monetary theory of the business cycle should at least match current wisdom about the relations between economic variables. In these scenarios, the following properties hold:

1 Increases in nominal money growth stimulate the economy in the short run.
2 Monetary tightenings bring immediate declines in output (Romer and Romer 1989).
3 Higher rates of inflation do not improve economic welfare in the long run, at least on average.
4 The long-run results of any particular instance of money growth cannot be predicted accurately.
5 Monetary policy appears not to matter when we include the nominal interest rate in a vector autoregression (Litterman and Weiss 1985).
6 Expected and unexpected increases in inflation do not bring fundamentally different results (Mishkin 1982).
7 Increases in the volatility of nominal money will induce the growth rate to fall (Mascaro and Meltzer 1983).
8 Stagflation (high inflation and low growth) is possible, but does not always occur.

The monetary scenarios presented above can account for both Keynesian and monetarist intuitions about monetary policy. On one hand, discretionary monetary policy can stimulate the economy in the short run, which accounts for the widespread intuitions behind Keynesianism and most forms of Fed-watching. The increase in investment, induced by monetary policy, will cause a greater output increase in the short run than in the long run. As discussed in Chapter 2, the high expected returns for risky investments and the decay of entrepreneurial forecasts over time create the likelihood of an initial boom, following an increase in investment. That is, monetary policy will initially stimulate the economy, at least on average.

On the other hand, expansionary monetary policy need not improve overall economic performance, at least not if we adjust for risk. By choosing information-sensitive, long-term investments, entrepreneurs invest for expected high returns today but cannot be certain that high returns will persist over time. Doses of monetary inflation will induce a riskier mix of investments. Sometimes monetary discretion will pay off and produce a sustainable boom. Other times the induced increase in investment will lead to clusters of entrepreneurial errors and a subsequent economic downturn. Both the advocates and opponents of monetary discretion will find historical ammunition to support their case. We will observe the same monetary policy, applied in similar circumstances but in different periods of time, producing opposing results. Monetary economics appears to be a subject of great mystery.

Increased monetary volatility, if combined with higher rates of money growth, may create stagflation. Two separate effects will occur at once. The lower real interest rate will encourage a shift towards long-term risky investments, while the increase in volatility will encourage a shift in the opposite direction. The net effect will be uncertain, and long-term investment may either contract or expand. Stagflation can arise when the negative real shocks caused by monetary volatility outweigh the increase in returns induced by higher rates of money growth. Low rates of economic growth, one component of stagflation, will result from the increased monetary volatility. High rates of price inflation, the other component of stagflation, result from the high rate of nominal money growth. Inflation and unemployment will be high simultaneously, as we saw in the 1970s, and contrary to the predictions of Keynesian economics.

Despite the possibility of stagflation, however, an inverse Phillips curve relation will not hold universally. Inflation and unemployment will be positively correlated only when high and volatile inflation occur together, and when the negative effect of volatile inflation on growth outweighs the positive effect of high inflation on returns. We should expect neither a stable Phillips curve, nor a stable inverse Phillips curve relationship over time.

Studies of discretionary monetary policy, if translated into econometric evidence, will present apparent anomalies. Either expected or unexpected money growth will appear to stimulate short-run output in a simple vector autoregression. Adding interest rate measures of monetary policy to that vector autoregression, however, will cause the effects of money growth on output to disappear. Changes in the Federal Funds rate, for instance, may pick up the explanatory power otherwise held by the money supply. Litterman and Weiss (1985), in their well-known econometric investigation of money and output, found a related result. Placing the nominal interest rate in the vector autoregression will cause the significance of money to disappear. Increases in short-term nominal rates will predict subsequent declines in output. The potency which Litterman and Weiss attach to the nominal interest rate therefore may be picking up the real effects of monetary policy (Bernanke and Blinder 1992). The cyclical story presented here potentially accounts for the Litterman and Weiss result, yet without requiring the conclusion that money does not matter (see Chapter 5 for more on this point).

Inflationary monetary policy does not necessarily raise or lower welfare, compared to a tighter monetary policy. Lower real interest rates do increase the likelihood of a cycle, but they also increase the rate of economic growth, on average. Inflation changes the distribution of wealth and moves the economy from one level of risk to another. Welfare economics implies no definite reason for preferring either the *ex ante* or the *ex post* level of risk. If the private sector tends to accept too little risk (perhaps because of imperfect insurance markets), the inflationary decline in real interest rates may improve welfare by encouraging private risk-taking. Conversely, if the private sector is already accepting too much risk, perhaps because of moral hazard problems, government should not use monetary policy to encourage further risk-taking. If we start at a first best situation, the government is choosing among different Pareto points with its monetary policy. We must use other considerations, such as the potential for real costs of inflation, to provide a case for lower rates of monetary growth.

Expected vs. unexpected money growth

Both expected and unexpected increases in money growth will stimulate the economy by lowering real interest rates. The two cases differ primarily with regard to the timing of the expansion. The expected spurt in inflation will bring an increase in risky investment before the rate of money growth actually rises. Entrepreneurs know a real sectoral shock is coming and will start adjusting to the shock before it arrives. Contrary to most rational expectations treatments of monetary policy, a dose of expected money growth can have greater short-run potency than unexpected monetary policy. The expected change in monetary policy induces a quicker increase in high-yield, long-term investments. In contrast, when money growth is unexpected, no initial boom arrives until the money growth actually comes to pass.

The well-known empirical results of Mishkin (1982) support the greater potency of expected inflation, compared to unexpected inflation (see Chapter 5). The theory presented in this chapter is consistent with such results. To the extent Mishkin's evidence holds up, the Fed may wish to announce its intentions when it wishes to engage in short-run stimulation. In the long run, however, expected and unexpected money growth should have roughly equal potency. Expected money growth will make the boom come sooner, but it will not change the risk–return opportunities embedded in the available array of real productive technologies.

HOW MONEY AFFECTS INVESTMENT WHEN BANKS RATION CREDIT

Credit rationing changes the mechanics but not the substance of the monetary scenarios outlined above. Credit rationing forces monetary policy to operate through the absolute availability of loanable funds, rather than through changes in measured real interest rates. When credit rationing is present, changes in the supply of loanable funds lower the real interest rate from infinity to the rate observed in the market, at least for the borrowers who had previously been excluded. I will first briefly consider the mechanics of credit rationing, and then examine how credit rationing could influence business cycle mechanisms.

Credit rationing arises when bank profit maximization implies interest rates below market-clearing levels. The expected profit on a given loan may vary non-monotonically with the real interest rate. Higher real rates may decrease the probability that the loan is ever repaid. First, higher real rates encourage borrowers to incur more risk. The higher the interest rate, the more some of the downside risk is borne by the lending bank, rather than by the borrower. Second, higher real rates may decrease the quality of the borrowing pool. Borrowers who do not expect to pay off their loans will be less deterred by high interest rates (Stiglitz and Weiss 1981). Under these conditions banks will not choke off excess demands for loans by raising interest rates; they will find it more profitable to ration credit. Banks will limit the amount of money any single individual can borrow (at any price), and will turn away some percentage of observationally identical borrowers.

The graph in Figure 3.1 portrays loan markets with credit rationing. Credit rationing corresponds to common-sense observations about borrowing constraints (Chapter 5 considers some of the evidence). Businesses typically cannot borrow unlimited amounts from lenders at a given interest rate. At high enough loan sums, demanders often cannot borrow at all. Unlike many other prices, interest rates represent a promise to pay in the future, rather than a price which is paid today. Simply offering to pay a higher price does not convince the loan supplier that the payment will actually be received, and may in fact create the opposite impression. Deadbeats, who do not expect to pay in any case, will not mind incurring greater obligations.

Non-market-clearing models are distinct from sticky price, wage, or interest rate models. Contrary to popular impression, credit rationing models (and efficiency wage and price models more generally) do *not* derive the existence of price rigidities. In these models real interest rates adjust freely as market conditions and credit risks change. Interest rates are sticky in the following sense only: an outward shift of the supply curve of loanable funds need not lower real interest rates. Rather than thinking of a sticky price or interest rate, credit rationing models generate flexible prices, but set at non-market clearing levels. Prices of this nature move in response to some economic variables, but not in response to all economic variables.

Banks need not hold excess reserves in credit rationing models. The lower real rate of interest, induced by credit rationing, discourages savings

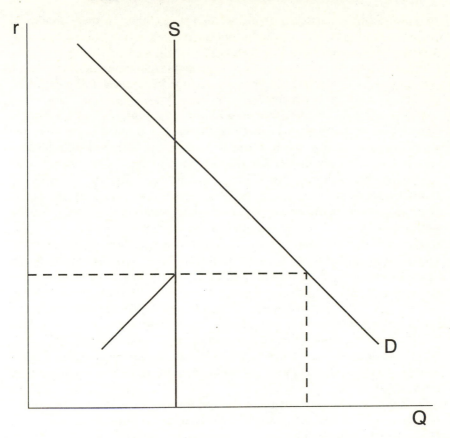

Figure 3.1 Loan markets with credit rationing

and therefore decreases the supply of loanable funds. Although investors would like to borrow more than financial intermediaries will lend, all saved funds are lent out.

Analysts of credit rationing, such as Stiglitz, sometimes imply that banks hold excess reserves or buy T-Bills with their 'surplus' funds (see Stiglitz and Weiss 1981; Greenwald and Stiglitz 1988a, 1988b). Monetary policy supposedly is ineffective, as banks simply hold excess reserves in response to a monetary expansion. Holding excess reserves or surplus funds, however, violates profit-maximizing equilibrium behavior, given the basic assumptions of the model. If banks find it profitable to lend at all, they will find it profitable to lend out surplus funds. Borrowers are observationally identical to banks, *ex ante*, even though they will differ *ex post*. If the last loan was profitable to make, the next one will be profitable too. All funds owned by the bank are lent out, after taking normal reserve demands into account. Greenwald and Stiglitz (1990, p. 22), in a later and clearer treatment of the matter, provide a correct account of the potency of monetary policy under credit rationing and reject the 'excess reserves' argument for monetary policy impotence.

Special assumptions are required to generate the excess reserves result. Banks will hold excess reserves, for instance, under the following conditions: borrowers are heterogeneous, the bank wishes to ration the quantity of funds per borrower in addition to the number of borrowers, the number of borrowers in favored classes is too small to exhaust the supply of loanable funds, banks have lent all the funds they wish to favored classes of borrowers, and banks do not wish to lend at all to the non-favored classes of borrowers. Under these assumptions, banks simply do not wish to make more loans; monetary expansions can lead to surplus reserves. I consider the more general case, however, where monetary policy has potency through a loanable funds supply effect.[1]

The 'full employment' of saved funds distinguishes credit rationing models from efficiency wage models for the labor market. In efficiency wage models (i.e., Shapiro and Stiglitz 1984) not all workers are hired, even though all funds are lent out in the credit rationing model. Hiring additional workers involves a diminishing marginal product of labor; hiring one laborer does not imply that all subsequent homogeneous laborers will be hired as well. Making more loans, in contrast, involves no such movement along a downward-sloping returns schedule. Efficiency wage models generate unemployed labor, but credit rationing models do not generate unemployed funds.

In the basic credit rationing model, expansionary open market operations bring an expansion of investment. Even though real interest rates need not fall, the new funds will be lent out and investment will increase. Lenders already had been willing to make more loans at prevailing real interest rates, but depositors were unwilling to supply more loanable funds at that price. An open market operation, by definition, supplies more reserves to the banking system either at the previous real interest rate or at a lower real interest rate. Following the increase in the money supply, banks will lend out the newly created reserves.

Within the very simple credit rationing framework presented above, expansionary open market operations will increase welfare. Additional investment has a shadow value higher than its social cost, which implies welfare losses from credit rationing. At non-market-clearing interest rates banks are unwilling to finance additional investment; banks do not wish to bear the private pecuniary losses resulting from deadbeats. The resulting non-market-clearing price implies an area of deadweight loss, as traditional microeconomic theory suggests. By supplying loanable funds to validate

---

[1] Stiglitz (1992) analyzes the special case where banks are at a corner, characterized by the assumptions discussed above in this paragraph.

the low real interest rate chosen by the private banks, an inflating central bank can move the market to a first-best, market-clearing Pareto optimal point.

If expected inflation involves no costs whatsoever, optimal monetary policy would shift the supply curve of loanable funds to the point where a market-clearing interest rate prevails once again, as illustrated in Figure 3.2. If bank profit maximization offers policymakers a constant real interest rate, the central bank should supply the quantity of loanable funds which validates this real interest rate as a market-clearing one.[2]

If the initial equilibrium has excess demand for loanable funds, monetary inflation will increase the quantity of loanable funds and investment, but will not lower real interest rates. Aggregate risk and economic cyclicality

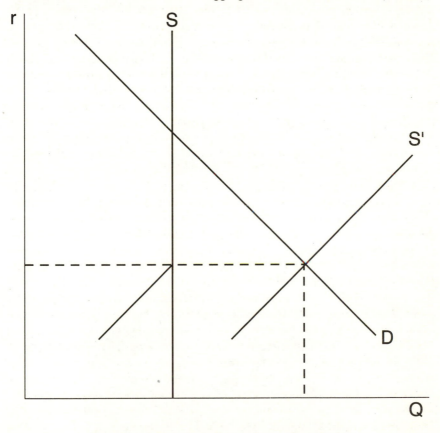

Figure 3.2 Monetary policy under credit rationing

---

[2] Of course, to the extent expected inflation involves real economics costs (tax system costs, shoe leather costs), the supply curve for loanable funds should not shift this far to the right.

will increase through the mechanisms outlined in the previous chapter. Unlike in the previous chapter, however, inflation tends to increase welfare, at least to the extent the inflation does not bring other social costs.

Increases in monetary volatility also have real effects in credit rationing models. The volatility of nominal money supply will imply a volatile availability of loanable funds. In other words, for some borrowers the cost of borrowing will fluctuate between a constant real interest rate and infinity, depending on whether or not funds are available. If credit rationing is not absolute, the infinite rate will be replaced by a very high risk rate, such as the rate a borrower would receive from a loan shark.

An increase in the volatility of monetary policies and loanable funds supplies will cause credit-intensive, long-term investment to contract, through the mechanisms discussed above. This volatility will impose high costs on those projects especially dependent on credit. The elasticity of response to this volatility may be higher in credit rationing models than in market-clearing models. The movement in loanable funds supply is absorbed entirely in quantities, rather than being spread across quantities and prices. Borrowers face a binary mix of potential costs – they either face the same real interest rate or they face a real interest rate of infinity – rather than facing a continuum of potential real rates.

Credit rationing and risk

Credit rationing models provide an independent justification of the claim that monetary policy leads to a riskier mix of investments. More complex credit rationing models drop the assumption that all borrowers are *ex ante* identical and consider different risk classes of borrowers. Risky borrowers, or borrowers with new risky project ideas, are more likely to be credit constrained than safe borrowers. Relatively safe borrowers, such as blue chip corporations, have higher credit ratings, enjoy independent access to credit markets through securitization, and have more to lose by pursuing go for broke strategies. At the margin they will have an easier time borrowing funds than will less established corporations. An easing of credit rationing constraints will therefore tend to have especially large effects on risky firms, or previously safe firms that are proposing new and risky projects. The central bank, by easing monetary policy, induces a higher percentage allocation of credit to riskier firms. We should expect the economy to become riskier and more susceptible to cyclical fluctuations. This effect will hold regardless of whether investment is riskier or less risky than consumption, an assumption discussed in the previous chapter.

MONETARY POLICY ISSUES

The analysis of this chapter does not yield direct policy implications. As discussed above, increases in the rate of nominal money growth increase economic cyclicality but do so by moving the economy from one Pareto point to another. Increasing the level of aggregate risk in this manner does not constitute a change to be either intrinsically preferred or avoided. In the absence of externalities, differing rates of money growth deliver different points on the Pareto frontier with varying degrees of riskiness and cyclicality.

Externalities may provide a case for preferring one level of *ex ante* risk to another. Business downturns may bring negative externalities through sticky wages and prices, or through a decline in the exploitation of increasing returns. Similarly, periods of high growth may bring positive externalities through increasing returns or through increasing market thickness and liquidity (Shleifer 1986). Such points, however, do not dictate any particular rate of money growth without empirical investigation. Even if externalities are present, highly cyclical economies will bring about both positive externality and negative externality states with greater frequency. We cannot easily determine which levels of *ex ante* cyclicality offer more favorable performance with regard to externalities. More generally, investment-based and risk-based theories necessitate heterogeneous agents, which makes welfare comparisons problematic, even within narrowly defined models, much less in the real world.

Some claims about government-engineered increases in economic volatility can be made. To the extent that monetary policy makes the environment more volatile, economic agents will respond by contracting investment, leading to a decline in the rate of growth. Risk will increase and output will decline, with no offsetting benefits in the form of higher returns. In essence, the government has forced the risk–return frontier to contract. The central bank therefore should attempt to minimize monetary volatility, but it is difficult to draw exact conclusions from this precept.

One option would apply a nominal money growth rule either to the monetary base or to the broader monetary aggregates. Constant rates of base money growth remove the central bank as a source of monetary volatility and eliminate all volatility in the monetary base, by definition of the policy. Whether we favor a money growth rule for the base or for the broader aggregates, however, depends upon how we view non-governmental volatility shocks to the loanable funds market. Under one view, increases in volatility coming from the private sector represent real changes in preferences and should be ignored by the central bank. Even if the economy shifts to lower-yielding investments, entrepreneurs presumably prefer their new investment positions, perhaps because they now have less tolerance for risk. This view implies that the central bank should stabilize the monetary base rather than any broader aggregate.

Under a second view, increases in volatility coming from the private sector represent exogenous forces that investors would prefer to avoid, if possible. We can imagine exogenous changes in real conditions, for instance, that would make loanable funds conditions more volatile. In this view the central bank can improve welfare by smoothing out these other sources of volatility in the loanable funds market. The central bank thus should target the broader monetary aggregates, rather than the narrow base. When exogenous forces put incipient volatile pressures on the broader aggregates, the central bank should manipulate the base to stabilize the loanable funds market. Models where monetary policy causes cycles also must allow for the possibility that monetary policy can smooth other sources of cycle-causing shocks.[3]

As an alternative to targeting a broader monetary aggregate, the central bank also could set a (loose) target for the real interest rate. That is, the central bank would intervene to offset market pressures tending to push real interest rates above or below a particular level. Central banks can influence real interest rates only imperfectly, but the evidence suggests monetary policy can exercise some control over real interest rates (see Chapter 5). We can imagine a central bank following an underlying monetary target, but deviating from that target whenever market pressures place incipient upward or downward pressure on the real interest rate. Real interest rate smoothing has received little systematic attention, although it is mentioned as a policy option by Christiano and Eichenbaum (1992a, p. 352).

The central bank almost certainly should not try to maintain an absolute peg of real interest rates. The central bank could find itself committed to massive inflations or deflations, or might not be able to achieve the targeted real rate at all. None the less some stabilization of the real interest rate may be preferable to no stabilization at all. If exogenous volatility shocks impinge on the loan market, the central bank could gently alter its monetary stance to smooth out market conditions.

The pitfalls of monetary policy

The capital market effects of monetary policy imply that some apparently stabilizing regimes may in fact produce destabilizing effects under some circumstances. As discussed above, money supply changes bring sectoral shifts for risky investment sectors. Whenever the money supply is used to stabilize some other target, such as the price level or the nominal interest

---

[3] Phillips et al. (1938, pp. 207–8) advance an Austrian theory of the trade cycle, for instance, and recommend a policy of smoothing per capita credit growth.

rate, external pressures on those targets induce offsetting changes in monetary policy. The change in monetary policy will offset one set of factors, but at the same time will create sectoral shifts towards or away from risky investment goods.

Price rules

A price rule requires money supply adjustments in responses to productivity changes in the real economy. High rates of productivity growth require high rates of money growth, and low rates of productivity growth require low rates of money growth. Volatile rates of productivity growth will imply volatile rates of money growth and thus volatile sectoral shocks across investment goods. In effect, the policy rule makes money supply behavior hostage to productivity shocks. The real sectoral shift of a productivity shock will induce, through the required monetary policy response, another real sectoral shift affecting risky investment goods as well.

Both Hayek (1967), writing from an Austrian perspective, and Jo Anna Gray (1976), writing from a Keynesian perspective, offer related arguments against price level stabilization. In Hayek's model a zero inflation rule does not reduce intertemporal coordination problems. A productive economy requires money supply growth to maintain a constant price level; otherwise prices fall in absolute terms. Volatile productivity growth therefore implies volatile behavior for the money supply, and volatile profitability for different kinds of investment. In the argument of Gray (1976), the maintenance of a stable price level requires adjustments to the *absolute* level of many prices. In her model a negative supply shock places upward pressure on the price level. To maintain the price level target the central bank must contract the money supply and force many other nominal prices to fall. Gray's problem arises because nominal prices are sticky and react poorly to nominal volatility; Hayek's problem arises because relative price volatility creates forecasting problems for entrepreneurs and induces costly malinvestments. Each argument points to a differing kind of real volatility created by central bank pursuit of a price level target.

Nominal interest rate targeting

Nominal interest rate smoothing produces volatile sectoral shocks, and poor macroeconomic results, when money demand is unstable. Nominal interest rate smoothing uses nominal money supply to match changes in money demand. When the demand for money increases, the monetary authority will accommodate with additional nominal money, rather than allowing nominal interest rates to rise. Nominal money demand therefore determines subsequent monetary policy, and determines the sectoral shocks that will hit risky investment sectors (similarly, a price rule allows productivity shocks to determine changes in monetary policy). An increase in money demand, for instance, will induce an increase in the money supply, lowering real interest rates and increasing the demand for long-term investment goods. A decrease in money demand will have the contrary effects. To the extent that money demand is volatile, the loanable funds market will be volatile as well, which will induce long-term investment to contract, as discussed above.

Nominal GNP rules

Nominal GNP rules adjust the rate of money growth to keep a constant M × V stream, thereby providing 'velocity-adjusted' monetary rules. McCallum (1985) has been the most prominent advocate of such a rule in recent times. Hayek (1967, pp. 122–4) wrote favorably about a related policy as a means of minimizing cyclical fluctuations of the Austrian type. He advocated freezing the nominal money supply, save to adjust for changes in velocity.[4]

Nominal GNP rules offer well-known macroeconomic advantages, but they do not minimize investment-based business cycles. Like price level or nominal interest rate smoothing, nominal GNP rules use the nominal money supply to stabilize some pre-specified economic variable. The nominal money supply, and therefore sectoral shocks in investment markets, will behave smoothly only to the extent that velocity is stable. When velocity is unstable, money supply responses will create volatility in the loanable funds market. Money and velocity have equivalent or symmetric effects upon the price level and aggregate demand; stabilizing the product of money and velocity therefore stabilizes aggregate demand. When new money enters the economy at a specific point, however, money supply and velocity do not have similar effects upon relative prices. Changes in the supply of loanable funds have an especially large effect on capital goods and long-term investments and, as a result, stabilizing nominal aggregate demand may increase the volatility of sectoral demands.

Commodity monies

The use of commodity monies, or free banking systems based on commodity monies, does not alter the logic of intertemporal coordination issues. Money supplies and demands may become more or less volatile,

---

[4] Contemporary proposals for stabilizing nominal GNP frequently choose M2 as the relevant monetary aggregate. Hayek's proposal did not define the relevant concepts of money supply and velocity. Haberler (1964, p. 61) interprets Hayek's proposal in terms of 'trade velocity.' Trade velocity covers all money exchanges against final goods or inputs, but excludes financial transactions, such as transactions on the stock exchange.

but a given set of changes in the loanable funds market will produce the same effects as under a fiat money regime. An increase in the supply of gold, for instance, will create sectoral shifts towards riskier investments if the new gold supply increase enters via the loanable funds market.

For the purposes of this discussion, free banking gold standards and government-run gold standards will have the same effects. In either case the quantity of base money is determined by the cost of producing the money commodity and the demand for that money. Whether the government or private sector issues the covering banknotes may affect other real variables, but it does not change the logic of a cycle driven by changes in the monetary base. Free banking systems do not necessarily stabilize the marginal cost of producing gold, even if they offer automatic checks against overexpansion of the broader monetary aggregates (White 1984b; Selgin 1988).

Even demand-driven changes in the supply of a commodity money can set off the business cycles discussed in the previous chapter. Changes in the demand to hold base money will induce corresponding changes in gold mining activity. If the new gold enters the economy through the banking system (more on that point shortly), credit expansion will still increase and the real interest rate will still fall. Entrepreneurs will choose investments of greater risk, thereby causing economic cyclicality to increase.

Commodity monies do alter the applicability of cyclical theory. Increases in commodity money, unlike open market operations, do not always enter the economy through the banking system. Increases in the supply of monetary gold, for instance, typically enter the economy through the portfolios of gold miners and through the portfolios of individuals who convert non-monetary gold to monetary uses. To the extent that gold mine owners have marginal expenditure patterns fully representative of the economy as a whole, changes in the gold money supply will not bring sectoral shocks.

Changes in the gold money supply do shift sectoral demands to the extent gold mine owners allocate their new gold in an unrepresentative manner. To the extent that gold mine owners have higher savings rates than the economy as a whole, the analysis follows the case of open market operations (see p. 64). Money supply expansions will increase the real supply of loanable funds and lower real interest rates. Conversely, if gold mine shareholders have higher spending rates than the economy as a whole, an inverted version of the story would hold. The real quantity of loanable funds is high when the rate of money growth is low, and vice versa. Increases in the rate of money supply growth would cause contractions and decreases in money supply growth would cause expansions.

A second difference between gold and fiat money arises from wealth effects. Changes in commodity money supply, unlike changes in fiat money supply, change real net wealth. Increases in fiat money do not themselves change the real productive capacity of the economy (at least not prior to subsequent adjustments, which may be either positive or negative). An increase in the supply of a commodity money, such as gold, brings an outward shift of the production possibilities frontier. Even if the new gold is used for monetary purposes, money holders retain the option of converting their gold into commodity uses.

Increases in the rate of gold money growth therefore might bring a more intensive boom than increases in the rate of growth of fiat money. If the new gold enters the economy through the banking system, the economy experiences both an increase in real wealth and an increase in loanable funds supply. The boom will be wealthier. Conversely, the downturns resulting from decreases in the rate of money growth will be even poorer, as the rate of gold wealth creation also is falling. The changes in real wealth associated with changing commodity money supply may magnify the other real effects of a changing money supply.

Commodity monies decrease economic cyclicality only to the extent they decrease the volatility of the real economy. The backing of 'real wealth' behind the monetary unit does not itself prevent or sustain unprofitable malinvestments. Long-term investments may be undertaken, for instance, in the hope that initially high rates of gold discovery will be sustained for future periods. If gold discoveries cease or decelerate, the chosen investments may turn out to be unprofitable. Volatile money supply behavior still will induce economic contractions.[5]

One hundred percent reserve banking

Some defenders of traditional Austrian business cycle theory have evinced a strong preference for 100 percent reserve banking. These economists argue (correctly) that 100 percent reserves would prevent Austrian-style cycles from being generated through the banking system. Monetary policy, however, can still induce changes in capital investments through other, non-bank lending institutions.[6]

The imposition of 100 percent reserve banking eliminates the distinction between the monetary base and the broader monetary aggregates. Banks can no longer create credit based on their reserves, and the monetary base becomes the only relevant measure of the money supply. Banks also lose their central position in the loanable funds market. Thus, 100 percent reserve banks serve as money warehouses who guard or maintain funds but cannot lend them out. Lending and deposit-taking become separate functions.

[5] Rothbard (1975, pp. 37–8) argued that Austrian-style business cycles, of the traditional kind, are not possible with commodity monies.

[6] For Austrian defenses of 100 percent reserve banking, see, for instance, Rothbard (1975, pp. 30–3) and Skousen (1990, Chapters 8–10).

Despite these fundamental changes to financial institutions, 100 percent reserve banking does not alter the logic of investment-driven business cycles. Changes in the real supply of loanable funds, or volatility in that supply, will still induce changes in capital investment. Thus, 100 percent reserve banking merely changes the conduit for the loanable funds market. The central bank can no longer manipulate the loanable funds market by dealing with banks; banks now serve as money warehouses and do not lend out funds. Nonetheless the central bank still can affect the loanable funds market by engaging in open market operations with non-bank, non-deposit-taking, lending institutions. The monetary authority can create new reserves and use those reserves to buy real assets from lenders. The lenders, now holding more real liquidity, will expand their loans. Fractional reserve banking is not required for this result; the change in monetary policy will give lenders a higher real quantity of liquid funds, and these funds can be lent out, just as with traditional banking. Lenders need not take deposits for this mechanism to operate.

New monetary economics systems

The phrase 'New Monetary Economics,' coined by Hall (1982), refers to a variety of alternative scenarios for monetary and financial institutions. Most typically money's medium of exchange and medium of account functions are separated into two or more different assets. Financial assets are used as exchange media, while prices are reckoned in terms of a real commodity or real commodity bundle. Monetary services are supplied competitively, leading to the total or partial displacement of government currency and non-interest-bearing base money.[7]

In this section I will consider a scenario where privately issued interest-bearing securities serve as settlement media and base money. Transactors might settle clearing-house claims, for instance, by transferring a basket of commercial paper claims; such a basket also might serve directly as an exchange medium. Consumers would hold the basket of assets in their checkable money market fund accounts; checks would be cleared by the appropriate transfer of shares. For purposes of simplicity, I refer to IBM commercial paper as the relevant asset, without ruling out the possibility that more than one asset would be used. If one share of IBM commercial paper was priced at three commodity basket units at settlement day, and a check was written for nine commodity basket units, three shares of IBM commercial paper would be transferred. Currency might still be used for small retail transactions, but the bulk of the money supply would consist of privately supplied financial assets. I assume away the transactions costs

---

[7] See Fama (1980, 1983). Cowen and Kroszner (1994a) provide an overview of some relevant scenarios.

issues raised by White (1984a, 1987) and others, and consider how such a regime might affect the incidence of investment-based business cycles.

The separation of medium of exchange and medium of account functions does not itself alter the course of the cycle. The direct pricing of liquid medium of exchange and settlement claims does not eliminate the link between conditions in the loanable funds market and changes in the quantity and kind of investment. For a New Monetary Economics system to arise in the first place, the real quantity of commercial paper must expand relative to the real quantity of (traditional) base money. The volatility of commercial paper borrowing costs becomes more important, relative to the volatility of interest rates on borrowing traditional base money, but the business cycle takes a similar course.

New Monetary Economics systems affect cyclicality only by changing the principles governing exchange media supply. The replacement of traditional base money with financial securities effectively institutes 100 percent reserve banking, using debt and equity securities as the new 'monetary base.' Changes in this 'monetary base' now directly represent changes in the quantity of lending activity, without the intermediation of banks. Like 100 percent reserve banking, securitized exchange media decrease or eliminate the role that banks play in the cyclical story, but they transfer the cyclical impetus to other markets rather than eliminating cyclical factors altogether.

Concluding remarks on policy options

The above survey of policy options indicates no automatic remedy for risk-based business cycles mechanisms. Fixed money growth rules avoid monetary shocks but money growth rules do not eliminate volatility in the loanable funds market more generally. The other policy options examined all increase sectoral volatility under at least some circumstances. Despite the pessimistic or at least ambiguous practical implications of this result, we should take some theoretical comfort in the results. If business cycles truly are complex, we should not be able to eliminate them with simple or uni-dimensional policy options. If business cycles could be remedied so easily by a mere change in policy, the market would have already handled the problem by providing some proxy for the needed good policy, by providing some kind of insurance against bad policy, or by developing some means of avoiding the systematic cluster of errors which brings on the downturn.

TRANSMISSION OF CYCLES ACROSS CURRENCIES

Open economy considerations may affect the monetary transmission of business cycles in at least two ways. First, the presence of a mobile pool of international capital may limit the importance of money supply fluctuations in any single country. In that case the theory applies to changes in international supplies of loanable funds. Second, the effect of money on real interest rates may spread from one country to another and transmit sectoral demand shifts on an international scale. I will focus on this second linkage and provide an account of how cyclical transmission might occur.

International transmission requires that the money supplies, real interest rates, or relative prices of countries be linked. The pattern of cyclical transmission depends upon the exchange rate regime and the degree of economic openness.

Fixed exchange rates

Under permanently fixed exchange rates, the relevant countries effectively share a common money. Increases in the money supply in one country will spill over to other countries; more generally, real money balances will be distributed in accordance with regional demands. Monetary policies must accommodate these changes in relative money demand to maintain the stated exchange rate peg. In this case we may speak of a common monetary area. Traditional single-economy analyses of business cycles apply directly to this broader economic region.

Under managed fixed exchange rate systems, central banks manipulate money flows by influencing nominal interest rates, using either open market operations, jawboning, or legal controls on capital flows. Increases in the nominal rate are used to restrict money outflows, and decreases in the nominal rate may be used to hinder money inflows. Some economists have argued that the nineteenth-century classical gold standard operated on such a basis; more recent systems of exchange rate pegging, such as the European Monetary System, also have used nominal interest rates to sustain currency values.

If the relative demand for gold rises in Germany, relative to the United Kingdom, gold will start to flow from the United Kingdom to Germany, provided the gold export points are surpassed. In a world of imperfect capital mobility, the UK central bank can 'manage' the gold standard by raising interest rates and weakening the pressure to export gold. In effect, central banks can use interest rate policy to reshape the geographic distribution of money demand and sustain currency values. The German central bank might lower nominal interest rates while the UK central bank raises nominal interest rates. In so far as these changes in nominal interest rates are achieved through monetary policy, cyclical forces may be set off in both countries.[8]

---

[8] On related criticisms of the managed gold standard, see Meulen (1934), and Hayek (1971). Imperfect capital mobility is required for these results. Massive capital inflows would otherwise push UK interest rates back down again.

Floating exchange rates

International transmission of interest rate effects under floating exchange rates brings considerable theoretical complications. Domestic investment depends on real interest rates, but international demand for a currency depends upon its nominal interest rate. Foreign investors, dealing in a different numeraire, find their total net *real* return on another currency is given by that currency's *nominal* interest rate. The international links between real interest rate changes and nominal interest rate changes, however, are indeterminate outside of a fully specified model. A change in real interest rates, in one country, may or may not be transmitted internationally, depending upon price and exchange rate behavior.

Throughout the analysis I assume that covered interest parity holds. That is, if one currency pays a higher nominal interest rate than the other, the high nominal interest rate currency must sell at a forward discount; the currency must be expected to depreciate. Covered interest parity follows directly from arbitrage and has been confirmed empirically. I do not, however, assume that real interest rates must be equalized across different countries. Capital mobility alone does not imply equalization of real interest rates. A German investor who will purchase a German bundle of goods cares only about the nominal interest rate on Japanese yen, not the real rate. Real rate equalization occurs only when goods are fully mobile, or if the German investor can move to Japan at zero cost and purchase his or her goods bundle there. Real interest rate equalization is most definitely not supported by the empirical evidence (Mishkin 1984a).[9]

Consider first an unexpected increase in German inflation, causing German real interest rates to fall. German entrepreneurs will increase long-term investment, increasing economic cyclicality. Similar results will be transmitted to Japan to the extent that real rates in Japan follow the German path. By assumption, the Japanese have not changed their monetary policy, but Japanese economic variables may react to the change in German real interest rates.

The real effects in Japan depend upon the course of German nominal interest rates. If the unexpected increase in German nominal money has its full effect on prices immediately, nominal interest rates in Germany will fall rather than rise. The Fisher effect will not operate, and the greater supply of loanable funds in Germany will push down German real and nominal interest rates. Dornbusch's overshooting model (1976) presents a related scenario where nominal interest rates fall; in his analysis Keynesian liquidity effects on interest rates outweigh Fisher effects, causing both real and nominal interest rates to fall in the country with the inflation.

---

[9] If real interest rate equalization did hold, we would be back to the case of a single currency area and effectively a single economy.

Alternatively, the German inflation will raise German nominal interest rates to the extent that German commodity prices are expected to rise with a lag. In that case German nominal interest rates will rise through a Fisherian inflationary premium.

When German nominal interest rates fall, the demand for mark-denominated assets will fall relative to yen-denominated assets. Equilibrium requires some mix of the following: Japanese nominal interest rates must fall, or forward exchange rates must reflect expected appreciation of the German mark. Without these adjustments the relative returns on yen-denominated and mark-denominated assets do not stand in equilibrium. To the extent Japanese nominal interest rates fall, Japanese real interest rates will fall as well. (Recall that monetary policy in Japan, and thus the Japanese price level path, has not changed.) Cyclical pressures are transmitted partially, but not fully, depending upon how closely the two sets of real interest rates move together.

Analogous results hold when German nominal interest rates rise. Japanese nominal interest rates must rise, or forward exchange rates must reflect expected depreciation of the German mark. To the extent that Japanese nominal interest rates rise, Japanese real interest rates will rise as well. Again, interest rate changes are partially transmitted from one country to another.

In either of the cases discussed above, the monetary policy action of one country affects investment demand in the country with the passive monetary policy. To the extent investment demand in the passive country rises, the economy of the passive country becomes more cyclical. To the extent investment demand in the passive country falls, the passive country becomes less cyclical. The Germans can make the Japanese economy more cyclical to the extent that they can lower their own nominal interest rate and induce capital flows into Japan.

In these scenarios transmission from Germany to Japan is based upon a change in Japanese nominal interest rates. If the mark/yen forward exchange rate adjusts in lieu of an interest rate move, a different kind of sectoral shock, an exchange rate shock, transmits real effects to Japan. To the extent forward and spot exchange rates move in lieu of interest rate movements, we return to more standard accounts of cyclical transmission operating through export and import sectors.

Now consider the comparative statics experiment of an unexpected increase in monetary volatility in Germany. Long-term investment and aggregate riskiness in Germany will decline as discussed in the first section of this chapter. The nominal interest rate effects created in Germany then will be transmitted partially to Japan, as discussed above. Either the forward exchange rate must adjust or Japanese nominal interest rates must adjust. The Japanese economy may contract as well. In addition, the real effects of monetary volatility on the German economy will be transmitted to Japan as well, in the form of traditional real shocks.

FOUNDATIONAL ISSUES: WHY DOES MONEY MATTER?

The monetary scenarios presented earlier in this chapter simply have assumed that increases in the nominal money lower real interest rates. This final section turns to fundamental issues and asks why money matters at all. Since the real interest rate effects of monetary policy are not universally accepted, I will defend in some detail the view that money is non-neutral with respect to capital markets. The outlined link between money and real interest rates is sometimes called the 'Wicksell effect.' Knut Wicksell, in his *Interest and Prices* (1936) argued that the non-neutral nature of monetary injections would cause expansionary monetary policy to lower the real interest rate. Wicksell and his successors, however, did not outline the exact mechanism through which a change in the financial policy of banks might affect real economic variables and real interest rates.

A closer analysis of the non-neutrality of money also bears on the differences between traditional and revised versions of the Austrian theory, as will be discussed in Chapter 5. In this chapter I will show that monetary shocks can be decomposed into changes in the fiscal position of the government. Therefore we should think of monetary policy as a real sectoral shock, rather than as a purely nominal event, or as an inevitable source of signal extraction problems, as sometimes portrayed in Austrian and monetarist writings.

The subsequent discussion of monetary policy assumes a unique, stable, well-behaved equilibrium in the loanable funds market. The rate of interest equals the real rate of return on investment, adjusting both magnitudes for transactions costs and risk, and assuming that no credit rationing occurs. Lenders will provide funds if the price is right, and rates of interest reach their market clearing levels.[10]

The supply and demand for loans, taken together, determine a market rate of interest. The loanable funds theory attempts to capture the monetary, time preference, and productivity elements emphasized in competing interest rate theories. At its most basic level, the loanable funds theory provides a generalized description of the supply and demand curves that determine interest rates. Specification of these supply and demand curves simultaneously pins down nominal and real rates of interest. Historically the loanable funds theory has been developed by Irving Fisher, Carl

---

[10] For some general remarks on how we should regard multiple equilibria, see the discussion of capital reswitching in Chapter 5.

Menger, Arthur Marget, Herbert Davenport, and T. S. Tsiang. Meir Kohn (1981) and Lars Svensson (1985) offer modern treatments.[11]

Arbitrage establishes an equality between interest rates and rates of return on capital, again adjusting both magnitudes for appropriate risks. Entrepreneurs seek to borrow funds if the real rate of return lies above the real interest rate. The increased demand for funds will push up the loan rate of interest and bid up input prices, thereby bringing rates of return and rates of interest to equality. If the real rate of return lies below the interest rate, the demand to borrow funds will fall. Interest rates will fall, and the capital stock will decline over time through depreciation, thereby raising marginal rates of return. Once again, the relevant equality between rates of interest and rates of return is established.

The comparative statics of monetary change

Even with flexible, market-clearing prices and rational expectations, changes in the supply of money will affect real variables through injection effects. That is, money supply increases enter the economy at specific points in space and time; changes in the money supply occur through individual portfolios. Real demands will shift if the expenditure patterns for the new monetary injection do not replicate the expenditure patterns for previously available funds.

These real effects of monetary changes do not require any price stickiness or adjustment rigidities. A counterfeiter, for instance, creates sectoral shifts towards his or her favored basket of goods even when prices are perfectly flexible. Changing prices constitute part of the mechanism that reallocates resources to the newly favored sectors. The particular direction of the real effects depends upon how the new monetary claims are deployed. If the new increases in liquidity enter through loanable funds markets, investment will be favored at the expense of consumption.

---

[11] Marget (1926) surveys the history of the loanable funds tradition. I read Hayek (1941, e.g., Chapter XVII, Appendix I) as using a version of Fisherian theory, despite his convoluted presentation. Hayek (1975, pp. 413–14, 420) does criticize some interpretations of Fisher for laying too much stress on the time preference element, relative to productivity concerns, but he does not charge Fisher himself with this confusion. Later Hayek (1945) admitted he had previously underestimated the importance of time preference factors. Again, he made this point within a Fisherian framework. Other Austrian economists, such as Mises, Rothbard, and Kirzner, have advocated a 'pure time preference' theory of interest. Most advocates of the pure time preference theory, however, do not dispute that real world interest rates are determined by many of the features identified by the loanable funds theory (Kirzner 1993; see also Pellengahr 1986). The advocates of the pure time preference theory wish to isolate one component of the interest rate – the time preference component – as 'essential' to the nature of interest. In this regard the Misesian theory is consistent with the loanable funds approach, even if non-essentialists, such as myself, find the special emphasis on time preference to be tautologous or superfluous.

Changes in monetary policy bring injection effects when increases and decreases in the money supply occur through banks. By assumption, changes in the money supply enter the economy through changes in banking system reserves. I consider the case where a central bank increases the monetary base through open market operations. The analysis does not require the central bank to control the monetary base with any degree of precision, only that the base varies due to central bank action. The central bank, for instance, may decide to engage in expansionary open market operations, and purchase treasury securities from primary dealers. I use the word 'banks' to refer to the financial intermediaries that both extend credit to private borrowers and serve as conduits for government monetary policy.

The central bank creates new money to buy treasury securities (T-Bills) from financial intermediaries. The increased demand for T-Bills will raise the prices of those bills. Bank shareholders had previously decided to buy T-Bills with their funds, but now the higher price of T-Bills will push their subsequent expenditures towards other assets. In the traditional account of monetary policy, banks use their new liquid reserves to lend to the private sector.

The increase in bank lending to the private sector does not follow *a priori* but, rather, represents one of a series of possible equilibria. In principle, the open market operation may disturb the initial real equilibrium in such a manner to induce bank shareholders to shrink the size of the bank, for instance. Shareholders could contract both loans and deposits, and convert the new funds to dividends and spend them on consumption. Or banks may use the new reserves to repay short-term borrowings at the discount window of the central bank (Black 1987). While these possibilities cannot be ruled out, I assume that the standard analysis of monetary policy holds and that real factors do not induce a shrinking of the banking sector.

Three separate effects may induce private banks to shift their portfolio towards private lending, following an expansionary open market operation. First, the central bank has bid up the price of T-Bills, causing private sector expenditures to spill over to related or similar assets. Given the new, lower yield on T-Bills, some funds will now be allocated to loans. Portfolio effects will transmit the higher demand for T-Bills into higher demands for other return-bearing assets. This effect, of course, does not hold *a priori*. Banks may find that holding non-interest-bearing reserves provides a closer substitute to T-Bills than does lending to the private sector.

Second, legal reserve requirements may contribute to the potency of monetary policy. To the extent reserve requirements are economically binding, banks would like to make additional loans but do not find it profitable to bid for the necessary reserves. Monetary policy injects those reserves into banks at a price below the previous market price, and therefore can stimulate lending.[12]

The recent literature on the 'bank lending channel' of monetary policy emphasizes a third effect. Banks may be liquidity-constrained in their ability to raise reserves through the outside market. Banks would like to make additional loans, but banks cannot bid for the necessary reserves at profitable prices, usually due to credit rationing. Expansionary monetary policy eases banks' liquidity constraints, and thus enables these loans to be made. Similarly, contractionary monetary policy will make credit constraints more binding (Kashyap et al. 1993).

Combinations of these three effects will establish links between money and real variables. Expansionary monetary policy increases the supply of loanable funds to the private sector and induces real interest rates to fall and finance constraints to ease. The demand to borrow funds will increase, and economic activity will rise in interest-sensitive and borrowing-sensitive sectors. In similar fashion, if the central bank created new money and spent it on ice cream, the supply of ice cream and its substitutes would rise.

If the inflation does not continue over time, open market operations do not necessarily lower real interest rates in the long run. Consider a one-time open market operation. The relative demand for T-Bills has increased in the short run but will not increase in the long run. Once the inflation ceases, the flow demand for T-Bills will return to its previous levels, as will T-Bill prices, real interest rates and loanable funds activity. The central bank demanded T-Bills at a higher rate than before, but the eventual recipients of the new money have not increased their demand for T-Bills; by assumption preferences are constant. The next round of market expenditures will bring a real demand for T-Bills no higher than before the open market operation. Once the new money ends up in the portfolios of individuals with representative expenditure patterns, real interest rates will return to previous levels. The lower real interest rates will persist only to the extent that subsequent recipients of the new money spend money on T-Bills, or related assets, at a higher rate than before. Otherwise the old expenditure flows will re-establish themselves over time.[13]

Real interest rate effects will persist, however, if the central bank continues the inflation. Ongoing inflation increases the flow demand for T-Bills

---

[12] Reserve requirements also do not allow derivation of an *a priori* effect on lending. In the case of continual and expected inflation, the nominal interest rate will rise. The tax created by reserve requirements will become more binding, and inflation may cause total lending to decline.

[13] In this case the persistence of inflationary real effects depends upon the velocity of money. To the extent the velocity of money is high, the initial real effects of inflation will be reversed relatively quickly; previous real expenditure patterns will establish themselves quickly. To the extent the velocity of money is low, the real effects of the initial inflationary burst will persist for longer. Previous demand patterns will take some time to re-exert their influence on prices.

permanently, giving rise to a permanent real interest rate effect. Similarly, if in each period the government purchases a certain quantity of cheese, the price of cheese will rise permanently. Ongoing open market expansions will fail to lower the real rate permanently only to the extent that other real effects of inflation kick in. Output, for instance, may decline if inflationary monetary policy brings real costs, perhaps through a nominally based tax system or through menu costs. These output declines will produce further real interest rate effects over time, which will intermingle with the initial real interest effects of open market operations.

The relevance of Modigliani–Miller and Ricardian equivalence theorems

Both the quantity theory and financial asset theories of money can offer support for the claim that changes in monetary policy affect real rates of return. These two approaches to monetary theory, if specified properly, do not provide contrary results. The Modigliani–Miller approach to monetary theory does not imply that all monetary policy operations are fully neutral. Rather, the Modigliani–Miller approach offers the more defensible proposition that monetary policies which also involve changes in fiscal policy, and only such monetary policies, will bring definite real (and nominal) effects.

The Modigliani–Miller theorems for open market operations (e.g., Wallace 1981; Smith 1984, 1988) link real and monetary theories of the business cycles. Open market operations, while commonly defined as a form of monetary policy, can be interpreted as a change in fiscal policy as well. Open market operations, as traditionally defined, do not involve a balanced budget change in government or central bank policy; the central bank spends fiat money at a value higher than its marginal cost of production. The central bank runs a 'surplus' vis-à-vis the remainder of the economy, and is spending this surplus to exert net pressure on expenditure flows and real interest rates. The government/central bank, taken as a consolidated entity, has confiscated more resources from the private sector, using monetary policy, and has spent those resources in a particular direction.

Barro's Ricardian equivalence theorem, or more broadly the Modigliani–Miller theorems, imply only that changes in debt or finance, *for a given level of government spending*, will prove neutral with respect to real variables. The Ricardian theorem does not imply that increases in the central bank/treasury surplus, if allocated to change the economy's net expenditure patterns, will be neutral with respect to real interest rates or other real variables.

Modigliani–Miller theorems do not imply that the private sector will offset the real change in expenditure flows created by the central bank. If a robber steals money from my house and increases his expenditures on investment goods, I do not decrease my savings to 'offset' that action. (The income effect of the theft may induce my savings to decline, but I do not act to restore the initial real equilibrium.) For similar reasons, if the central bank confiscates real resources from the economy by spending its seigniorage surplus on T-Bills or other financial securities, it can create real effects on interest rates.

Proponents and critics of Modigliani–Miller propositions have usually taken opposing positions on the applicability of the propositions to monetary policy. Defenders of the Modigliani–Miller approach, such as Smith (1984, 1988) claim that some kinds of open market operations will have no effects on real or nominal variables. Smith cites open market operations where the government promises to repurchase the money later, supposedly creating a balanced budget open market operation. Critics, such as McCallum (1983), claim that the policy irrelevance results come from models which ignore the medium of exchange function of money. Recognizing that medium of exchange function supposedly will reinstate the traditional quantity theory view of monetary policy.

I stake out a middle ground between these two positions. The Modigliani–Miller approach is correct in the following sense: balanced budget open market operations, if we define them with sufficient precision, do involve full neutrality. A fully balanced budget policy must reverse any initial asset exchange; it is no surprise that such policies bring no real or nominal effects. Hoover (1988) gives the example of a balanced budget monetary policy which trades in two five dollar bills for a ten dollar bill.[14]

The critics of Modigliani–Miller theorems are also correct, however, in arguing that real world open market operations will not be neutral. The Modigliani–Miller models imply correctly that balanced budget open market operations are neutral, but the models do not imply that the real world phenomenon called an 'open market operation' in fact satisfies the balanced budget assumption. Expansionary open market operations are not typically accompanied by changes in expected tax rates; therefore the open market operation, taken alone, implies a net fiscal drain from the private sector to the central bank/government. Real world open market operations

---

[14] Wallace's model (1981) also satisfies the balanced budget requirement. In this model bonds are held for their higher pecuniary return, and money is held for its greater safety. The monetary authority starts by swapping money for bonds. The government's budget position has become riskier, however, and the balanced budget requirement implies that the initial swap ends up being reversed. The monetary authority reverses the initial asset swap by refunding the difference in risk/return profiles between money and bonds securities to the private sector. The private sector ends up with the same net asset position it started off with. In some Modigliani–Miller models (Bryant and Wallace 1979, 1980), balanced budget open market inflation can even cause the price level to *fall*, if initial market imperfections exist and the government can trade or intermediate assets more cheaply than the private sector can.

have real effects because the change in central bank policy can be decomposed into an equivalent change in fiscal policy.

The liquidity premium of money does make a fundamental difference to Modigliani–Miller theorems, as McCallum suggests. Exchanges of liquid money for financial or real assets cannot satisfy the balanced budget assumption, even when the government tries to make offsetting changes in fiscal policy. The non-pecuniary convenience yield of money cannot be packaged separately from the money asset itself. When the central bank swaps money for bonds, banks (i.e., bank shareholders) suddenly hold more liquidity. There is no offsetting fiscal policy which will soak up or absorb this excess liquidity. The difference between the assets exchanged cannot be refunded to taxpayers. The fiscal authority cannot, even in principle, require taxpayers to give up 'the liquidity of their money' without taking the value of the money itself. Yet the change in the government's fiscal position consists precisely of the difference between pecuniary returns (bonds) and non-pecuniary returns (money).

Some assets can be broken down into component parts; witness the separate markets for the principal and coupon payments on government securities. Unlike coupon payments, however, convenience yields cannot be distributed separately from the assets to which they are attached. Individuals cannot enjoy the liquidity services of money without holding money itself. Likewise, we cannot hold the purchasing power of money without also holding its liquidity services. Even if money's liquidity services could somehow be severed physically from money's purchasing power, the purchasing power would fall to zero without attached liquidity; money is dominated as a pure store of value. This indivisibility of money's services prevents the balanced budget assumption from ever holding when liquid monetary assets are swapped against financial assets. The indivisible nature of money's purchasing power and liquidity therefore provides the ultimate microfoundations for why monetary policy matters.

Defenders of the neutrality theorem sometimes postulate an issuance of more nominal money, combined with a government promise to retire the money in the future (Smith 1984, 1988). Individuals supposedly hold the new money to pay off the forthcoming taxes, à la Barro, rather than spending the money with inflationary effects. Even in this case, however, the liquidity premium of money will induce real and nominal effects. Barro (1976) himself admits, and even emphasizes, that debt neutrality does not hold when government bonds offer liquidity services; a similar conclusion holds for monetary policy as well.

When the central bank injects more liquidity into individual portfolios, individuals will spend that liquidity, even when they face forthcoming tax payments. The real balance effect of inflation sets off a *scramble for goods*, as analyzed by Friedman (1969) and Burstein (1986, p. 126). The money supply increase implies that the marginal value of holding money for liquidity services is now less than the marginal value of spending that money. Each individual attempts to capture more goods or assets by increasing his or her nominal spending. Market participants scramble for assets, as the nominal quantity of liquid claims has increased while the supply of goods and services is constant. Spending increases until prices rise enough to restore the real supply of exchange media balances to an equilibrium level. At the end of this process portfolio equilibrium is restored, yet no individual faces a higher future tax burden. Portfolio readjustment effects will increase the price level, but they will not reverse the non-neutral effects of the original asset purchase of the central bank.[15]

Why do we use money in open market operations?

Central banks typically use money when conducting open market operations because of the special liquidity of the money asset. Philip Cagan, in his 1958 essay, asked why central banks sell money and purchase T-Bills when they wish to stimulate the economy. Cagan asked, for instance, why did central banks not conduct open market operations by buying T-Bills with apples, or by buying T-Bills with Old Master paintings? Cagan was not suggesting that these alternative procedures were practical in terms of transactions costs, but rather he was asking whether the asset of money holds some special power to produce real effects.

The Modigliani–Miller decomposition of monetary policy into fiscal policy suggests an answer to Cagan's query about why money holds an especially potent power for open market operations. The ability of the central bank to print fiat money at low marginal cost allows it to break balanced budget constraints. Since effective monetary policy can be decomposed into changes in fiscal policy, money creation represents one obvious means of changing fiscal policy – the central bank creates a surplus and spends it. If the central bank took a comparable tack with apples or Old Masters, the central bank would have to confiscate those assets from the private sector. Unlike paper dollars, the central bank cannot produce those assets at a value below their marginal cost, the critical assumption needed to break the balanced budget constraint. If the central bank first bought those assets before selling them, we would move closer to the case of a balanced budget open market operation, and thus closer to policy neutrality.

In addition, the liquidity of money provides an indivisible service, or 'coupon,' that cannot be separated from the underlying security, as discussed above. If, in contrast, the central bank sold IBM securities for T-Bills, the private sector will have received a more risky asset for a less

---

[15] On the real balance effect, see Friedman (1969), Burstein (1986, p. 126) Sweeney (1988, Chapter 5), and Cowen and Kroszner (1994, Chapter 2).

71

risky asset. The differences between these two assets might be refundable, at least in principle, through the tax system.[16]

Cagan's (1958) explanation for the use of money in open market operations focuses on the zero elasticity of supply for money. That is, the central bank can 'sell' money without discouraging the production of the money asset. The central bank cannot, however, produce a free lunch through this mechanism. If central bank sales of money favor the relative price of T-Bills, capital goods, or whatever, the relative prices of some other assets must fall. The production of those assets will fall as well. Even if money production does not decline, some other assets must decline in production, if monetary policy encourages the production of one set of assets. With unemployed resources, a demand shock might increase the production of all assets, but that assumption does not support the use of money for open market operations. If stimulation of one set of outputs need not discourage the production of another set (due to unemployed resources), then the supply elasticity of money would not matter within the logic of Cagan's argument. Regardless of the assumptions made about full employment, money's zero elasticity of supply does not give it special stimulative powers.

Comparison with other views of money and real interest rates

In recent times, contemporary theorists have outlined a number of other mechanisms, both alternative and complementary, for how money might affect real interest rates.

Cash in advance models (Grossman and Weiss 1983; Rotemberg 1984) provide two related accounts of how distribution effects may change real interest rates. In the Grossman and Weiss paper agents replenish their cash balances every two periods; at any given point in time, half of the population is at the bank and the other half is not. When the monetary injection arrives, it must be held by those agents currently at the bank. The real rate of interest falls to induce those individuals to hold, and to spend, the increase in real balances.

The assumption of staggered trips to the bank plays a critical role in generating real effects for monetary policy. Monetary injections change the budget constraints of the relevant marginal traders. These marginal traders, rather than the market as a whole, must pick up the entire increase in

---

[16] The importance of asset indivisibility, however, does suggest one reason why Old Master paintings could, in principle, produce some of the effects of open market operations conducted with money. Old Master paintings offer a non-pecuniary 'viewing' return which is inseparable from the asset itself. If the central bank sold Old Masters to the private sector, this non-pecuniary viewing return – really a kind of liquidity premium – could not be refunded through the tax system. We would again have an indivisible asset service, making it impossible to decompose the open market operation into a fully balanced budget change in fiscal policy.

nominal money; in other words, those marginal traders must be willing to hold a greater quantity of real balances, and the real interest rate must fall. The assumption of staggered trips to the bank, while not fully realistic, can be interpreted as representing the differences between the marginal trader and the representative trader. Some set of marginal traders, rather than the economy as a whole, must undertake portfolio adjustments in response to monetary injections. Rotemberg (1984) postulates a similar cash in advance technology and generates non-neutral real interest rate effects from staggered bank trips, this time in the context of a production economy with varying output.

A separate class of liquidity effects arises in addition to the distributional effects of inflation discussed directly above. Lucas (1990), Christiano and Eichenbaum (1992a and 1992b, 1995), and Fuerst (1992, 1994a) consider models where agents cannot equalize the marginal utilities of allocating funds to different markets, following a monetary shock. Lucas (1990) was the first to explicitly separate this liquidity effect from the distribution effect occasioned by monetary policy. Drawing on the work of Lucas, Fuerst (1992, 1994a) postulates an explicit imperfection in the market for 'liquidity risk.' Households would prefer to contract for loans after all monetary shocks are realized, but they cannot do so by assumption. Monetary shocks therefore bring unexpected liquidity shocks to firms; when money shocks are positive, firms end up with more liquid funds for investment than they had planned. The demand for capital rises, lowering the real interest rate. Those liquidity shocks remain even after adjusting for changes in the distribution of wealth. Christiano and Eichenbaum (1992a and 1992b) rely on mechanisms similar to those specified by Fuerst, but also add small costs of reallocating funds across sectors, to increase the persistence of real interest rate effects through time. Christiano and Eichenbaum (1995) add inflexibilities in the production process (firms cannot adjust their production plans, once a surplus of cash arises) to drive real interest rate effects.[17]

The mechanisms specified by Tobin (1969) and Mundell (1963) also generate changes in real interest rates. Tobin argues that higher rates of expected inflation induce shifts out of currency and into bonds, thus lowering the real rate of interest on real assets. Whereas Tobin focuses on a substitution effect occurring through portfolio holdings, Mundell focuses on income effects (the Tobin and Mundell effects are often confused in casual discussions). Mundell argues that inflation lowers private sector wealth, which may induce a savings increase, again lowering real rates of return. These effects, however, have fallen out of favor in recent times. The elasticity of currency demand with respect to inflation is relatively low, at least for moderate rates of inflation; furthermore the capital stock

---

[17] For another recent treatment, see Dotsey and Ireland (1995).

is large in value relative to shifts in the supply of currency (Summers 1983). The Mundell effect neglects the relative stability of private savings and does not account for changes in the government budget constraint. Society as a whole does not feel poorer, following an inflationary redistribution of wealth. For these reasons, the mechanisms postulated by both Tobin and Mundell have fallen out of favor.[18]

Do long rates or short rates matter?

The increase in investment, following the decline in real interest rates, does not presuppose any particular assumptions about the relative elasticities of investment with regard to short- and long-term interest rates. Keynesians frequently have argued that monetary policy cannot stimulate investment. Monetary policy supposedly lowers the short rate alone, while the long rate supposedly regulates investment demand. This perspective, however, is misleading and does not imply irrelevance of the short rate for investment decisions.

Entrepreneurs might make investment decisions by comparing the current long rate to the expected long rate for the next period. This expected difference in the long rate is given precisely by the current short rate. Forward-looking investors therefore may pay greater heed to short rates than to long rates, even if they are planning long-term investments. If we assume that capital is homogeneous and entrepreneurs will never wish to disinvest, looking at the short rate alone suffices to determine optimal investment (Hall 1977). While these assumptions are clearly unrealistic, Hall's analysis does show that the primacy of the long rate in determining investment demand cannot be taken for granted. Altug (1993), who considers an explicit 'time to build' technology, shows that investment decisions typically ought to depend upon all parts of the term structure. Short rates also will affect investment to the extent that short-term borrowing helps finance long-term projects; short-term working capital and long-term investment capital may be complements (Machlup 1940, pp. 256–7). Short-term borrowing is especially important for small firms, who do not typically have access to securities issues or established lines of credit. The data, the final arbiter, provide at least partial support for the importance of a monetary channel on investment, as will be discussed in Chapter 5.

A reasonable consensus exists in the empirical literature that the Federal Reserve can influence short-run real interest rates. Whether monetary policy also will induce long real rates to fall depends on expectations.

---

[18] See also Fried and Howitt (1983), who provide a generalization of the Tobin effect in terms of which assets are most easily substitutable for money. Cagan (1972) also interprets the real interest rate effects of money in terms of portfolio effects.

Changes in long rates will reflect the expectations that entrepreneurs hold about future short-term rates, and thus reflect expectations about future monetary policy. If entrepreneurs expect short-term rates to remain low, long rates will fall with short-term rates.[19]

Theory cannot predict whether the immediate increase in investment is greater when both long and short real rates fall, or when short rates fall alone. A low long rate implies expectations of permanently low real short rates; conversely, a relatively high long rate implies expectations of only temporarily low real short rates. Two offsetting effects will operate. On one hand, relative price effects which are perceived as permanent spur demand less than relative price effects which are perceived as temporary (Lucas 1981). The immediate interest-elasticity of investment may be higher from a fall in the short rate alone. On the other hand, the expectation of a permanently low real rate may favor an immediate boost in long-term investment if entrepreneurs must undertake complementary borrowing in future periods. For that reason, the interest elasticity of a fall in the short rate may be higher when it is accompanied by a fall in the long rate as well.

---

[19] The above argument draws upon the so-called 'expectations theory' of the term structure of interest rates. Although the available data appear to contradict the expectations theory of the term structure, this result may be an artifact of short-run nominal interest smoothing by the central bank. With short-term interest rate smoothing, observed variations in the short rate signal only central bank unwillingness to target the short rate on an absolutely continuous basis. Such short-rate variations will have little or no predictive power for long rates; when short rates are currently high, for instance, market participants will not expect future long rates to be falling. Nominal rates will either be stationary, or if the Federal Reserve changes its targets over time, will mimic a random walk. These supposed empirical refutations of the expectations theory do not actually discriminate against it (Rudebusch 1995). Consistent with this point, Mankiw and Miron (1986) find that the expectations theory, as traditionally conceived, applies more clearly before the founding of the Federal Reserve.

4

BUSINESS CYCLES WITHOUT RATIONAL EXPECTATIONS:
The Traditional Approach of the Austrian School

THE TRADITIONAL AUSTRIAN CLAIM

The traditional Austrian claim: Positive rates of nominal money growth induce unsustainable increases in long-term investment.

Traditional Austrian business cycle theories focus on the overexpansion of long-term investment as the relevant intertemporal coordination problem. We find this emphasis in the writings of Mises, Hayek, Rothbard, Garrison, and other presentations of Austrian cycle theory. Competing presentations of the Austrian theory offer differing accounts of exactly how and why these malinvestments cause business downturns, but the initial overexpansion of long-term investment is central to all versions of the theory.[1]

This chapter examines the signal extraction problems behind the traditional Austrian theory in detail and considers whether entrepreneurs will, in fact, overexpand long-term investment in response to an inflation-induced decline in real interest rates. I will attempt to draw out the underlying expectational assumptions behind the traditional Austrian theory and examine whether these assumptions are plausible and whether they generate the stated conclusions. I also contrast the traditional Austrian theory with the risk-based approaches of the last two chapters; the final section of this chapter explicitly compares and contrasts the two approaches, and asks whether some synthesis or rapprochement might be possible. Similar to the risk-based theory presented above, the traditional Austrian account views investment as the transmission mechanism for the cycle, starts with the assumption of full employment, links the monetary and real sectors of the economy, uses a loanable funds theory of interest, and builds on Wicksellian themes.

---

[1] See the writings of Mises, Hayek, Rothbard, and Garrison, as cited in the bibliography. O'Driscoll (1977, 1980), McCulloch (1981), O'Driscoll and Rizzo (1985), de Long (1990), Skousen (1990), McCormack (1992), van Zijp (1993), Laidler (1994), and Colonna and Hagemann (1994) offer recent treatments of the Austrian theory.

The traditional Austrian theory attempts to link monetary policy to a very specific set of expectational errors; in this regard the Austrian theory is more ambitious than the risk-based theory outlined above. The risk-based theory focuses on the likelihood of errors in general, rather than postulating a specific kind of error. This chapter should be read as both a commentary on the traditional Austrian theory, and a more general critique of attempts to pin down the exact signal extraction problems behind the business cycle.

The expectational assumptions behind the traditional Austrian theory

The postulated entrepreneurial mistakes in the traditional Austrian theory, which are systematic, violate the rational expectations hypothesis. Entrepreneurs with rational expectations will sometimes choose unprofitable term-lengths of investment, but they will not err systematically towards excessive term-length. The expectational assumptions behind the Austrian claim, while they never have been fully specified, appear to consist of two separate concepts:

1 Naïve expectations: entrepreneurs underestimate the probability that monetary inflation is responsible for observed changes in the economic data.
2 Elastic expectations: entrepreneurs overestimate the permanence of observed price and interest rate changes.

Both naïve and elastic expectations differ from adaptive expectations, a commonly used alternative to rational expectations. Under adaptive expectations, individuals initially underestimate the impact of monetary changes, but gradually converge to rational expectations over time. The naïve expectations assumption postulates initial ignorance of monetary conditions, but neither implies nor rules out eventual convergence. Elastic expectations differ from both adaptive expectations and naïve expectations. Individuals overestimate the permanence of the real effects of monetary policy.[2]

Naïve and elastic expectations, although two separate and distinct assumptions, imply similar kinds of perceptual errors. Entrepreneurs are placing too much weight upon immediately available observations, without worrying sufficiently about the underlying causes of those observations or whether the observations will persist. Visible signals are given too much weight, relative to less visible pieces of information, or relative to general caution about the information communicated by visible signals.

The expectational errors postulated by traditional Austrian theory imply that signal extraction problems will induce resource misallocation. My

---

[2] On the Austrian assumption of elastic expectations, see Lachmann (1943) and Mises (1943). Garrison (1989, p. 10) refers to the Austrian theory as assuming 'static' expectations.

discussion will refer repeatedly to three kinds of signal extraction problems:

1 Signal extraction problem one: entrepreneurs may confuse real and nominal price changes.
2 Signal extraction problem two: interest rates may provide entrepreneurs with misleading information about forthcoming expenditure streams.
3 Signal extraction problem three: entrepreneurs may incorrectly estimate the permanence of observed price or interest rate changes.

The Austrian claim is based upon signal extraction problems two and three. The government engineers an exogenous increase in the money supply, increasing the supply of loanable funds and prompting real interest rates to fall. The decline in real interest rates then brings both kinds of signal extraction problems to bear on entrepreneurial decisions. First, entrepreneurs mistakenly believe consumers have increased their rate of saving. The demand for consumption goods in the far future is expected to rise, relative to demand for consumption goods in the near future. Rothbard (1975, p. 18), for instance, writes: 'Businessmen, in short, are misled by the bank inflation into believing that the supply of saved funds is greater than it really is.'[3]

Second, entrepreneurs believe the decline in real interest rates is permanent. They invest under the expectation of continuing low rates, and are later disappointed by a higher real rate increase. At least since Hayek (1939), the Austrian theory has emphasized the first expectational error rather than the second. I consider both for the sake of completeness; in fact the first kind of expectational error may be more problematic than the second kind.

Note that lending out the new inflationary funds does not itself suffice to set a business cycle in motion. In principle, entrepreneurs could borrow the funds and reinvest them in safe, short-term production processes, or perhaps use the funds to pay off previous debts. Generation of the cycle requires that entrepreneurs borrow the funds to undertake long-term, risky investment projects. For the theory to hold, entrepreneurs must be fooled by incorrect price signals emanating from the interest rate.[4]

An alternative version of the Austrian theory may arise if monetary policy and real interest rates are constant, and the real rate of return on investment shifts, leading to a discrepancy between market and 'natural' rates of interest. Without intending any prejudice against these real scenarios, I will focus on the argument which blames monetary policy for

---

[3] See Garrison (1986), for instance, for another example of this claim.
[4] For two Austrian discussions of mistaken expectations about real interest rates, see Rothbard (1975, p. 21), and Mises (1978, p. 130).

the business cycle, to examine if the Austrians have developed a coherent monetary scenario.[5]

According to the traditional Austrian theory, each effect implies that entrepreneurs read the lower real rate incorrectly and respond by over-expanding long-term investment. The eventual unprofitability of these investments provides a negative shock and sets off the downward phase of the business cycle. Appendix C to this chapter will consider the complications involved with defining 'capital-intensity' and 'long-term investment' in detail, but for the time being I accept the traditional Austrian use of these concepts without question. I use the two concepts interchangeably throughout the discussion.

Rothbard (1975, p. 19) provides a clear summary of the traditional Austrian theory:

> In sum, businessmen were misled by bank credit inflation to invest too much in higher-order capital goods, which could only be prosperously sustained through lower time preferences and greater savings and investment; as soon as the inflation permeates to the mass of the people, the old consumption/investment proportion is reestablished, and business investments in the higher orders are seen to have been wasteful. Businessmen were led to this error by the credit expansion and its tampering with the free-market rate of interest.

For purposes of clarification, consider how the traditional Austrian theory differs from the business cycle mechanism specified by Lucas (1972, 1981). In the Lucas model, agents commit only the first kind of signal extraction problem – they confuse real and nominal shocks. Agents produce on different 'islands,' and cannot observe demand conditions elsewhere in the economy. They confuse increases in nominal prices with increases in the real demand for their product, and expand labor supply to produce more real output. Intertemporal substitution of leisure gives rise to a pattern of boom and bust. The relevant mistake is made through labor supply rather than through the capital market. In fact incorporation of an economy-wide capital market into the model will tend to eliminate real–nominal confusions, as emphasized by King (1983). The traditional Austrian approach, in contrast, starts with capital market effects. The confusion between real and nominal variables is left out of the story, but individuals make two kinds of errors about real interest rates. Individuals assume too much permanence to observed price changes, and individuals assume that

---

[5] Mises had originally believed that excessively low real rates of interest could be caused by exogenous real shocks. Later he revised his opinion and blamed increases in the quantity of money relative to demand (1978, pp. 135–6). He appears to have included fractional reserve banking, government discount rate policies, and government pressures on banks to lower their discount rates under this rubric (e.g., 1978, pp. 139, 144–5, 167–8, *passim*). For some other real scenarios, see Hayek (1966); Cottrell (1994) discusses this strand in Hayek's work.

all changes in real interest rates are caused by changes in private saving.

Two other business cycle theories postulate signal extraction problems through capital markets, but they also differ from the traditional Austrian theory. Grossman and Weiss (1982) build a real business cycle model based on capital market imperfections. Malinvestments occur because agents cannot use the nominal interest rate to distinguish between aggregate and idiosyncratic shocks to productivity. Uncertainty about money demand prevents entrepreneurs from reading the appropriate real interest rates from observed nominal rates. In the model of Barro (1980), unexpected increases in the money supply enter through output markets, thereby raising the prices of consumer goods and increasing expected rates of return. Output and employment will increase as part of an erroneous response to this change.[6]

Outline of the critique

I consider eight reasons why the traditional Austrian claim does not fully establish the plausibility of the specified entrepreneurial errors. First, the Austrian claim requires that entrepreneurs make systematic errors in the most costly possible direction by choosing excess capital-intensity. Second, the volatility associated with inflation might discourage rather than encourage long-term investments. Third, entrepreneurs will confuse monetary inflation with an increase in private savings only if private savings is volatile. Fourth, entrepreneurs might confuse monetary inflation with declines in investment demand, rather than with increases in private savings. Fifth, confusions about real vs. nominal interest rates may imply that chosen term-lengths are too short rather than too long. Sixth, the Austrian claim requires that interest rates provide relevant and significant signals about the composition of consumer demand. Seventh, the Austrian claim requires special (and implausible) assumptions about how investors interpret interest rate signals, combined with special assumptions about the term structure of interest rates. Eighth, constant or roughly constant rates of nominal money growth may validate newly chosen long-term investments to some degree. Volatile money growth, not positive money growth, provides the more likely monetary culprit for intertemporal coordination problems.

None of these eight arguments requires the assumption of rational expectations, or implies that money does not have real effects. In each case, non-RE assumptions can provide results contrary to those stated in the

---

[6] Barro also postulates a curious interest rate mechanism. On one hand, the unexpected money supply increase will lower nominal interest rates through a liquidity effect; on the other hand, increased nominal demand pressure in output markets implies that expected real rates have risen. Barro reconciles these two results by postulating that individuals (mistakenly) expect the rate of price inflation to fall.

Austrian claim. Even if we accept the premise that monetary inflation fools entrepreneurs, it is difficult to generate the specifics of the Austrian claim about systematically excessive long-term investment. For this reason, the criticisms outlined in this chapter also are robust to reinterpretations of the Austrian theory. For instance, defenders of the Austrian theory might cite additional reasons, which I have not considered, in support of the Austrian claim. Such new arguments, if they could be adduced, would not answer the overall thrust of my criticism. I do not deny that we can cite many distortionary forces operating in a single direction; rather, my claim is that we cannot rule out the contrary forces which induce distortions in other directions as well.

The arguments of this chapter also illustrate two more general themes: First, postulating systematic deviations from rational expectations does not improve the prospects of monetary theories of the trade cycle. Second, the original Austrian claim does not specify the relevant signal extraction problems with sufficient clarity and logical rigor. Under various auxiliary assumptions, outlined in the text, the Austrian claim may still be valid. Nonetheless the eight arguments, taken collectively, show that the Austrian claim lacks generality and requires very special assumptions about knowledge and expectations for its support. The injection of inflationary funds into the loanable funds market does not, without numerous auxiliary assumptions and effects, lead to excess long-term investment.

POSTULATING ESPECIALLY COSTLY ERRORS

The Austrian claim postulates systematic entrepreneurial errors in the most costly possible direction. Entrepreneurs do not merely err in their choice of term-length; entrepreneurs choose excessive investment term-length when confronted with inflation. More specifically, the theory does not allow entrepreneurs to overestimate the dangers of an inflationary boom and to respond by keeping investment term-length too short.

Excessive caution may be just as likely as excessive boldness. We can imagine a 'mirror image' version of Austrian theory in which entrepreneurs live in great fear of inflation. They do not understand inflation very well, and cannot observe the money supply, but they do know inflation sometimes brings negative consequences for their businesses. As price theory predicts, the real rate of interest will fall when private savings have increased. Yet in this mirror image theory, entrepreneurs do not respond with a significant increase in long-term investment, as they ought to. Entrepreneurs believe that the increase in private savings is in fact an increase in monetary inflation. The rate of growth is low, but the economy never experiences a business cycle.

Austrian theorists do not address why the mirror image scenario is less plausible than the case they emphasize. In fact we might expect the mirror image scenario to be more plausible. Austrian business cycle theory implies that excessive investment term-length brings especially high costs – a business cycle downturn. According to the Austrian claim, entrepreneurs deviate from rational expectations in the least advantageous direction; we might instead expect them to deviate in the more cautious direction.[7]

Under rational expectations, if excessive term-length has higher costs than insufficient term-length, risk-averse entrepreneurs will play it safe and more likely err on the short side. Expected utility maximization implies individuals will take special care to avoid an especially costly outcome. The Austrian claim not only violates rational expectations but requires an especially severe *naïveté*. Even entrepreneurs without rational expectations have some tendency to avoid erring in the more costly direction.

Some Austrians have argued the following: even if entrepreneurs realize that long-term investment will prove unprofitable, they will undertake the investment anyway and sell that investment to more foolish entrepreneurs before the downturn arrives. Viewed more generally, this argument suggests that the more foolish and overly optimistic entrepreneurs will bid to own the relevant investment resources in the first place. A 'winner's curse' will operate to place resources in the hands of the most overly optimistic entrepreneurs.[8]

Such a maneuver does not rescue the Austrian claim. Winner's curse arguments imply that the market economy already possesses a systematic tendency to make overly optimistic investments; monetary inflation is not needed to set off this effect. Presumably a winner's curse effect would operate even in the absence of inflation. In addition, excessive entrepreneurial optimism does not imply a systematic distortion in the direction of excess long-term investment. Entrepreneurs can be overly optimistic about the prospects for short-term investment as well, even in the presence of monetary inflation. Following an inflation, for instance, entrepreneurs may believe the lower real interest rate does not discriminate against short-term investments much at all. These entrepreneurs will bid for resources to increase short-term investment. Excess optimism will induce resource dis-

---

[7] Some commentators on the Austrian claim have questioned how the theory generates the postulated asymmetry between boom and bust (I discuss this issue in Chapter 2). The original Austrian theory, for reasons not fully explicated by its advocates, associates the move from long-term investments to short-term investments with an economic bust. Within the same framework, entrepreneurial moves from short-term to long-term investments cause an economic boom, at least temporarily. Whatever the microfoundations for the boom/bust distinction, the move to longer term-lengths involves greater precariousness and greater risk. Entrepreneurs therefore should err more likely on the side of caution than on the side of boldness, given the asymmetry assumption. Hummel (1979, pp. 43–5) surveys some (brief) Austrian attempts to address the issue of asymmetry; see, for instance, Hayek (1967, p. 93n). On the critical side, see Durbin (1935, pp. 242–6), and Gilbert (1955, pp. 55–6).

[8] I have heard such arguments frequently in the Austrian oral tradition, although I have not seen them in print.

tortions in all directions; the question remains open why distortions should appear systematically in the most costly direction possible.

INFLATION VS. INFLATIONARY VOLATILITY

The economic volatility associated with inflation provides one reason why entrepreneurs might respond to monetary shocks by decreasing rather than increasing long-term investment. Chapter 3 presented unexpected money growth and increased monetary volatility as two distinct cases with opposing effects on long-term investment. The Austrian claim focuses on only one of the two scenarios – unexpected money growth and lower real interest rates. Entrepreneurs, however, also might read inflation, or low real interest rates, as a signal of a more volatile economic environment. Even naïve entrepreneurs who underestimate the presence of inflation might attach some probability to the presence of a volatile inflationary environment. The traditional Austrian theory itself claims the government cannot maintain a steady rate of inflation over time, and must at some point introduce inflation volatility (see pp. 96–100).

An increase in economic volatility decreases the reliability of current information and induces entrepreneurs to shy away from long-term projects. In other words, the added volatility increases option value, or the value of waiting. Entrepreneurs will be less inclined to make long-term commitments, and will be more inclined to move to short-term assets, such as cash or T-Bills. Inflation therefore may lead to an immediate contraction of long-term investment.

Inflation and the perception of inflation volatility have opposite effects on long-term investment, and the negative effect of volatility may well be stronger. Under plausible choices of parameter values, moderate amounts of uncertainty may more than double the required expected rate of return for a project to be undertaken (McDonald and Siegel 1986). Such an increase in required rates of return may more than counteract the stimulating effects of lower real interest rates.

The Austrian claim requires at least one of two conditions. Either the stimulating effect of lower real interest rates must outweigh the discouraging effect of inflation volatility, or inflation might not be correlated with inflation volatility. In the latter case, increasing the rate of inflation would not bring an accompanying volatility effect. The first possibility has received no empirical investigation, and the second claim appears to be empirically false; in any case volatility effects show that naïve expectations do not suffice to induce excess long-term investment.[9]

---

[9] Evans (1991) finds that inflation and inflation volatility are correlated positively; for a theoretical account, see Ball (1992). On the effects of economic volatility on investment, see Chapter 5.

IS INFLATION CONFUSED WITH CHANGES IN CONSUMER SAVINGS?

The Austrian claim, like all monetary misperceptions theories, must specify the confusion that inflation creates. In other words, what exactly do entrepreneurs misperceive a monetary change to be? The major statements of the Austrian claim provide a common answer to this question. Entrepreneurs confuse nominal money supply growth with increases in private savings.

The plausibility of such a confusion, even under naïve and elastic expectations, requires that private saving be volatile and unpredictable. To the extent that private saving is either stable or predictable, the postulated monetary misperception will not occur. In the limit, a totally stable rate of private savings implies that entrepreneurs will never associate real interest rate moves with changes in the savings rate. When savings are relatively stable, the postulated Austrian confusion appears especially implausible. Entrepreneurs should not confuse monetary policy with changes in savings when savings changes only slightly or not at all.

The Austrian claim therefore requires savings to be a relatively volatile, unpredictable economic variable. Yet empirical macroeconomists traditionally have found savings to be one of the most stable variables over time, using a variety of tests, and in a variety of developed economies. At least on the surface, the Austrian claim specifies an implausible signal extraction problem. Signal extraction problems tend to be greatest when *both* potential causes for a given event – real or monetary causes of low real interest rates, in this case – exhibit considerable variation.

Volatile savings behavior can rescue the Austrian claim, but only at a cost. If savings were more volatile, monetary factors could not provide the sole explanation of business cycles. Unstable private saving implies that misperceptions of the savings rate will cause business cycles even in the absence of distortive monetary policy. Entrepreneurs would incorrectly forecast current and future private savings rates with reasonable frequency. Incorrect forecasts of that nature would induce entrepreneurs to choose inappropriate term-lengths for investment; Hummel (1979, p. 41) argues for the possibility of such a real cycle through volatile savings behavior.

The price signals generated by market interest rates do not suffice to eliminate the difficulty of forecasting future rates of savings. Even if interest rates correctly signal the current quantity of savings, entrepreneurs still will err in correctly forecasting future rates of saving, provided the savings rate is volatile and unpredictable.

The Austrian claim therefore is caught in a bind. To the extent that entrepreneurs can forecast current and future rates of consumer saving, monetary policy will not induce malinvestments. To the extent entrepreneurs cannot forecast current and future rates of saving, monetary factors cannot be the sole or primary source of malinvestments.

More generally, all monetary misperceptions theories imply a corresponding real theory of the business cycle; monetary misperceptions cannot be the sole causes of cycles. Monetary misperceptions arise only when a monetary shock is confused with a real shock. The monetary shock has significant effects on behavior only to the extent that the same real shock also can produce significant cyclical effects. In other words, when money is postulated as the only potential cause of significant plan discoordination, that plan discoordination becomes implausible. When some other potential cause of significant plan discoordination exists, that other source also will cause business cycles.

The potential for real business cycles, based on forecast errors in non-inflationary environments, is heightened by the expectational assumptions behind the Austrian claim. If entrepreneurs have elastic expectations, for instance, they will overestimate the likely future duration of observed changes. Temporary changes in market conditions will induce systematic malinvestments in all cases, not just inflationary scenarios. Entrepreneurs in volatile environments will systematically over-react to period-by-period changes in their information set. Economy-wide increases in real economic volatility will induce over-adjustments that will prove unprofitable in the long run, thereby inducing correlated clusters of error.

CONFUSING INFLATION WITH CHANGES IN INVESTMENT DEMAND

The Austrian claim assumes that entrepreneurs attribute a lower real interest rate to a shift in the supply curve for loanable funds rather than to a shift in the demand curve. The Austrian literature, however, does not address why one kind of confusion might be more likely than the other. At least three factors may lower real interest rates: higher non-inflationary savings, inflationary injections into the loanable funds market, and declines in investment demand. The Austrian claim implicitly assumes entrepreneurs confuse the first and second of these causes, and does not consider the alternative possibility of a confusion between the second and third causes.

The postulated confusion between money growth and a private, non-inflationary savings increase arises only to the extent that entrepreneurs perceive private investment demand to be stable. Otherwise, entrepreneurs may read lower real interest rates as a signal of lower investment demand, rather than as a signal of greater private savings supply. Lower real interest rates may (mistakenly) signal that potential investors have lowered their demand for loanable funds.

Confusing money growth with declines in investment demand, while it may induce significant distortions, limits the potential for a business cycle of the specifically Austrian kind. The real interest rate falls, and entrepreneurs are tricked by this fall, but they do not believe consumer savings have increased. Entrepreneurs therefore will not expect demanders to shift their expenditures into the relatively distant future. The signal extraction problem of the second kind, forecasting the temporal distribution of forthcoming expenditure streams, no longer supports the Austrian claim. The only cyclical force remaining is entrepreneurial overestimation of the permanence of observed interest rate changes (elastic expectations); that is, entrepreneurial overestimations of how long lower real interest rates will last.

If entrepreneurs can observe supply and demand curves in the loanable funds market, they will not confuse an inflationary decline in the real interest rate with a decline in investment demand. Postulating the observation of supply and demand curves, however, does not help establish the Austrian claim. If entrepreneurs can read underlying supply and demand curves, they probably also can ascertain the quantity of private savings. Monetary misperceptions of all kinds become less likely. The Austrian claim also assumes investors cannot properly read or interpret money supply figures. If the current money supply is difficult to observe or interpret, we might expect current data on loanable funds supply to be difficult to observe or interpret as well.

Alternatively, we might assume that potential investors observe only market prices (i.e., interest rates) and do not know the supply and demand curves behind this price. In that case lower real interest rates may again be confused with declines in investment demand, rather than be confused with increases in private non-inflationary savings.

Economic theory offers no *a priori* indication of whether entrepreneurs will confuse the real interest rate move with a shift in loanable funds demand or with a shift in the supply of non-inflationary savings. The process of expectations formation remains a black box from the point of view of economic theory. Intuition nonetheless suggests the greater likelihood of a confusion with the more volatile variable. That is, whether entrepreneurs confuse inflation with shifts in investment demand or with savings supply depends upon which is more volatile.

The available evidence strongly suggests that loanable funds demand is far more volatile than loanable funds supply; in other words, investment demand is far more volatile than savings. Entrepreneurs will therefore tend to read interest shifts as signaling changes in investment demand, rather than as signaling changes in non-inflationary savings. To that extent, the specific signal extractions problems behind the Austrian theory simply do not apply.[10]

---

[10] On the greater relative volatility of investment, see, for instance, Sherman (1991, p. 111).

Digression on the paradoxes of information

When entrepreneurs associate lower real interest rates with declines in investment demand, the question remains what conclusion they draw from their (potentially mistaken) inference. The inference of lower investment demand might none the less induce more long-term investment if entrepreneurs assume that the lower real interest rate represents an *erroneous* contraction of investment on the part of other entrepreneurs. Each entrepreneur might expect future supplies of goods and services to be lower than profitable and they will perceive a profit opportunity in producing for the more distant future. In other words, if entrepreneurs second-guess the validity of a perceived decline in investment, excess long-term investment may arise through another mechanism, a mechanism not specified by the traditional Austrian theory.

This source of malinvestment remains a potential scenario, but invoking this argument alters the informational assumptions behind the traditional Austrian theory. In other contexts the Austrian theory assumes that investors read price signals naïvely rather than strategically. Entrepreneurs believe that price signals represent real changes in opportunities rather than errors on the part of other market participants. Entrepreneurs observe prices, and then use those prices to update their priors about the real opportunities out in the world; in other words entrepreneurs 'free ride' on the information suggested by the price. If we apply the assumption of naïve price-reading behavior consistently, the lower real interest rate will signal a lower demand to invest, and will induce entrepreneurs to believe investment prospects have declined in attractiveness. Despite the lower real interest rate, entrepreneurs reading a signal of widespread pessimism may be reluctant to significantly expand long-term investment. Increased entrepreneurial wariness will raise the option value of remaining liquid or will raise the relative expected returns to choosing safer short-term investment projects.

This discussion raises the well-known paradoxes of information associated with Grossman and Stiglitz (1980). Not all market participants can read prices naïvely. If all market participants read prices naïvely, the prices themselves will contain no information and naïve price-reading behavior will yield no gains. More realistically, some entrepreneurs behave naïvely and some entrepreneurs believe price signals are erroneous and prone to successful arbitrage. This outcome, however, does not necessarily bode well for the Austrian claim. The entrepreneurs who behave naïvely will free ride on observed price information. They may interpret a decline in real interest rate as a decline in the desirability of long-term investment, and will not necessarily expand their operations. On the other hand, the investors who do market research and who question observed prices will not necessarily be tricked by the monetary inflation.

DO INTEREST RATES PROVIDE USEFUL INFORMATION ABOUT CONSUMER DEMAND?

The Austrian claim requires that entrepreneurs use interest rates to forecast the content of consumer demand. Following a decline in real interest rates, long-term investment rises for two distinct reasons, according to the Austrian claim. First, the lower real rate increases the relative present value of long-term projects. Second, the lower real rate provides a signal about the composition of future demands. In other words, entrepreneurs expect demand to be high for the outputs of long-term projects, and expect demand to be relatively low for the outputs of shorter-term projects.

The available evidence does not lend much credence to this second signal extraction problem. In reality, the real interest rate appears to play only a weak role in signaling how demands will be distributed across time. Expectations about income and employment provide more important information about the intertemporal variation in future demands.

The Austrian claim postulates not only that the interest-elasticity of investment decisions is high, but that the interest-elasticity is high for a particular reason. When entrepreneurs are forecasting whether demand for product A or product B will be higher, entrepreneurs supposedly examine the real interest rate to resolve the question. The real interest rate has importance above and beyond its effect on present value calculations; the real interest rate signals information about future demand curves for products in the Austrian world. To the extent the real interest rate does not signal information about demand curves, one of the two signal extraction problems behind the Austrian claim does not apply. Lower real interest rates will not induce entrepreneurs to conclude that demand for long-term outputs has risen (the second signal extraction problem).

Real interest rates do have significant predictive power for the demand for debt-financed consumer durables, such as homes and automobiles. Consumers often cannot save enough to buy houses, and must rely on mortgages. Demand curves for homes will depend on real interest rates. Mistaken expectations about future borrowing rates therefore may induce entrepreneurs to produce unprofitable outputs, such as homes, when consumers cannot afford mortgages.

The Austrian claim, however, specifies a different mechanism through which low interest rates signal high consumer demand in the future. The low real interest rate signals that savings are high today, and that consumption demand therefore will be strong in the relatively distant future. Debt-intensive purchases, as discussed above, imply the following chain of reasoning: entrepreneurs use current real interest rates to forecast future real interest rates, and use their estimates of future real interest rates to forecast future demand for debt-intensive purchases (e.g., real estate). The Austrian claim implies a different and less plausible chain of reasoning:

today's real interest rates, completely apart from any extrapolation about future real interest rates, help predict future demands by predicting forthcoming expenditure flows.

Several factors suggest that real interest rates will be poor predictors of future demand curves. The preponderance of evidence on consumption indicates great stability over time and with respect to the real interest rate (e.g., Carlino 1982; Christiano 1987a, 1987b; Campbell and Mankiw 1989). The Austrian claim, in contrast, requires that significant changes in the intertemporal distribution of consumption be correlated with observable changes in the real interest rate. For a change in the real interest rate to significantly alter expected project profitability through demand-side effects, interest rate changes must imply relatively large shifts in expected demand across time. If the real interest rate is low today, consumption in some future period must then be especially high. This prediction, however, contradicts the available data.[11]

To the extent consumption is stable over time, entrepreneurs will not use or need interest rates to forecast the temporal distribution of forthcoming expenditure streams. The stream of consumption will be easy to predict from past values, without examining interest rates. Even theories which imply varying consumption over time do not tend to support the Austrian claim. Some Keynesian theories claim that consumption varies considerably with current income and employment, and the life-cycle theory postulates that consumption varies with demographics, but neither theory assigns a critical role to the real interest rate.

Furthermore, changes in real interest rates signal only that the temporal distribution of demand has shifted. Real interest rates do not signal which particular goods will be in high demand at a given point in time. To the extent that the number of different outputs is high, the profit variance on a particular project arises primarily from product-specific factors, rather than on the overall intertemporal distribution of demand. Changes in the real interest rate will have only small effects on expected demand curves for particular products, relative to the other sources of variation behind entrepreneurial forecasts.

Somewhat ironically, the Austrian claim implies a central role for aggregate demand in determining project profitability, and downplays the importance of relative demands in a particular time period. The Austrians typically have criticized other aggregate demand theories for neglecting the

---

[11] In the post-war American economy, consumption has absorbed over 90 percent of personal disposable income and 60–65 percent of gross national product. From 1952 to 1980, the ratio of consumption to GNP has never fallen below 61.5 percent and never risen above 64.5 percent; see Sherman (1991, p. 83) and Christiano (1987a, 1987b). On consumption as a random walk, see Hall (1978). Hall (1986) has tried to argue for the cyclical importance of shocks to aggregate consumption, but this argument has not found favor; see the accompanying comments by Deaton (1986) and King (1986). Temin (1976) argues that consumption shocks were a significant contributing force behind the Great Depression.

particular content of consumer demands. Yet within the Austrian theory itself, the real interest rate, at most, signals the distribution of aggregate demand over time; the real interest rate does not signal how that demand will be distributed across particular products once that time period arrives. Success of the Austrian claim therefore requires that signals about aggregate expenditure flows play a large role in determining the success of investment forecasts, relative to signals about demands for particular products.

Decision-making strategies outlined in managerial texts do not suggest using real interest rates to infer future consumer demand. Investment theory assigns interest rates importance as borrowing costs, or as means of calculating present value, but neglects interest rates as signals of the content of future expenditure streams. Managers do not generally treat real interest rates as significant predictors of future demand curves. The validity of the Austrian claim not only requires a revision of investment theory, but also requires that entrepreneurs already have made such a revision in their decision-making practices, and that business school education lags behind.

DO OTHER SIGNAL EXTRACTION PROBLEMS COUNTERACT THE AUSTRIAN CLAIM?

The naïve expectations assumption may operate against the Austrian claim, once all signal extraction problems are specified fully. As explained above, the Austrian claim relies on signal extraction problems of the second and third kinds (forecast of expenditure streams, and temporary vs. permanent changes). Yet the naïve expectations assumption also implies confusions about real and nominal variables (signal extraction problems of the first kind). Real vs. nominal mistakes counteract the tendency for chosen invest-ments to be excessively long term, and raise the likelihood of investments which are insufficiently long term.

To the extent investors have naïve expectations, they do not fully antici-pate the forthcoming effects of money supply growth. Incipient price inflation will not raise nominal interest rates through a Fisher effect. Future price increases will arrive unexpectedly, and *ex post* real rates of interest will be lower than currently observed nominal rates would indicate. In other words, entrepreneurs will have overestimated forthcoming real rates of interest on borrowing. *Ex post* real borrowing rates will be especially low, perhaps even negative.

Investments financed with medium- to long-term debt will reap an unexpected windfall from the arrival of unexpected inflation. Entre-preneurs, by initially overestimating the real rates of interest that will prevail, will have been too reluctant to borrow money. To that extent, entrepreneurs will choose too little short-term investment. Real vs. nominal confusions thus counteract the traditional Austrian claim, which suggests that entrepreneurs choose too much long-term investment.[12]

Unexpected price inflation of even a few percent will make *ex post* real interest rates zero or negative in most cases (Summers 1983). Most *ex ante* real rates do not exceed a few percent. Unexpected inflation will in any case cause *ex post* realized borrowing rates to be lower than expected, not higher.

As long as the inflation continues, the real vs. nominal confusion counteracts the permanent vs. temporary confusion. If unperceived inflation continues, so will the unexpectedly low realizations of real interest rates. The Austrian claim therefore requires the relative insignificance of real vs. nominal signal extraction problems. Ironically, when it comes to real vs. nominal variables, the Austrian claim implicitly attributes information-processing skills to agents that even some rational expectations theorists, such as Lucas, do not.

If entrepreneurs come to anticipate the inflation, or if the inflation stops, the real vs. nominal confusion ceases. In those cases, however, the other signal extraction problems disappear as well, limiting malinvestment. Entrepreneurs will not necessarily assume that consumers have decreased their nominal spending, or that declines in the real interest rate are permanent.

More generally, welfare losses do not increase monotonically with the number of signal extraction problems facing entrepreneurs. A greater number of signal extraction problems can produce better forecasts than a smaller number of signal extraction problems. In the example given above, one signal extraction problem offers a kind of insurance against another signal extraction problem. Entrepreneurs underestimate the rate of money growth and conclude that a lower real interest rate is permanent when in fact it is temporary. Entrepreneurs may borrow too much for long-term projects. An error of this nature, however, will be partially remedied by the decline in borrowing costs brought on by unexpected inflation. The two postulated errors tend to offset each other.

Net expansion of long-term investment, as postulated by the Austrian claim, requires that signal extraction problems of the second and third kind (forecasts of expenditure streams, and temporary vs. permanent) outweigh real vs. nominal confusions. Entrepreneurs must place great emphasis on interest rates as a means of forecasting future expenditure streams, and place relatively little emphasis on the interest cost of debt. The above arguments (see pp. 88–89), however, implied that real interest rates play a relatively minor role in signaling future consumer demand.

---

[12] Austrian economists have recognized the possibility of a Fisher effect from almost the beginnings of their work in monetary theory (e.g., Mises 1978, pp. 93–4), but have not considered whether imperfect Fisher effects might counteract traditional Austrian business cycle theory.

DOES THE TERM STRUCTURE OF INTEREST RATES SIGNAL INFLATION TO INVESTORS?

The term structure of interest rates may communicate information which limits the ability of monetary inflation to induce excessive investment term-length. Monetary inflation tends to lower short-term real rates more than it lowers long-term real rates; the resulting signals limit entrepreneurial tendencies to malinvest.

Savings has both a quantity or value dimension and a time dimension. The value dimension refers to the stock of saved funds at a given point in time. The time dimension refers to how long these savings are held before being spent. Entrepreneurs use real interest rates as signals of how much individuals are saving in the current period, and as signals of how long individuals wish to save for, two distinct variables of import.[13]

The short rate signals how much individuals are saving now, while the long rate signals how long entrepreneurs expect savings to last before being converted into consumption. Current long-term rates represent the market forecast of expected future short-term rates, adjusting for risk, liquidity, and frictions. If entrepreneurs expect future short rates to be low, the current long rate will be low as well. A low current long rate implies that entrepreneurs expect savings to last, i.e., that currently saved funds will not be spent on consumption until the distant future.

The Austrian claim, as commonly presented, does not specify whether investors misread short-term interest rates, long-term rates, or both. The Austrian claim assumes that all real interest rate decreases are interpreted as signals of demand shifts towards the future. In fact, declines in the (real) short rate indicate only that the supply of savings has increased for the moment; short rate declines do not indicate that individuals have an especially long time duration of saving. Only declines in the long rate signal an expected shift of expenditures to the relatively distant future.

The actual effect of a money supply increase on the term structure of interest rates depends on how the new inflationary funds are allocated across short-term or long-term loan markets. Short-term fund allocation lowers the short rate, and long-term fund allocation lowers the long rate. Banks will allocate the new funds to loan markets on the basis of which market offers the most promising set of loans, on the margin.

Incorporating term structure considerations decreases the plausibility of the Austrian claim. The available evidence suggests money supply inflation

---

[13] Previous arguments raised questions about the significance of interest rate signals for demand projections, and whether interest rates sent signals about savings supply or investment demand. For the remainder of this section, I will grant the Austrian claim the strongest possible case by setting these problems aside.

has greater effects on short-term than on long-term real interest rates. (Chapter 5 surveys this evidence in more detail.)

Declines in the short rate, unaccompanied by comparable declines in the long rate, signal relatively impermanent or temporary increases in the supply of loanable funds. Entrepreneurs will not respond to these signals by undertaking excessive long-term investment. Even entrepreneurs who are totally or partially unaware of monetary inflation may understand the distinct signals sent by long-term and short-term rates. The long-term interest rate, which serves as a direct indication of savings permanence, correctly signals entrepreneurs not to mistakenly assume the time duration of saving has risen.

The Austrian hypothesis that entrepreneurs overestimate the permanence of interest rate changes (elastic expectations) implies definite predictions about the term structure of interest rates. Money supply increases ought to decrease long-term real interest rates, not just short-term rates. Yet the available data do not provide strong support for this prediction (again, see Chapter 5).

The volatile and unpredictable nature of monetary policy may account for why inflation tends to have greater impact on short rates. To the extent inflation is high and volatile, banks will tend to place funds in the short-term loan market. Banks are lending specialists with a strong incentive to forecast the permanence of future fund flows. To the extent that subsequent monetary policy may cause real rates to rise in the future, banks will not wish to lend long, keeping long rates relatively high.

The term structure provides a mechanism through which the best-informed market participants communicate their expectations of monetary policy to all others. To the extent banks see inflation as a volatile source of fluctuations in the supply of loanable funds, they will increase only short-term lending in response to inflation. The term structure of interest rates will reflect this judgment accordingly. The lower short-term rates again reflect a message of 'temporariness' to potential lenders, allowing them to free ride upon the knowledge held by bankers. Even if investors as a whole do not have rational expectations about permanence, lenders and security market participants might. The term structure of interest rates tends to contain the best information available in the market about the likely permanence of observed interest rate changes.

Banks generally will not be fooled about current monetary policy – banks themselves receive the new inflationary monetary reserves. Under the Austrian claim, *someone* – at the very least the new money recipients – must know inflation has taken place rather than an increase in private savings. Banks can communicate this information to their customers either by allocating new loans through short-term markets (i.e., through the term structure of interest rates), or by directly advising their customers about the new inflationary environment.[14]

If the term structure does not communicate the appropriate information about interest rate permanence to investors, systematic arbitrage profits will be available. If the mistaken expectations behind the Austrian claim continue, systematic arbitrage profits can be reaped through trading in the term structure in the following manner. Currently low long-term real rates will not be validated by forthcoming short rates. Given that entrepreneurs are overestimating the permanence of currently low short rates, short rates will end up higher than had been expected. Traders can earn supra-normal expected profits by shorting medium-term bonds. Traders could complete a hedge by buying long-term instruments, if they wish to protect against exogenous changes in forthcoming short rates. To the extent monetary policy provides the relevant variation in interest rates, however, even the unhedged position would not be very risky to an investor who understands the Austrian theory.

ARE THE NEW INVESTMENTS SUSTAINABLE?

Even if an initial burst of money growth increases the term-length of investment, it remains an open question whether these new investments are necessarily malinvestments. Constant rates of nominal money growth, or nominal money rules, may sustain the new long-term projects to some degree. Some of the earliest and strongest criticisms of Austrian business cycle theory focused on whether the new investment would become malinvestments. The following discussion focuses on an initial burst of unexpected inflation, followed by maintenance of that inflation rate for the foreseeable future.[15]

A steady rate of money growth will increase loanable funds supply by a predictable amount each period. To the extent nominal money growth lowers real interest rates, real interest rates will remain low over time, or if not, market participants presumably may understand that real interest rates are subject to mean-reversion. Why should the newly undertaken investments prove to be mistakes?

---

[14] Analogous problems plague other monetary misperceptions models. In the Lucas (1972) model, an overlapping generations assumption is used. The old get the new money, and the young are confused about whether they observe real or nominal price increases. Young individuals do not receive the new money and thus cannot estimate the new money supply by examining their own portfolios. The Austrian model does not resort to this artifice, which is in any case implausible.

[15] Issues of sustainability have been raised, for instance, by Haberler (1964, Chapter 3), Sraffa (1932), Hansen and Tout (1933), Neisser (1934), Wilson (1940), Hansen (1964, p. 390), Hummel (1979), Haberler (1986), Tullock (1988, p. 73), and Laidler (1994), who also surveys the historical debate on the matter and offers the clearest statement of the problem.

The 'natural rate of interest'

Some expositions of Austrian business cycle theory use the concept of a 'natural rate of interest,' an idea dating at least as far back as Wicksell. According to these expositions, the new investment must be malinvestments because the market rate of interest does not correspond to the natural rate. Equality of the market rate and natural rate is required to maintain equilibrium for the chosen mix of capital goods and investment projects.

Earlier writers defined the natural rate of interest concept in various ways. Hayek originally defined the natural rate as the rate of interest that would prevail if savings and investment were made *in natura*; that is, without any distortionary monetary effects. Mises (1978, p. 124) defined the natural rate of interest as the equilibrium rate for the capital structure. Later treatments defined the natural rate as the real marginal productivity of capital or as the interest rate which equalizes *ex ante* savings and investment.[16]

The modern focus on signal extraction problems enables us to sharpen the natural rate of interest concept. I see the 'natural rate of interest' as an incomplete concept; the more important relation is whether investors' expectations are consistent with forthcoming market demands and supplies. In Austrian models the interest rate *always* clears the market for loanable funds. In that sense the market rate is always a 'natural' rate or an 'equilibrium' rate. If expectations are sufficiently sophisticated, this real interest rate will not induce disequilibrium, even if it has been lowered by monetary inflation. If entrepreneurs know that inflation caused the lower real rate, they do not necessarily respond with malinvestments. They can simply borrow the new funds and make safe, short-term investments. I am not suggesting that entrepreneurs always see through inflation, but the example shows that we cannot blame the level of the interest rate *per se*. Intertemporal discoordination arises, not when interest rates are at 'incorrect' levels, but when entrepreneurs misinterpret the information contained in interest rates and other market signals. Inflation may increase the likelihood of incorrect forecasts, but business cycle theory should focus on the derived expectational errors, rather than assuming that any inflation-induced interest rate movement necessarily creates distortions of a particular kind.

---

[16] On different definitions of the natural rate of interest, see also Marget (1938). Critics of the early Austrian theory made the concept of a natural rate of interest one of their prime targets. Sraffa (1932) criticized extant natural rate definitions for referring to a hypothetical barter or 'neutral money' economy. First, the relative prices of a barter economy may be irrelevant to a monetary economy. Second, in a barter economy a different natural rate of interest will prevail for every commodity. Keynes (1936) claimed savings and investment could be equilibrated at various levels of income and employment; a different natural rate of interest prevailed for each potential level of aggregate income. Hayek (1975, p. 35n), in his later and most systematic statement of capital theory, appears to accept this criticism of Sraffa's and to abandon the strict *in natura* definition he had offered in earlier writings.

The interest rate that minimizes signal extraction errors, or the 'minimum-noise' interest rate, provides an alternative interpretation of the natural rate of interest. The minimum-noise interest rate concept, however, does not apply to a particular level of interest rate. An interest rate will be minimum-noise when it is determined by a process which is easy to predict and understand. Noise in the interest rate will increase when the process behind those interest rates becomes more volatile and difficult to predict. The concept of a minimum-noise interest rate applies more properly to a policy or institutional regime, rather than to a particular level of a particular price.

Some Austrian writers also claim that malinvestments necessarily occur because investment has increased without a concomitant increase in consumer savings (e.g., Rothbard 1975). Such a claim, however, does not establish the existence of malinvestments without a further signal extraction problem. New inflationary funds, if they are lent out, do increase the supply of loanable funds and lower real rates of interest. Long-term investment *ought* to increase by some degree.

We can even interpret the new lending as an act of saving on the part of the new money recipients, the bank shareholders. The owners of the new money must abstain from a potential act of consumption and increase the supply of loanable funds instead. Although nominal consumption expenditures have not declined, the real quantity of savings and lending has risen none the less. The total rate of monetary savings consists of two factors: savings from previous monetary income and savings from new, inflationary monetary income. Savings from new inflationary income may or may not produce the same real effects as savings from previous income, but investment expansions must none the less be accompanied by some kind of real savings increase.[17]

Defense of the Austrian claim requires one of two responses, neither of which succeeds fully. First, entrepreneurs still may be plagued by signal extraction problems about forthcoming expenditure streams, even when money growth is constant. Second, constant nominal money growth may have varying effects over time when adjustment frictions or sticky prices are present.

Signal extraction problems under constant money growth

Proponents of the Austrian claim offer a primary argument why constant rates of money growth may not sustain new investments. Once the new inflationary funds spread through the economy, old spending/saving patterns will reassert themselves. Banks channeled the entirety of the inflationary burst into the loanable funds market, but the recipients of

---

[17] On this point, see Hawtrey (1952, p. 236), Hummel (1979), and Tullock (1988).

the invested funds probably will not save the entirety of their new income. These fund recipients will demand goods and services in accordance with their previously expressed market-place demands. The Austrians argue consumers will demand goods and services consistent with the pre-inflation structure of production, rather than with the post-inflation structure.

I would define first-round fund recipients as the banks who receive inflationary reserves and lend them out in the funds market. Second-round recipients are those who borrow the lent funds and invest them. Third-round recipients are those who own the factors of production that the second-round recipients purchase or hire.

Third-round recipients of the new inflationary funds will allocate the money in different ways from the first-round recipients. Rather than placing the entirety of the new income in the loanable funds market, they will spend the funds in accordance with their marginal propensities to consume. Notice that since the constant rate of inflation is a recent innovation in the example, we do not have all three rounds of spending happening at once, at least not in the early stages of the inflation.

The Austrian claim requires that this subsequent spending on consumption will make the new long-term investments unprofitable. The new long-term investments will prove unprofitable, however, only if entrepreneurs commit another set of systematic expectational errors. Entrepreneurs must mistakenly overestimate the correlation between observed first-round spending effects and subsequent latter-round spending effects. Discrepancies between the preferences of first- and third-round fund recipients do not themselves induce resource misallocation.

Entrepreneurs can avoid being fooled if they recognize that expenditure patterns do not remain constant across differing rounds of received funds. When entrepreneurs notice shifts in market demands (whether inflation-induced or not), they presumably realize that latter-round recipients of the newly spent funds need not allocate those funds in the same manner as the first-round recipients. Such a realization checks the tendency to over-commit resources in the direction of first-round spending. This same understanding might check malinvestment in the traditional Austrian story.

The Austrian claim requires that inflation worsens the ability of entrepreneurs to predict the forthcoming demands of latter-round fund recipients. Traditional arguments for fixed money growth rules emphasize their contribution to a relatively stable economic environment and their ability to diminish signal extraction problems. The Austrian claim implies that for one kind of forecast – inferring the spending and saving preferences of latter-round fund recipients – fixed positive rates of money growth may increase the volatility of the environment. Several hypotheses attempt to explain why this signal extraction problem might become worse; each hypothesis is plausible, but none is necessarily compelling. In each case the validity of the Austrian claim relies on the postulation of yet another set of signal extraction problems.

One hypothesis notes that inflation disrupts the link between the rate of interest on loanable funds and consumers' intertemporal marginal rate of substitution. Investors no longer have free access to a price signal which directly expresses the prevailing intertemporal marginal rate of substitution on non-inflationary funds. Positive rates of money growth create a wedge between the savings rates of first-round funds recipients and latter-round funds recipients. Price signals reflect marginal rates of saving – those of bank shareholders – which are not representative for the economy as a whole.

A second hypothesis claims that a volatile wealth distribution over time increases the difficulty of inferring third-round demands from first-round demands. Even if entrepreneurs do not crudely and directly extrapolate third-round demands from first-round demands, they nonetheless may use first-round demands as an input for estimating third-round demands. The more volatile the distribution of wealth, the less reliable the first-round demands are as an informational input about latter-round demands. Money supply growth might increase the errors in entrepreneurial forecasts of latter-round demands by making wealth distribution more volatile over time.

A third hypothesis claims that a fixed rate of nominal money growth does not provide a constant supply of real loanable funds through time. The real quantity of loanable funds will be higher in the first period than in subsequent periods. Latter-round funds recipients have higher spending propensities than do early-round funds recipients. Policy rules, such as nominal money growth rules, eliminate signal extraction problems only to the extent they bring constant *real* effects, and not merely constant nominal effects. Yet constant nominal money growth may bring a volatile real savings rate over time.

Frictions of adjustment

Frictions of adjustment may provide other reasons why constant nominal growth does not fully preserve the value of new long-term investments. Entrepreneurs do not care about money supply growth *per se*; they care about the effects of money supply growth on real variables. Frictions will cause the real effects of constant money supply growth to vary over time. These frictions become successively more 'unstuck' as time passes, reflecting the greater magnitude of long-run elasticities of adjustment relative to short-run elasticities. Again, constant nominal policies may have varying real effects over time, giving rise to signal extraction problems.[18]

Rates of price adjustment may vary over time under constant money supply growth. For a given rate of money growth, prices will rise more each year. Perhaps the first year of money supply growth produces a 2 percent increase in capital goods prices, the second year brings a 3 percent increase, the third year brings a 4 percent increase in prices, and so on. Sticky nominal prices eventually change as aggregate demand pressures increase, contracts are rewritten, periodic price-resetting occurs, and entrepreneurs move to more flexible price-adjustment technologies.[19]

When the rate of price inflation increases over time, money supply growth translates into relatively high loanable funds supply increases in early periods. Recipients of the new money face relatively low rates of price inflation and enjoy an especially large edge in purchasing power. Real investment will be high, compared to subsequent periods. As prices adjust more rapidly, however, a given nominal money supply increase will translate into successively smaller increases in real loanable funds supply. The diminishing increments of real loanable funds supply will produce rising real interest rates.

Adjustments in money demand produce analogous effects. Inflation, which taxes real currency balances, increases monetary velocity more in the long run than in the short. Continued and steady rates of nominal money growth will have increasing impacts on the price level, again producing varying real effects on real loanable funds supply over time.

Market participants presumably understand that long-run elasticities are greater than short-run elasticities. Entrepreneurs do not expect constant rates of money growth to have constant real effects, and invest with this knowledge in mind. None the less, accurate forecasts of the real effects of inflation require a knowledge of the relevant long- and short-run elasticities. Residual signal extraction problems will remain, even if nominal policy is constant. Entrepreneurs will sometimes forecast the real effects of inflation incorrectly, and will sometimes choose unsustainable long-term investments.

---

[18] For Hayek (1967, pp. 150–2), increasing price adjustment over time implies constant nominal money growth still gives rise to malinvestments. Hayek presented two other arguments which imply that even constant credit expansion will have varying real effects over time. First, real rates of interest may increase with the debt–equity ratio. Second, the increased demand for cash during a boom may push real rates up. See Trautwein (1994, p. 76) on these arguments. Hayek (1969, p. 288) appears to have made partial concessions to the view that indefinite sustainability is possible. He does, however, mention the formation of price expectations as a factor which might prevent indefinite sustainability.

[19] For a modern treatment of increasing price adjustment over time, see Sheshinski and Weiss (1976). In addition, entrepreneurs move to more flexible price-setting technologies. Department stores issue catalogs more frequently, and restaurants move away from printed menus and to chalkboard posting of prices.

If policymakers know the relevant elasticities, they might attempt to sequence money supply growth rates to maintain approximately constant real effects. Gently rising rates of money supply growth could, for a while, maintain roughly constant real effects in response to increasing elasticities of adjustment. Real loanable funds supply might remain approximately constant rather than diminish. Even omniscient policymakers, however, cannot avoid an eventual dilemma. Rates of inflation cannot rise forever without either approaching asymptotic stability or terminating in hyperinflation. At some point the rate of inflation must fall or remain constant, which brings us back to non-constant real policy effects through time, and signal extraction problems.

Summary remarks on constant nominal money growth

The Austrian claim can call upon a variety of arguments why constant nominal money growth will not fully sustain new long-term investments. These arguments partially succeed if we are willing to postulate additional signal extraction problems. Nonetheless constant nominal money growth does sustain longer-term investments to some degree. The Austrian claim requires a complex set of additional and highly contingent arguments to establish positive rates of money growth as the culprit, rather than volatile rates of money growth.

Even then, the remaining degree of unsustainable investment may be small. Under the Austrian claim, only those entrepreneurs who make new investments during an inflationary boom will misallocate resources; previously invested resources should not become unprofitable. According to the Austrian claim, the subsequent, post-bust equilibrium restores the real interest rates that would have prevailed without the initial burst of inflation. Previous investment decisions, which were based on expectations of these earlier rates, should remain intact in value to a large degree; only investments made within a particular time frame should become unprofitable. To the extent that the flow of new investment is small relative to the capital stock, only a small fraction of total resources will be mal-invested. If some of this investment value is sustained by constant monetary policy, the resulting distortions may not be large enough to generate cyclical behavior.[20]

---

[20] Tullock (1988, p. 75) makes a similar point about the Austrian claim. The oral Austrian tradition does address the general decline in investment values with the aid of such constructs as the 'secondary deflation' which occurs during a downturn. To this extent, however, the Austrians must resort to other business cycle constructs to generate negative comovement among investments.

CONCLUDING REMARKS ON THE TRADITIONAL AUSTRIAN THEORY

This chapter has examined the signal extraction problems behind the traditional Austrian theory in some detail. A close look at the issues does not rule out the Austrian theory as one possible scenario, following an increase in money supply growth, at least if we are willing to reject the rational expectations assumption. The Austrian claim, however, does require a number of specific additional postulates about expectations and informational imperfections. The Austrian claim not only assumes the rejection of rational expectations, but also requires that deviations from rational expectations take some very particular forms. More specifically, the Austrian claim requires the following:

1 Entrepreneurs have naïve expectations and underestimate the presence of monetary inflation.
2 Entrepreneurs overestimate the permanence of observed interest rate changes.
3 Entrepreneurs commit systematic errors in especially costly directions.
4 The effects of positive inflation and lower real interest rates encourage long-term investment more than increased volatility and increased option value discourage it.
5 The supply of saving is relatively volatile and unpredictable.
6 Entrepreneurs confuse monetary inflation with increases in consumer savings, rather than with declines in investment demand.
7 The real interest rate is a significant factor in forecasting demand curves for future outputs.
8 Inflation increases long-term investments on net because the first signal extraction problem, real vs. nominal, is outweighed by the second and third kinds of signal extraction problems.
9 Consumption is relatively variable through time.
10 Systematic profit opportunities on trading in the term structure of interest rates persist through time.
11 The term structure of interest rates does not effectively communicate bank estimations of monetary policy.
12 Entrepreneurs systematically overestimate the correlation between first-round spending effects and latter-round spending effects.
13 Constant rates of nominal money growth involve considerable volatility in the real supply of loanable funds over time.

Even if these suppositions are sometimes plausible, the Austrian theory is left as a considerably more contingent proposition than its advocates have claimed. The Austrian theory does not follow directly from the ability of inflation to distort market price signals, or from the injection of new inflationary funds into the loanable funds market. Yeager (1986, pp. 380–1) notes correctly that: 'The Austrian scenario of boom and downturn is hardly the only conceivable scenario . . . the Austrian theory . . . is no more than a conceivable but incomplete scenario.'

COMPARISON WITH THE RISK-BASED THEORY

The monetary scenarios presented in Chapter 3 were designed, in part, to avoid the criticisms of the traditional Austrian theory made in this chapter. Let us review the list of problems with the traditional Austrian theory once more, and see how a risk-based investment theory may help avoid those difficulties. The risk-based theory is my attempt to reconfigure the traditional Austrian theory in response to the criticisms of this chapter.

Most importantly, the risk-based theory offers different basic scenarios from the traditional Austrian theory. As discussed above, the Austrian theory, if it succeeds, requires volatile inflation rather than a steady rate of positive inflation. Under the risk-based theory, however, volatile inflation produces an immediate contraction and downturn, rather than an expansion of malinvestment. The risk-based theory is not committed to pinpointing the nature of expectational errors from inflation, as does the traditional Austrian theory. When positive inflation occurs, without inflationary volatility, the risk-based theory postulates an initial boom and an increase in risk, but does not require that a bust always follows, as discussed in Chapters 2 and 3.

Let us now go through each criticism in the list on p. 101, and then offer commentary on the risk-based theory with regard to that same point.

1 Entrepreneurs must have naïve expectations and underestimate the presence of monetary inflation.
   Risk-based theory: Rational expectations are assumed. Monetary shocks do not always bring downturns, even though the real effects of money will increase economic cyclicality.
2 Entrepreneurs must overestimate the permanence of observed interest rate changes.
   Risk-based theory: Discoordination comes from forecast errors more generally, and not from incorrect forecasts of future real interest rates.
3 Entrepreneurs must commit systematic errors in directions that are especially costly.
   Risk-based theory: Errors will be made in all directions. To the extent that making errors in a particular direction is especially costly, entrepreneurs will tend to avoid that kind of error.
4 The effects of positive inflation and lower real interest rates must encourage long-term investment more than increased volatility and increased option value discourage it.
   Risk-based theory: Either increases or decreases in long-term investment

may set off downturns. Increases in risky, long-term investments will increase cyclicality, and lead to sustainable booms some of the time and subsequent busts other times. Increased monetary volatility will induce an immediate downturn. These two scenarios both follow from a theory of investment risk and return.

5 The supply of saving must be relatively volatile and unpredictable.

Risk-based theory: Entrepreneurs do not necessarily confuse monetary inflation with changes in private savings. No particular assumptions are required about the volatility of private saving. Forecast errors involve supplies and demands more generally, not the intertemporal distribution of demand as predicted by interest rates.

6 Entrepreneurs must confuse monetary inflation with increases in consumer savings, rather than with declines in investment demand.

Risk-based theory: Entrepreneurs need not be confused by monetary inflation at all.

7 The real interest rate must be a significant factor in forecasting demand curves for future outputs.

Risk-based theory: Entrepreneurs do not commit particular signal extraction errors concerning interest rates. Furthermore, the real interest rate need not be a significant factor in forecasting demand curves for future outputs, or for predicting the intertemporal distribution of demand.

8 Inflation must increase long-term investments on net because the first signal extraction problem, real vs. nominal, must be outweighed by the second and third kinds of signal extraction problems (temporary vs. permanent, and real interest rates as predictors of future consumer demands).

Risk-based theory: Inflation increases long-term investments on net because entrepreneurs respond rationally to real sectoral shocks, not because they are fooled by monetary policy.

9 Consumption must be relatively variable through time.

Risk-based theory: No particular assumptions are required about the stability of consumption over time.

10 Systematic profit opportunities for trading on the term structure of interest rates must persist through time, even after adjusting for risk and transactions costs.

Risk-based theory: No systematic profit opportunities are available through time, after adjusting for risk and transactions costs.

11 The term structure of interest rates does not effectively communicate bank estimations of monetary policy.

Risk-based theory: The term structure of interest effectively communicates rational expectations estimates of future conditions in the loanable funds market, including the relatively informed estimates of banks about monetary policy.

12 Entrepreneurs must systematically overestimate the correlation between first-round spending effects and latter-round spending effects.
   Risk-based theory: No such overestimation is required or assumed. The new long-term investment sometimes will prove profitable, giving rise to a sustained boom.
13 Constant rates of nominal money growth must involve considerable volatility in the real supply of loanable funds over time.
   Risk-based theory: Positive and constant rates of nominal money growth will increase economic cyclicality, relative to zero money growth, but they do not necessarily bring a business downturn or a decline in welfare.

Can the two approaches be reconciled?

Although the above comments weigh against the traditional Austrian theory, the traditional and risk-based theories need not stand so far apart if we modify the traditional approach. First, if the traditional Austrian theory adopted more explicit assumptions about expectations, and accounted for risk more explicitly, it would move closer to what I have labeled the risk-based approach. Even barring this change in methodological orientation, a partial *rapprochement* between the two theories might be arranged.

The traditional Austrian theory focuses on positive rates of money growth as the culprit behind business cycles, but some versions of the old theory emphasize the negative effects of *volatile* rates of money growth instead of blaming positive rates of money growth *per se*. Hayek, in particular, can be read as endorsing either (or both) of these two views, as emphasized by Laidler (1994, pp. 12–13). Most modern Austrian school writings blame positive money growth, but shifting the emphasis to monetary volatility allows us to keep much of the initial spirit of the theory.

Focusing on volatile rates of money growth, rather than positive rates, remedies some of the problems with the traditional Austrian theory. Rather than having to argue for systematic overexpansions of capital-intensity, a more modest claim could be made – chosen levels of capital-intensity sometimes will not accord with subsequent levels of nominal money growth. This change in doctrine, however, already moves us towards the risk-based theory outlined in Chapters 2 and 3. If positive nominal money growth does not create problems *per se*, we must drop the claim that entrepreneurs are fooled by any positive level of money growth. We are already moving closer to a rational expectations assumption. Furthermore, the emphasis on monetary volatility would bring the Austrians closer to the 'monetary disequilibrium' approach of Warburton (1966), modern monetarism, the work of Mascaro and Meltzer (1983), the volatility of intermediation analysis of McCulloch (1981) (see Chapter 2), and the volatility scenarios analyzed in Chapters 2 and 3 of this book.

Volatile money growth remains a potential culprit for cycles under both the traditional Austrian theory and the risk-based theory, but the risk-based view offers a more plausible account of how volatility matters. Unlike the traditional Austrian theory, the risk-based approach emphasizes that uncertainty about future rates of money growth brings an immediate negative shock to the economy. Long-term investment will more likely contract than expand, and the economy will experience a downturn with no preceding boom.

APPENDIX A: FORCED SAVINGS

Analyses of intertemporal discoordination often have stressed a concept known as 'forced savings.' Both Hayek and Dennis Robertson analyzed this phenomenon, or more properly phenomena, since different definitions of the concept have been used.[21]

According to one common definition (e.g., Bresciani-Turroni 1936, p. 171), forced saving occurs when the inflation enters the banking system and bids resources away from consumption and towards capital goods production. This concept arises from the first-order real distributional effects of inflation discussed in the final section of Chapter 3. The more controversial definitions of forced saving refer to second-round effects resulting from inflationary credit expansion.

Some economists have used the term forced saving to refer to the second-order substitution effects created by inflationary injections into the loanable funds market. When inflationary funds are injected in the loan market, the (nominal) prices of consumer goods will rise. Entrepreneurs bid resources into longer-term investments and away from the production of immediate consumer goods. The declining supply of consumer goods supposedly induces a price increase for those goods; this price inflation occurs even apart from the effects of the new inflationary funds on prices in general.

Consumers, facing a higher price for tomatoes, buy fewer tomatoes and end up being 'forced' to save more. 'Induced saving' is perhaps a more accurate label for the concept. Haberler (1964, p. 43) refers to

> a restriction of consumption and the release of productive resources for the production of additional capital goods. In other words, the real capital which is needed for the increased investment is extorted from the consuming public by means of rising prices.

Mises (1978, p. 121) refers to consumer good prices rising faster than wages, an assumption criticized by Hicks (1967, p. 208).

The Austrian theory does not require forced saving of this kind to occur.

---

[21] On different definitions of forced saving, see, for instance, Haberler (1964, pp. 43–5), Mises (1978, p. 121), and Presley (1979).

In fact, forced saving of this kind tends to mitigate the kind of cycles postulated by the Austrian claim. If rising consumer good prices do induce a higher rates of private savings among consumers, the additional savings will partially validate the new, longer-term investments that entrepreneurs have undertaken.

I see forced savings as an unlikely second-order effect during an inflationary credit expansion. Forced saving requires that the prices of consumption goods rise faster than the nominal disposable incomes of consumers. If nominal incomes rise faster than consumption prices, consumption is encouraged rather than discouraged. The increase in consumption prices, induced by the decreasing supply of consumption goods, will depend upon elasticities, which may be either small or large, and upon the speed of price adjustment.

Individuals employed in producing long-term investment goods may find that their nominal incomes have risen more than the prices of consumption goods. These individuals will not face a substitution effect that induces forced savings; rather, these individuals will face lower prices for the consumption basket. If consumption prices do not adjust upwards immediately but are expected to rise in the future, individuals may be induced to spend their higher incomes on consumption rapidly, before prices rise.

Furthermore, the second-order effects of inflation may lower, not raise, the relative price of consumption goods. During the boom, resources leave the production of consumption goods only because the prices of capital goods have been bid *up*. The price of consumption goods relative to the price of capital goods may fall, not rise. Factors of production will move from short-term to long-term production, but this movement along a demand curve may not offset the initial shift of demand curves in favor of long-term outputs. If the price of consumption goods falls, relative to investment goods, induced consumption will occur rather than induced saving. If the stock market appears expensive, why not buy a vacation instead?

Consider an individual who receives higher nominal demand for his services late in the inflationary process, after many prices have risen. The prices of both consumer and capital goods have increased more than that individual's wage. But according to the Austrian theory capital goods prices have increased more than consumer goods prices have. Tomatoes are now cheaper relative to investment goods, and these individuals may purchase more tomatoes. *Lifetime* consumption for these individuals will go down; they now find equities too expensive and will therefore save less for their retirement. Nonetheless, consumption in the immediate future may still rise, due to the relative price effects of inflation.

In summary, the concept of forced saving requires an arbitrary specification of the second-order relative price effects of inflation. Forced saving may or may not occur, but in any case the concept is inessential to the intertemporal coordination problems facing market participants.

APPENDIX B: THE RICARDO EFFECT

The Ricardo effect, or the substitution of labor for machinery, has sometimes played a role in Austrian business cycle theory. Hayek, in some of his later statements of his trade cycle theory, relied on the Ricardo effect to explain why new, inflation-induced investments might prove unsustainable.[22]

The Ricardo effect, in its earliest statements by Ricardo, referred generally to capital–labor substitution. Rising real wages induced entrepreneurs to substitute machinery for labor. Alternately, falling real wages would induce substitution of labor for machinery. Hayek, however, invoked the Ricardo effect for a very specific purpose. He used the Ricardo effect argument to explain why inflation-induced shifts in resource allocation eventually will be reversed.

In the Austrian theory, monetary inflation lowers real rates of interest and induces expansion of long-term capital goods at the expense of immediate consumption goods. Using Ricardo's terminology, Hayek argued that entrepreneurs will substitute capital for labor. This substitution, however, must eventually be reversed, at least according to Hayek. As resources move into the production of long-term production goods, the nominal price of consumption goods will rise, even apart from the higher nominal money supply (see the above discussion of forced savings). The higher nominal price for consumption goods implies a lower real wage. The lower real wage induces entrepreneurs to substitute labor for machinery, reversing the earlier move towards longer-term processes of production.[23]

I reject the Ricardo effect as an account of cyclical dynamics. Some real wages may rise during the move towards longer-term investments, as discussed above in the section on forced savings. Workers in capital-intensive industries may find that their wages rise more quickly than do the prices of consumption goods (Hicks 1967); the net effect depends on the relevant elasticities. To that extent the Ricardo effect does not reverse the capital-intensive investments.

More fundamentally, the Ricardo effect confuses a shift of the demand curve with a movement along that curve. To the extent that real wages do fall, they fall because resources have been bid away from immediate consumption to other opportunities. The price of consumption opportuni-

---

[22] See, for instance, Hayek (1939, 1969). Moss and Vaughn (1986) provide a good survey of the Ricardo effect debate.
[23] See, for instance, Moss and Vaughn (1986) and Hayek (1939).

ties will therefore rise. But the increased price of consumption, even when all of its secondary effects are considered, should not reverse the initial shift of resources. The rise in the price of consumption is part of the new equilibrium arising from the initial shift of the demand curve towards longer-term investments.[24]

Finally, changes in the price level, in and of themselves, do not create direct substitution effects which affect the capital–labor ratio. When entrepreneurs choose a capital–labor ratio, they compare the relative price of labor to the relative price of capital. The relevant real wage of labor, for the issue of capital substitution, is $(w/p)/(k/p)$, not merely w/p. The Ricardo effect notes that changes in p, the price level, alter w/p. Changes in w/p, when occurring through the p variable, are accompanied by corresponding changes in k/p, keeping constant the relative price of labor *vis-à-vis* capital.

In addition to these fundamental objections, the Ricardo effect encounters some other problems. The Austrian theory emphasizes the distinction between short-term and long-term capital goods. Even if long-term capital becomes cheap (or dear) relative to labor, the price of short-term capital may be moving in the opposite direction. Rather than leading to a displacement of labor, the Ricardo effect may simply reallocate labor from long-term processes to short-term processes, or vice versa.[25]

The Ricardo effect also identifies machinery with relatively long-term production processes and labor with relatively short-term production processes. When we consider human capital, the necessity of training laborers, and worker-specific investments made by firms, labor may be the long-term resource and capital may be the short-term resource. In that case the initial move towards long-term investments would induce a shift into labor and away from capital, not vice versa. The resulting price effects could not induce a shift back to labor – there had never been a shift away from labor in the first place.

Finally, the Ricardo effect assumes that substitutability, rather than complementarity, characterizes capital and labor. The Austrian theory, however, emphasizes the complementarity of capital in other contexts. To the extent that capital and labor are complements, the demand for capital and labor may move together, rather than in opposite directions.

APPENDIX C: CAPITAL-INTENSITY AND THE CAMBRIDGE DEBATES

Although Chapters 2 and 3 emphasize changes in risk, the traditional Austrian approach analyzes business cycles in terms of a switch from less

---

[24] Kaldor (1942) criticizes the Ricardo effect on these grounds. See also Desai (1991) on this debate.
[25] I am indebted to Sarah Jennings for this point.

capital-intensive projects to more capital-intensive projects. Here I will examine whether the concept of capital-intensity is meaningful. The Cambridge capital debates have challenged the claim that declines in the real interest rate will necessarily increase capital-intensity, and have questioned the coherence of the concept. Since the concept of capital-intensity lies behind the traditional Austrian theory, the Cambridge critique suggests that the traditional Austrian theory does not even get off the ground.

The risk-based theory outlined in Chapters 2 and 3 does not require the concept of capital-intensity and therefore sidesteps the Cambridge critique altogether. The concept of capital-intensity nonetheless might prove useful for a risk-based business cycle theory as well. The Austrian concept of 'long-term' and 'short-term' investments (i.e., capital-intensity) offers another potential justification of the claim that declines in the real interest rate will increase aggregate riskiness. Declines in the real interest rate might, for instance, increase the orientation of economic activity towards the more distant future. Orienting economic activity towards the more distant future might also be more risky. As implied by the assumption of informational decay (see Chapter 2), projects bear increasing risk over time, at least on average. We have better information about the relatively near future than about the relatively distant future. A 10-year project might, on average, involve a greater spread of possible outcomes than a 5-year project. Austrian capital theory therefore might provide further support for a focus on changes in the level of risk.

No single definition of capital-intensity, or investment term-length, has commanded universal acceptance. In very rough or general terms, capital theorists often have interpreted the idea of capital-intensity as referring to the quantity of capital which is invested, the amount of time for which project inputs are invested, or both. The difficulty of providing a satisfactory definition is evident from the multi-dimensional nature of capital. Capital investments involve both a value dimension (how much money has been invested?) and a time dimension (for how long is the money invested?). Aggregation of these time and value dimensions into a single globally transitive metric has proven problematic.[26]

The Cambridge theorists have argued for two related points. First, rankings of capital-intensity are not independent of the real interest rate. One

---

[26] Hayek (1975, p. 76) tried to avoid problems of multi-dimensionality by defining capital-intensity in terms of how long particular inputs are invested. This concept of capital-intensity applies only to particular inputs, not to production processes in general. Capital-intensity increases if a given input is invested for a longer period of time rather than a shorter period. Hayek is examining the value and time dimensions of the problem but holding the value dimension constant. Hayek achieves a one-dimensional measure of capital-intensity only by assumption, and even this one-dimensional measure holds only for a single input. Hayek's measure does not apply when the value dimension of capital is being determined (i.e., which inputs will be produced?), or when the investment time horizons change for a series of inputs, rather than just a single input.

project may be more capital-intensive at one interest rate, with the ranking reversed at another interest rate. Second, measures of capital-intensity do not vary monotonically with the real interest rate. A project of given capital-intensity can be favored at two widely disparate interest rates, but not in between ('capital reswitching'). These ideas, in earlier forms, also can be found in the writings of Wicksell, Fisher, and Knight.[27]

The Cambridge claims can be interpreted as a case of multiple equilibria. For a given set of quantity variables, a 'project,' we can find two sets of prices that will support that project as the most profitable alternative. Examples of capital reswitching illustrate this point about multiple equilibria clearly. The quadratic or exponential functions used to determine discounted present values may have more than one root. Investment 1 may be more profitable than investment 2 at two disparate real interest rates, but not in between. One classic reswitching example is often presented as shown in Table 4.1.

Table 4.1 Two productive processes

Period	T1	T2	T3
Technique			
1		7 units input	
2	2 units input		6 units input

Table 4.1 represents two different productive processes, each of which produces one unit of output after three periods of investment. Technique 1 applies seven units of input in period two, and technique 2 applies two units of input in period one and six units of input in period three.

Solving for the equiprofitable interest rate gives the equation:

$$7(1 + i) = 2(1 + i)^2 + 6$$

This equation has two roots, $i = 1.0$ and $i = 0.5$, at which reswitching occurs. Technique 1 is more profitable at all interest rates below 50 percent and all interest rates above 100 percent, but technique 2 is more profitable at those rates in between. If we perform a partial equilibrium thought experiment and vary the real interest rate, project demand curves will not be downward-sloping with respect to the real interest rate.

Capital reversing, another phenomenon analyzed by the Cambridge theorists, follows from the same logic behind reswitching. If we convert the choice of investment projects into measures of capital value, a decline in the real rate of interest could lead to a decline in the absolute value of the capital stock. Capital reversing is essentially the same phenomenon as reswitching but expressed in a different metric.

---

[27] For a survey of the Cambridge criticisms, see Harcourt (1972). I have found the exposition of Yeager (1976) to be especially helpful.

Dealing with the Cambridge critique

The reswitching examples illustrate the difficulty of deriving transitive, monotonic rankings for multi-dimensional concepts such as capital-intensity. The problems with defining capital-intensity, however, illustrate only one example of a broader issue. The logic behind reswitching applies also to other rank order definitions of multi-dimensional economic concepts; capital-intensity metrics simply illustrate the relevant difficulties with clarity, due to the relative ease of defining the time and value dimensions of capital investment.

The multi-dimensional nature of capital implies we cannot derive unambiguous comparative statics predictions about how real interest rates affect investment. Multi-dimensional effects, however, can invalidate nearly any comparative statics claim found in economics, whether in capital theory or not. Income effects, transactions costs, imperfect markets, and risk aversion all can overturn traditional comparative statics results, if we incorporate these additional dimensions into the problem under consideration. These phenomena can complicate an apparently simple case of demand analysis and produce counterintuitive results.

Reswitching now has been added to the list of potential complicating factors, but the consequences for comparative statics analysis are not necessarily fatal. Typically economists proceed by taking a multi-dimensional problem and by assuming it can be collapsed into a tractable number of dimensions. The number of relevant dimensions is limited either by ignoring some factors, or by assuming that the additional dimensions do not counter the basic effect being postulated. The reduction of relevant economic dimensions to a manageable scale is not objectionable *per se*. Economists typically submit comparative statics claims to empirical testing to ascertain whether the chosen simplifications do excessive violence to reality.

The available empirical evidence, while sparse, does not support the importance of reswitching. The one empirical study I have found on the time and value dimensions of capital, Mayer (1960), finds that the time and value dimensions of capital investments tend to be positively correlated, supporting traditional comparative statics accounts.

The Cambridge examples are designed to play up the importance of the multi-dimensionality of capital. The likelihood of reswitching increases to the extent that the time and value dimensions of capital investments either conflict or cannot be ranked without ambiguity. In the example presented above, for instance, technique 1 uses a smaller quantity of inputs (defined in physical terms) but distributes those inputs through time earlier, on average. The conflicting time and value dimensions create the possibility of reswitching. In contrast, when the time and value dimensions of capital strongly complement each other, reswitching becomes less likely or impossible. If project 1b invests one unit of input for one period and project 2b invests five units of input for five periods, project 2b will be ranked as more capital-intensive across all real interest rates, under any reasonable definition of capital-intensity. In these cases traditional comparative static intuitions will hold up well. A decline in the real interest rate, for instance, will tend to encourage project 2b across all ranges of that price change.

Reswitching also raises the broader issue of whether different capital projects can be distinguished or compared with regard to their qualitative properties. The techniques compared in Figure 4.1 cannot easily be ranked in terms of their capital-intensity. The multiple solutions to the exponential equations verify what a simple eyeballing of the diagram suggests. The two projects 1b and 2b discussed above, however, can be differentiated easily with regard to their qualitative properties. One of these two projects is unambiguously more capital-intensive than the other.

Some project comparisons postulate investments of a qualitatively different nature and other comparisons consider investments which cannot be qualitatively distinguished with accuracy or coherence. To the extent the latter comparisons predominate, we cannot make meaningful qualitative statements about changes in capital structure or investment. A shift from one set of capital projects to another would not bring fundamental changes in the economic properties of the economy's capital structure, at least not in terms of easily characterizable properties.[28]

To the extent the reswitching critique is empirically significant, we should not be able to significantly correlate changes in real interest rates with important economic events of any kind. Changes in real interest rates simply would cause shifts from one set of projects to another set, but the two sets of projects could not be qualitatively distinguished in meaningful fashion. Chapter 5, on empirical tests of cyclical theory, examines precisely this question – do changes in real interest rates have any systematic effects or predictive power at all? Although the evidence is again far from conclusive, changes in real interest rates do appear to affect real variables in systematic fashion.

The significance of the Cambridge critiques is blunted by two further issues: first, have the Cambridge theorists identified a paradoxical result in a consistent model?, and second, how should we interpret findings of multiple equilibria more generally?

The Cambridge critique does not demonstrate the existence of paradoxical results in a general equilibrium model. The Cambridge reswitching diagram treats interest rates as free variables which vary without changing other real determinants of relative project profitability. In a full general equilibrium model, each of the Cambridge reswitching interest rates will

---

[28] Orosel (1979) considers the possibility of partial capital-intensity rankings from a neo-Austrian perspective.

be associated with different rates of saving, different consumption patterns, and different relative prices. Real interest rates measure only one aspect of project profitability, the cost of funds. Project profitability depends upon an entire set of funds, flows and prices, of which real interest rates are only one component. Once we allow other values to vary with the real interest rate, the Cambridge demonstration of project equiprofitability at two distant real interest rates disappears (Garrison 1979).

To return to Table 4.1, technique 1 may be most profitable at two disparate real interest rates *if we vary the real interest rate alone*. Technique 1 is not necessarily the most profitable alternative at both interest rates if we also specify the changed expenditure patterns and changed relative prices which, in a general equilibrium, must accompany differing real interest rates. In other words, the reswitching interest rates represent multiple equilibria only in a partial equilibrium framework; the Cambridge critique treats the rate of discount as the only relevant determinant of project profitability. It has not been shown that reswitching will occur in a more realistic context.

Even if multiple equilibria persist, we do not know that the multiple roots of exponential equations, as specified by reswitching, will remain the relevant source of multiple equilibria. The partial equilibrium Cambridge construct does not necessarily capture the relevant aspects of investment multi-dimensionality in a general equilibrium world.

In a more fully specified model multiple equilibria may still exist and may even be likely. Demonstrations of multiple equilibria have become increasingly common in economic theory. Yet demonstrations of multiple equilibria do not typically support sentiments that standard price theory is inapplicable. Rather, economists view multiple equilibria as puzzles to be solved with the tools of standard price theory.

The significance of the Cambridge critique rests upon a very particular methodological interpretation of multiple equilibria – the Cambridge critique requires that we take multiple equilibria as a description of a real world indeterminacy. An alternative perspective suggests that the inability to solve for a single solution represents the incomplete nature of a given model; it does not represent an intrinsic indeterminacy in real world economic activity. The existence of multiple equilibria therefore does not necessarily invalidate or overthrow standard comparative statics experiments.

Multiple equilibria result from models constructed by the economist; they are not features of the real world. Short of the quantum level, or perhaps human free will (both outside the scope of traditional economics), real world economic outcomes involve no indeterminacy. What happens must have happened, and nothing else could have happened, given the initial conditions. A model which finds multiple equilibria therefore is underdetermined as a model. The model cannot account for, or 'explain,' a given state of affairs. If we attempt to use the model to explain the real world, unmodeled factors must be driving which outcome actually comes to pass.

Findings of multiple equilibria provide useful heuristics which draw our attention to the importance of unmodeled factors. We attain a better sense of the limitations of our models and the need to eventually incorporate previously unmodeled factors into those models. In the meantime, however, the mere existence of multiple equilibria – that is, unmodeled causal factors – should not suffice to refute any particular economic theory or hypothesis. Whenever we see the phrase 'multiple equilibria' we should reread the relevant argument substituting the phrase 'unmodeled causal factors.'

To sum up, the Cambridge capital critique has demonstrated the importance of multi-dimensionality for concrete problems in capital theory. Claims about changes in the composition of capital investment will sometimes prove problematic and may require empirical support. The multi-dimensionality problem, however, does not create special difficulties for investment-based business cycle mechanisms. First, the risk mechanism operates through factors separate from the Cambridge critique. Second, all macroeconomic theories face problems of multi-dimensionality. Third, the Cambridge theorists have not unlocked the fundamental nature of the capital multi-dimensionality problem. Their demonstration of multiple equilibria requires a partial equilibrium framework, and leaves open the question of which causal factors induce determinate results in the real world.

5

EMPIRICAL EVIDENCE

INTRODUCTION

Empirical evidence, taken alone, cannot conclusively confirm a business cycle theory. Pieces of positive evidence can be given alternative interpretations, or may provide support for more than one theoretical explanation. The evidence, in some clear-cut cases, *can* conclusively falsify a theory, but even negative evidence usually admits of competing interpretations. Whether or not we accept or reject a business cycle theory therefore depends upon a variety of considerations, including logical consistency, the reasonableness of the assumptions, theoretical persuasiveness, and the ability of the theory to account for stylized facts. Statistical evidence provides only one piece of the relevant picture. Nonetheless the evidence should strongly influence our estimation of the plausibility of a theory, and for that reason I examine the statistical evidence of relevance to investment-based and Austrian business cycle theories.

I focus on modern statistical tests involving the US economy, usually in the twentieth century or post-war period. I hold no particular belief that the US economy provides a superior or more appropriate 'laboratory,' but most of contemporary empirical macroeconomics, for better or worse, has taken an American slant. For reasons of space and my own linguistic constraints, I do not survey writings published in languages other than English, even though much of this material is relevant.

Most of the writings discussed below do not set out to test any version of Austrian theory at all. Typically these writings are testing some other set of propositions about macroeconomics or finance. I will try to show how these tests also apply to the theories discussed in this book. I will focus my discussion and interpretations on the risk-based investment theory, although most of the tests apply to the traditional Austrian theory as well.

I will limit the presentation to statistical evidence and neglect the considerable historical and case study literature on business cycles. More specifically, I do not examine the literature which seeks to explain the

Great Depression in terms of the traditional Austrian theory of the business cycle (Robbins 1934; Rothbard 1975). Although I am not persuaded by these historical accounts (see Cowen 1989, 1991 for further commentary), I will exclude such treatments for other reasons. Austrian theories of all kinds have received a relative surfeit of historical treatment and a severe deficit of statistical and econometric treatment. I seek to redress that balance. Nonetheless, a reader seeking a fuller picture should consult the historical literature as well.

The tests which follow concentrate on the monetary scenarios outlined in Chapter 3. The focus on these tests does not imply that the monetary scenarios are more important or more likely than the real scenarios of Chapter 2. Rather, the monetary scenarios are easier to test because they involve well-specified, empirically measurable shocks – changes in monetary policy or the money supply. Although money supply measures themselves involve ambiguity (for instance, which measure of monetary policy should be used?), measuring real shocks involves even greater identification problems. Chapter 2 identified a variety of real shocks as potential causes of a cyclical investment boom, including declines in time preference, increases in risk tolerance, resolution of uncertainty about irreversible investments, and positive shocks to retained earnings. We can, to various degrees, measure the effects of such shocks, but the shocks themselves remain difficult to isolate. Exogeneity and simultaneity issues pose serious econometric problems for current econometric methods of testing real business cycle theories of all kinds, not just the risk-based versions.

We should find some methodological comfort in the difficulty of testing business cycle theories. If the causes and mechanisms of business cycles were easy to identify and isolate, the business cycle itself probably would be easy to prevent or at least to ameliorate. In reality, business cycles are unpredictable, difficult or impossible to control, and involve multiple causes and propagation mechanisms. We should not expect tests of business cycle theory to be easy. All good business cycle theories should predict that business cycles are complex, highly unpredictable, and difficult to test.

Consistent with previous chapters, I will use the following terminology in the subsequent discussion:

- *Risk-based theories*: Business cycles result from changes in the quantity and kind of investment. Initial booms arise when investors choose a greater real quantity of risky, high-yielding projects. The greater risk of these projects, however, increases economic cyclicality and the chance of a subsequent downturn.
- *The monetary scenario*: Unexpected increases in the money supply will lower real interest rates or ease finance constraints, inducing entrepreneurs to increase the real quantity of risky investment projects, thereby increasing economic cyclicality.

- *The monetary volatility scenario*: Increases in money supply volatility will increase economic risk and induce entrepreneurs to shift to lower-yielding resource allocations. The economy will experience a downturn without a preceding boom.

I will consider seven predictions, or areas of investigation, where empirical results might conceivably falsify the monetary scenarios of the risk-based approach. I examine the following questions, each of which corresponds to a section in this chapter:

1 Do increases in the money supply lower real interest rates?
2 Does monetary policy affect bank lending?
3 Does monetary policy induce sectoral shifts?
4 Does unexpected money growth increase expected stock returns and stock return volatility?
5 Does monetary policy have predictive power over investment?
6 Does money supply or interest rate volatility discourage high-yielding investments or predict output declines?
7 Are capital-intensive sectors more cyclical than other sectors?

The chapter concludes with some brief remarks about where risk-based approaches and related Austrian ideas are strongest and weakest with regard to the evidence.

DOES MONEY AFFECT REAL INTEREST RATES?

If monetary policy does not affect real interest rates, the data would militate against some versions of the monetary scenario. The monetary scenario could still remain relevant through credit rationing mechanisms, as analyzed in Chapter 3, but at least one channel for monetary policy would be ruled out.

Overall, the data on real interest rates provide partial but not complete support for the monetary scenario. On the plus side, a variety of careful and sophisticated studies have found a monetary effect on real interest rates. On the minus side, monetary factors do not necessarily provide the dominant source of the variation in real rates. The variation in real rates sometimes appears to come from real shocks; this fact discriminates against the monetary scenario, although it does not discriminate against risk-based approaches more generally.

A wide variety of studies have found evidence that real interest rates vary over time, and that real interest rates vary with money growth. Mishkin (1981b) adds data to Fama's (1975) sample set and rejects the null hypothesis of no variation in the real rate over time. He also finds a strong and significant negative correlation between rates of price inflation and real interest rates. Mishkin uses a Chow test to confirm the generality of that effect. Mishkin also finds that money growth, and not just price inflation, is associated with lower real rates of interest. Price inflation outperforms money supply growth as a predictor of real rate declines, however, contrary to the monetary transmission mechanisms examined in Chapter 3.

Rose (1988) finds that nominal interest rates have a unit root but that inflation does not, thereby implying the real rate exhibits a unit root and varies over time. Cochrane (1989) finds that money growth lowers even nominal interest rates for periods up to a year. The results of Mishkin (1990) suggest that much of the variation in the term structure is due to changes in real rates rather than variation in expected inflation and the Fisherian premium. Mishkin (1992) finds a long-run Fisher effect when inflation has a long-run trend, but no short-run Fisher effect at all in the absence of trends. Grier and Perry (1993) use ARCH techniques to adjust for heteroskedasticity and find liquidity effects on real interest rates where others had not. Lastrapes and Selgin (1995) find liquidity effects using vector autoregression techniques. Siegel (1992) finds considerable real rate variation over the last two centuries, for both the US and the UK; he does not, however, examine the causes of this variation. Mishkin (1984b), using international data, finds a very weak Fisher effect for France, Germany, the Netherlands, and Switzerland, and a stronger Fisher effect for the US, Canada, and the UK[1]

Huizinga and Mishkin (1984) find that inflation lowers the *ex ante* real returns on all categories of assets over a 3-month holding period, including long-term bonds and common stock. In addition to using the consumer price index to measure inflation, as do most studies, they produce similar results for other price indices as well.

Summers (1983) uses band spectral techniques to filter out high frequency variance in the data and finds strong evidence favoring real interest rate effects of inflation. Starting with the 1860s, he finds that nominal interest rates rise systematically less than realized rates of price inflation would suggest. To the extent that the Fisher effect holds at all, the period 1965–1971, where inflation was accelerating, accounts for most of the success. Evidence for the full Fisher effect is weak in other sections of the sample. The full tax-based Fisher effect, which predicts a greater than one-to-one increase in nominal interest rates with inflation, is refuted even more strongly by the data.[2]

---

[1] Carmichael and Stebbing (1983) take the anti-Fisher effect argument furthest; they claim evidence for an inverted Fisher effect, whereby nominal rates remain roughly constant and real rates move inversely with the rate of inflation. For criticisms of their econometric work, see Amsler (1986) and Graham (1988).

[2] Barsky (1987) challenges Summer's pre-World War I results on the grounds that inflation was close to white noise in that earlier period. The apparent inflationary effects on the real rate may in fact reflect errors in particular forecasts of inflation each period.

Shiller (1983) provides one of the more detailed defenses of the view that the central bank can influence real interest rates. He considers a variety of measures of the *ex ante* real rate, using either survey data or optimal linear forecasts of inflation rates. In both cases increases in monetary variables are negatively correlated with real interest rates. These results also pass Granger and Sims causality tests. Shiller also looks for identifying restrictions to isolate exogenous changes in Fed policy, such as the 1951 decision to abandon the peg of security prices; he finds that such exogenous changes in monetary policy do have predictive power over real rates of interest.

The definition of the money supply affects whether monetary variables influence real rates of interest. Christiano and Eichenbaum (1992b) argue that non-borrowed reserves provide a relevant measure of Federal Reserve monetary policy; non-borrowed reserves are the policy instrument that the Fed controls most directly. They find that changes in non-borrowed reserves bring systematic and persistent effects on both real and nominal interest rates. The downward movement in nominal rates can last for as long as a year (Christiano and Eichenbaum 1992b, p. 345). Christiano and Eichenbaum also find that innovations in non-borrowed reserves serve as a leading indicator for increases in real GNP. These effects are masked when broader monetary aggregates are used to study the question.

In contrast to these results, some studies have found that real interest rates have held roughly constant over time. The best-known of these studies is Fama (1975), who studies the time period from 1953 to 1971. He cannot reject the hypotheses that the *ex ante* real rate of interest is constant, and that nominal interest rates provide efficient predictions of the forthcoming inflation rate. A number of critics, however, have challenged Fama's results. Carlson (1975) uses survey data to measure the *ex ante* rate, and finds considerable variation over time. He also challenges Fama's conclusion on the grounds that unexpected movements in the price level will be correlated with movements in the real interest rate; the pure Fisher effect may appear to hold in the data even if the *ex ante* rate varies over time. Nelson and Schwert (1977) question the power of Fama's test and respecify the econometrics; they find that the real rate does vary. Garbade and Wachtel (1978) provide further criticisms and revisions. Both Shiller (1983) and Mishkin (1981b) note that Fama used an unrepresentative sample with insufficient variation. Fama (1977) offers a response to some of these criticisms, and defends his original results.[3]

---

[3] Fama, however, later moved away from the hypothesis of a constant real rate of interest. Several articles (Garbade and Wachtel 1978; Nelson and Schwert 1977; and Fama and Gibbons 1982) have raised the possibility that *ex ante* real interest rates follow a random walk. Our observation of *ex post* rates results from a combination of random walk *ex ante* rates and inflation forecast errors. Given that we only observe *ex post* rates, statistical tests will have difficulty distinguishing between movements in the *ex ante* real rate and inflation forecast errors.

Other researchers, following Fama's lead, also find support for a pure Fisher effect. Once data from the 1970s and beyond are considered, some studies find that the liquidity effect on real interest rates vanishes (Dwyer 1981; Melvin 1983). Evans and Lewis (1995) argue that real rates appear to decline only because of a small sample problem which causes us to miss shifts in the process generating inflation. The data show permanent shocks to *ex ante* real rates of interest even when none are present; a Markov switching process for inflation is at work instead. Leeper and Gordon (1992) emphasize that most of the results in literature on real rates, on both sides, are highly sensitive to choice of sample period, the exogeneity of money growth, and the definitions of anticipated and unanticipated monetary changes.

Expectational, tax, and heterogeneity effects

Tests involving real interest rates typically use *ex post* real interest rates when we wish to measure *ex ante* real rates; for that reason, these results should be interpreted cautiously. Any given test involves a joint hypothesis both about the effects of inflation and about how well we can infer *ex ante* interest rates.

Real interest rate proxies typically assume all individuals experience the same rate of inflation. This uniformity assumption will tend to bias real interest volatility measures downward, especially at higher rates of inflation. The dispersion of relative prices tends to increase at higher rates of inflation, as much of the literature indicates (see Golob 1993, and pp. 131–34). As inflation increases, differing market participants will face a spread of real interest rates, even when the data indicate constancy of some average real rate. Even when average real rates appear constant in the data, an inflationary environment is lowering real rates for some individuals and raising real rates for others. To the extent the dispersion of relative prices is high, uniform measures of the real rate will underestimate the variance of the real rate experienced across individuals.

Tax effects may cause the true real rate to move even when it appears stationary in non-tax-adjusted data. Under US tax law, corporate borrowers can deduct their nominal interest payments, rather than their real interest payments. Observing a one-to-one Fisher effect therefore implies a decline in post-tax real rates for corporate borrowers (Feldstein 1976; Summers 1983). The higher nominal rate of interest increases the real value of the tax deduction. For the Fisher effect to hold for these borrowers, nominal rates would have to rise approximately 1.3 percentage points for every 1 percent increase in the inflation rate (ibid.); the data refute this prediction unambiguously. Tax effects therefore strengthen the case for real rate effects of monetary inflation.

What do changes in real rates mean?

Some researchers have questioned whether finding a less than one-for-one Fisher effect demonstrates a monetary effect on real interest rates. Most prominently, Fama (1981) and Fama and Gibbons (1982) suggest that real rates may be linked to the rate of productivity growth. High rates of productivity growth tend to raise real interest rates and to increase money demand. Price inflation will be low when real rates are high, but monetary policy cannot necessarily influence the real rate.

The observed variations in real interest rates do not necessarily fit the monetary scenario. Although real interest rates appear to have varied considerably in the 1970s, one study of this period concludes that much of the variation was due to supply shocks (Wilcox 1983). Real interest rates appeared especially high in the 1980s, despite a relatively accommodating monetary policy throughout most of the decade. The upward shift in real interest rates started early in the 1980s, when monetary policy was tight, but has not been reversed through the 1990s. This same period has been associated with relatively good economic times.

Correlations more promising for Austrian approaches are presented by Hamilton (1985). He finds that post-war US recessions are associated with *ex ante* real interest rates twice as high as average. Butos (1993), in an explicit study of the traditional Austrian theory, argues that changes in monetary policy account for some of the changes in real rates through the 1980s and 1990s, although he notes some ambiguous results as well.

Economists have not found a fully satisfactory explanation for the real interest rate shift of the 1980s. Blanchard and Summers (1984) consider four explanations for higher real interest rates: increases in investment profitability, portfolio shifts, declines in savings (perhaps resulting from government deficits), and contractionary monetary policies. The third and fourth explanations, involving contractionary monetary policies and savings declines, suggest that higher real interest rates should have brought an economic downturn, but such a downturn was not observed. Blanchard and Summers conclude that all four cited factors possess some explanatory merit, but they do not believe that a final judgment can be provided.

Do real long rates vary with inflation?

The data provide less support to the claim that monetary inflation lowers long-term interest rates. *Ex ante* real long-term rates have received less study than short rates, primarily because they are more difficult to measure. *Ex post* measurements of thirty-year returns will not correspond closely to *ex ante* expectations of those returns. We therefore know much less about long rates than we do about short rates. Earlier Keynesian treatments typically have specified that monetary policy lowers long-run real interest rates, but that prediction has not been confirmed by recent studies.

Mishkin (1981a) tackles the estimation problem in measuring long rates by developing an efficient markets approach. If monetary policy affects long rates, measures of unanticipated monetary policy should have predictive power over changes in long rates. Mishkin could not reject the hypothesis that money growth and long real rates are uncorrelated. Mishkin's results, however, do require that the theorist can identify anticipated and unanticipated money growth *ex post*, and that the theorist can characterize money growth by a consistent time series process over time. The fragility of these assumptions implies inconclusive results once again.[4]

Huizinga and Mishkin (1984) consider the effects of price inflation on rates of return on longer-lived capital assets, not merely on T-Bills or short-term securities. Price inflation lowers the *ex ante* real returns most significantly on the longer-term assets. Using a modified version of the CPI, Huizinga and Mishkin find that a 1 percentage point increase in the inflation rate is associated with a 28 basis point fall in the *ex ante* real rate on T-Bills, a 65 basis point fall for long-term T-Bonds, and a 192 basis point decline for common stocks (ibid. p. 706). Real rates of return fall furthest for long-term instruments. Huizinga and Mishkin, however, do not control for real shocks (price inflation may be correlated with negative real shocks), do not control for inflation variability, and measure price inflation rather than changes in the money supply. Each of these distinctions may affect the interpretation of their results, as illustrated in the discussion of inflation and the stock market below. We do not know which factors are causing real returns on long-term instruments to decline.

Cyclical behavior of real interest rates

Real interest rates tend to follow a roughly pro-cyclical pattern over the course of the business cycle. Some economists (Cooper and Ejarque 1994) cite real interest rate pro-cyclicality as evidence against investment-based theories of the business cycle, but a closer look indicates no discrimination against the investment mechanism.

Many of the risk-based scenarios do not start with a decline in the real interest rate, as discussed in Chapter 2; real interest rate declines are central to only the monetary and time preference shift scenarios. In addition, the monetary scenario does not require or predict countercyclical real interest rates over the entire course of the cycle. The boom receives its first impetus when an exogenous shock (e.g., monetary policy) shifts out the supply curve for loanable funds. At first the real interest rate will fall, inducing

---

[4] For criticisms of the method of decomposing inflation into anticipated and unanticipated components, see Small (1979), Mishkin (1982), and Frydman and Rappaport (1987).

an increase in investment. According to the theory, the decline in real interest rates and the move to higher-yielding investments will create positive wealth effects and the expectation of a boom. The expected boom will shift out the demand curve for loanable funds, thereby putting upward pressure on real interest rates. When both the supply and demand schedules for loanable funds shift out, real interest rates may either rise or fall during the subsequent course of the boom. Similarly, real rates may move in either direction during the downturn.

Nor does the risk-based theory offer unambiguous predictions on whether declines in the real rate will, on average, precede booms. When economic volatility increases, or when a negative real shock hits the economy, entrepreneurs will move towards safer, lower-yielding investments. Real rates of return will fall, and the stock market and output will decline, all in conjunction. Lower real rates will precede a bust, rather than a boom. When both the volatility scenario and the monetary scenario operate in the data, it is difficult to receive a confirming result for either scenario. Tests for either effect, taken in isolation, will likely fail, even if both scenarios possess some explanatory power.

MONEY, CREDIT, AND THE BANK LENDING CHANNEL

A large and growing empirical literature seeks to determine whether monetary shocks offer statistical explanatory power over subsequent output movements. I do not intend to survey, or even cover, the bulk of this literature, but I will discuss a number of central pieces relevant to the monetary scenario. The monetary scenario requires that the statistical evidence shows some real effects of monetary shocks. I will consider the vector autoregression literature represented by Litterman and Weiss (1985), the literature on the 'bank lending channel' of monetary policy, and the literature on credit as a leading business cycle indicator.

Testing the monetary scenario involves at least two primary difficulties. First, monetary shocks do not bring the same results in all cases. Sometimes monetary shocks set off permanent booms and other times they lead to a boom/bust cycle. In terms of long-run statistical averages, money might appear to bring no effects at all, or appear to bring only slight effects. Second, money need not predict the turning points of the business cycle. Monetary shocks induce investors to accept greater or lesser degrees of risk, but the turning points themselves are brought on by the revelation of systematic forecasting mistakes. Real shocks, or perhaps some further monetary shock, might cause the business cycle in a more proximate sense.

Much of the current literature on money and output uses the technique of Vector Autoregressions (VAR). VAR studies attempt to find the statistical relations among macroeconomic variables without trying to estimate or test an underlying structural model. The VAR technique achieved a leading position in empirical macroeconomics through the rational expectations revolution and the Lucas critique, as well as through the general disillusionment with the arbitrary restrictions imposed by most structural models.[5]

The central VAR results have been provided by Sims (1980) and Litterman and Weiss (1985). In a vector autoregression money has no explanatory power over output once the nominal interest rate is included in the specification. Increases in the nominal interest rate statistically forecast forthcoming output declines, and eliminate the ability of nominal money shocks to forecast output. This relationship appears in post-war data for the US, Britain, France, and Germany, and has been cited as evidence against a wide variety of monetary theories of the business cycle, and in favor of real theories of the cycle.

The VAR results nonetheless provide partial evidence in favor of the monetary scenario, or indeed in favor of any theory where monetary policy operates through interest rates. The rise (fall) in the nominal interest rate might be proxying for an increased tightness (looseness) of central bank monetary policy. Money may be affecting output, but the nominal interest rate, by providing a measure of monetary policy and credit conditions, might pick up the relevant statistical significance (McCallum 1986; Bernanke and Blinder 1992). The Litterman and Weiss results therefore do not rule out the monetary scenario.

The Litterman and Weiss results nonetheless present an anomaly for the monetary scenario. Litterman and Weiss explicitly consider whether nominal interest rate changes have explanatory power over output by acting as proxies for real interest rate changes. They unambiguously reject the possibility of a real interest rate mechanism for a monetary influence over output; furthermore, they cannot reject the hypothesis that the real rate of interest is statistically exogenous with regard to money. Their VAR techniques thus produce results at variance with the literature on liquidity effects discussed above (see pp. 117–20). Real rates, when included directly in VARs, also have no explanatory power over output (Litterman and Weiss 1985, p. 144).[6]

To the extent we find the Litterman and Weiss exogeneity results convincing, the monetary scenario must rely on several options. First, changes in nominal interest rates might be providing proxies for changes in *ex ante* real rates, which cannot be measured directly in any case. Second, monetary policy might be operating through a credit rationing channel. With credit rationing we would not necessarily expect the real rate to vary with monetary policy, even if the supply of loanable funds varies.

---

[5] For a critique of the VAR technique, see Cooley and Leroy (1985).
[6] Litterman and Weiss (1985, p. 151), however, do reject the Fama hypothesis of real rate constancy, but cannot reject the hypothesis that the real rate is a random walk.

Third, movements in the nominal rate might be proxying for the real shocks which constitute the turning point of the business cycle. Once the relevant negative real shocks are on the horizon, bond prices fall in anticipation of a higher rate of price inflation or in anticipation of some other factor bearish for bond prices. The high nominal interest rates do not cause the decline in output, they merely forecast it. This sequence of events, while it may appear to support purely real theories of the cycle, does not rule out the monetary scenario. Money need not affect real output *on average*, but monetary policy still could induce greater vulnerability to real shocks, as the risk-based theory suggests. Whenever that increased vulnerability turns unfavorable *ex post*, the nominal interest rate will rise and forecast the forthcoming decline in output.

Isolating monetary policy innovations

An alternative strand of the macroeconomics literature looks for identifying restrictions to isolate monetary policy innovations and trace their effect on output. Romer and Romer (1989) examine the minutes of Federal Reserve Board meetings and identify six periods as contractionary monetary shocks. They show that output fell after each shock; according to their evidence money affects the real economy in some instances even if not always. While this result is consistent with the monetary scenarios, it is also consistent with a wide variety of other macroeconomic theories, including traditional Keynesianism and monetarism.

Other identifying restrictions can be drawn from innovations in the Federal Funds rate, as studied by Bernanke and Blinder (1992). They interpret the Federal Funds rate as an indicator of Federal Reserve policy, at least until the Volcker shift of regime in 1979. Prior to Volcker, the Fed often explicitly targeted the Federal Funds rate. Innovations in the Federal Funds rate therefore represent innovations in policy, and can be used to study the dynamic structural effects of monetary policy changes. Bernanke and Blinder find two central results: first, real output responds to shocks in the Federal Funds rate, even for the period after 1979; second, monetary transmission works through loans as well as deposits. (This second point is discussed in more detail in the subsequent section on bank lending.) The Bernanke and Blinder hypothesis, by specifying the Federal Funds rate as the transmission mechanism for monetary policy, does not contradict the VAR results of Litterman and Weiss (1985), discussed above.

The Federal Funds rate appears to forecast real output better than either monetary aggregates or other interest rates. Bernanke and Blinder interpret this finding as a challenge to Sims (1980) and Litterman and Weiss (1985). If the predictive power of nominal interest rates is due to real rather than monetary factors, as those authors suggest, we should not expect the Federal Funds rate to outperform other interest rates as a macroeconomic predictor. The Bernanke and Blinder result lends support to views which emphasize the real effects of money and postulate credit markets as the relevant transmission mechanism for business cycles.

Bernanke and Blinder also find that incorporating the interest rate spread between commercial paper and T-Bills eliminates the statistical significance of the Federal Funds rate. They interpret that interest rate spread as an alternative indicator of the tightness of monetary policy, and thus as further evidence for the potency of monetary policy acting through credit channels. Other interpretations of this spread will be discussed in further detail below, in the section on credit.

Does bank lending play a special role in the cycle?

Theories of the monetary transmission mechanism typically emphasize one of two channels. Monetary policy may affect the real economy by operating through bank liabilities, or deposits, or monetary policy may operate through bank assets, or loans. The classic Keynesian aggregate demand story emphasizes the nominal demand effects through bank deposits, but the bank lending channel has re-emerged as a source of study. The contemporary literature harks back to Wicksellian and post-Wicksellian writings, including Mises, Hayek, and the other Austrians (see Chapter 4).

Theories of the bank lending channel typically postulate two conditions. First, the supply of bank loans varies with central bank-engineered changes in monetary reserves; banks will reduce their supply of loans when the central bank contracts reserves. Second, borrowers cannot fully insulate their real investment and spending plans from changes in bank loans; in other words, non-bank means of finance do not provide perfect substitutes for bank loans, and/or the availability of non-bank means of finance moves with bank loans.[7]

The bank lending mechanism for monetary policy has received support from the empirical work of Kashyap *et al.* (1993). In their treatment tight monetary policy decreases the quantity of bank loans. Commercial paper issues will rise to (partially) offset the decline in bank lending, but the production of financial intermediation services, and thus output, will decline. Kashyap *et al.* present evidence that tight monetary policies typically precede declines in investment and output. To test their account of the transmission mechanism, the authors add the proportional mix of commercial paper and bank loans to traditional investment equations, and show that measures of that mix offer explanatory power for investment. The effects are strongest for inventories and equipment investment, but

---

[7] Kashyap and Stein (1994a) provide the best overview of the bank lending channel and the relevant literature.

weaker for investment in non-residential structures (Kashyap *et al.* 1993, p. 92).

The work of Bernanke and Blinder (1992) on the Federal Funds rate, discussed above, also finds a significant role for banks in the monetary policy transmission process. Tight money tends to reduce bank loan assets, and easy money tends to increase bank loan assets. Following a monetary contraction, the short-run effects first show up in terms of a decline in bank securities. Eventually the effects of the contraction spread to loans as banks rebalance their portfolios to reflect the lower quantity of deposits.

The primary criticism of the bank lending view comes from Romer and Romer (1990). Romer and Romer set out to address whether monetary policy has its greatest impact through bank liabilities (deposits), or through bank assets (loans). Following their 1989 piece, Romer and Romer isolate six instances when the Federal Reserve deliberately disinflated to slow the rate of price level growth. These instances are used to provide identifying restrictions for statistically exogenous monetary shocks. In the literature these episodes have come to be known as 'Romer shocks.'

Romer and Romer find strong evidence that Romer shocks have significant effects on transactions balances. The evidence for lending effects, however, is less clear. Loans do lead output, but the estimated impact of loans on production peaks after five months and returns to zero after seventeen months (Romer and Romer 1990, p. 179). This evidence suggests a nearly contemporaneous link between lending and output, which Romer and Romer find implausible. They interpret the evidence as suggesting that output drives lending, rather than vice versa (ibid., p. 186). Romer and Romer (ibid., pp. 195–6) do not deny that bank loans may be 'special,' but they question whether monetary contractions reduce the real supply of such loans in significant fashion, given that banks have access to alternative sources of funds.[8]

Several commentators have offered alternative interpretations for the findings of Romer and Romer. Goldfeld (1990) notes that the output-lending link is more stable outside of the 'Romer episodes' than is the output-money link; the bank assets transmission mechanism may be more robust than the bank liabilities transmission mechanism. Both Goldfeld (1990) and Friedman (1990) question whether the Romer results in fact reject the lending view when money and lending factors operate in tandem. The greater explanatory power attributed to the money view may be picking up some of the simultaneous effects of lending. Modigliani (1990) notes that the apparently excessively short time lags between lending and output may come from the use of loans to finance inventories, and do not

---

[8] King (1986) also finds evidence critical of the bank lending view, although he emphasizes the credit rationing motivation for the bank lending mechanism and tests for credit rationing. Bernanke (1986, pp. 64–5) provides a critique of some aspects of King's study.

discriminate against the lending view. In a variety of contexts, commentators (e.g., Eichenbaum 1994) have wondered whether any available empirical tests discriminate either in favor of or against the bank lending channel.

Valerie Ramey (1993) also produces an extensive criticism of the bank lending view of monetary policy. She finds that measures of M2 have greater predictive power over output than do measures of credit. Bernanke (1993b), however, does not accept her results as negative for the bank lending view. He notes that deposits change before loans in both accounts of the monetary transmission mechanism, the money view and the lending view. Furthermore, the leading indicator M2 can just as easily be interpreted as a 'credit aggregate' than as a 'money aggregate.'

Another criticism of the bank lending channel comes from Oliner and Rudebusch (1995). Like Kashyap *et al.* (1993), they also find that restrictive monetary policy increases the ratio of commercial paper to bank loans. Unlike previous studies, however, Oliner and Rudebusch consider other forms of non-bank debt, in addition to commercial paper, such as longer term securities, loans from finance and insurance companies, and trade credit. They find that contractionary monetary policy does not change the overall mix of bank and non-bank debt for either large or small firms, taken separately. Oliner and Rudebusch do find that restrictive monetary policy reallocates all types of credit from small firms to large firms. The share of bank lending declines in the aggregate because large firms, which are more likely to use commercial paper and other forms of non-bank debt, account for a larger share of total borrowing. Gertler and Gilchrist (1993, 1994) find confirming evidence that expansionary monetary policy increases the borrowing share of small firms, and that contractionary monetary policy decreases that same borrowing share. Along related lines, Kashyap and Stein (1994b) find that contractionary monetary policy has especially strong effects on small banks, who presumably do not have equal access to non-deposit sources of funds.

Oliner and Rudebusch emphasize that their results do not discriminate against credit-based views of the monetary transmission mechanism. Rather, their results discriminate only against credit-based views that assign a special role to banks. They do not deny that contractionary monetary policy may restrict the aggregate supply of credit, with credit restrictions falling on small firms the hardest.

The Oliner and Rudebusch interpretation may be especially conducive to the monetary scenario, which stresses total lending rather than the relative quantity of bank to non-bank lending. The Oliner and Rudebusch account also offers an independent explanation – distinct from the discussion of Chapters 2 and 3 – why expansionary monetary shocks might increase entrepreneurial risk-taking. If monetary expansion reallocates resources towards small firms, and if small firms tend to be riskier than large firms, monetary expansions may induce an increase in aggregate risk. Lang and Nakamura (1995), discussed in further detail below, provide evidence that monetary inflation increases the riskiness of loans.[9]

Is credit pro-cyclical?

The literature on credit as a leading macroeconomic indicator examines whether lending in general has predictive power for business cycles. This branch of empirical investigation has generated several results (see Friedman and Kuttner 1993a, especially p. 210, for a survey and overview). First, both prices and quantities in short-term credit markets serve as statistically significant leading indicators for subsequent output movements. Second, price and quantity variables in short-term credit markets offer independent information about output movements. Third, much of the relevant price information comes in the form of interest rate spreads (see also Romer and Romer 1990, p. 167, and Friedman and Kuttner 1992). Fourth, the volume of commercial paper is a better leading indicator than the volume of bank loans (see also Kashyap et al. 1993).[10]

While these results do not discriminate against all competing business cycle hypotheses, each is consistent with investment-based theories. The first result, the pro-cyclicality of credit, follows from the expansion of lending and investment which sets off the boom. The second result, the different information contained in price and quantity variables for credit, suggests that both the size of the initial real interest rate shock and subsequent market reactions to that shock have predictive power.

The third and fourth results require closer scrutiny. The third result, the predictive power of interest rate spreads, may be subject to a variety of interpretations. Researchers typically find that the spread between the T-Bill rate and the commercial paper rate will lead downturns; that is, increases in the T-Bill/commercial paper spread predict declines in output. Tight monetary policy will not necessarily imply this result, since the tightening presumably will raise rates on both T-Bills and commercial paper.[11]

According to some accounts, the T-Bill/paper spread may vary with default risk. Incipient negative real shocks may induce market participants to believe that the default risk on commercial paper has risen. Since credit market prices react quickly, the T-Bill/paper spread widens before the

---

[9] This conclusion does not follow, of course, if the marginal investments of small firms are significantly less risky than their infra-marginal investments.

[10] In addition to the cited writings, see Bernanke (1986), who provides evidence for the significance of credit using vector autoregression techniques.

[11] Kashyap et al. (1993) and Friedman and Kuttner (1993a, 1993b) both consider the hypothesis that monetary tightening pushes a higher proportion of lower-quality firms into the commercial paper. This hypothesis, while possible, neither supports nor contradicts investment-based mechanisms.

negative economic conditions arrive. Credit markets will appear to have predictive power across the cycle, but they only reflect other real causes of the cyclical turning points. This mechanism neither favors nor discriminates against risk-based theories.

Several criticisms have been raised against the claim that changes in the T-Bill/paper spread reflect changing default risk, rather than changes in monetary policy. Bernanke (1990, 1993a, p. 270), for instance, defends the claim that the spread measures the stance of monetary policy. The Bill/paper spread can swing as much as 300 basis points, yet defaults on high-grade commercial paper are rare. Bernanke also notes that the Bill/paper spread is nearly uncorrelated with other measures of default risk, such as the spread between Baa and Aaa corporate bond rates. Kashyap *et al.* (1993, pp. 94–5) also defend the claim that the predictive power of the Bills/paper spread reflects the influence of monetary policy. In addition to endorsing the arguments of Bernanke, they note the countercyclical nature of commercial paper volume. The increase in commercial paper issues, like the Bills/paper spread, also reflects the tight stance of monetary policy in a given period.[12]

The fourth result, the greater predictive power of commercial paper over bank loans, suggests that we should reject narrow, bank-centered accounts of the lending or credit mechanisms. Much of the cyclical fluctuation in credit comes in non-bank lending markets.

The strong predictive power of commercial paper issues over output movements does not itself yield decisive economic implications. Under one hypothesis, a tightening of monetary or credit conditions increases the difficulty of obtaining bank loans. Firms, at least large firms, turn to the commercial paper market to make up for that deficiency. Such an interpretation, however, fails to explain why credit should be easier to obtain through the commercial paper market than through banks, given that funds can flow from one sector to another. An alternative hypothesis suggests that firms resort to commercial paper issues to make up for deficiencies of cash flow (Friedman and Kuttner 1993a). Bad economic conditions might result, for instance, when firms choose output mixes unsuitable to consumer demand. Cash flow may decline before the downturn sets in fully; in that case we might observe commercial paper issues as a leading indicator for the downturn. Firms that issue commercial paper tend to be more creditworthy than firms that concentrate their short-term borrowing from banks. Credit rationing, which is applied most stringently to smaller firms, might prevent bank loans from rising in step with paper

---

[12] Romer and Romer (1990, p. 189) also find evidence supporting the view that the spread measures the tightness of monetary policy. Friedman and Kuttner (1993b) find evidence for both default risk factors and monetary policy factors related to the absolute height of interest rates. See also Cook (1981).

issues, following negative cash flow shocks (see the remarks of Gertler 1993, p. 274).

Overall, the econometric literature on credit and bank lending mechanisms is too recent to demonstrate definitive conclusions. A variety of studies, however, do show evidence that monetary policy affects the real economy through credit and bank lending channels. While extant interpretations of the evidence have not commanded universal assent, the positive results of this literature are consistent with investment-based business cycle mechanisms.

DOES MONETARY POLICY INDUCE SECTORAL SHIFTS?

The empirical literature on sectoral shifts arose in the early 1980s as a response to aggregate demand theories of the business cycle. Sectoral shift theories, which usually form a branch of real business cycle theory, attribute economic downturns to volatile demand and supply shocks across sectors. Output falls, not when aggregate demand is weak, but when planned sectoral supplies do not match forthcoming sectoral demands. The relevant 'productivity shock' comes from changing degrees of coordination across sectors, rather than from changes in technical knowledge.

The modern literature on sectoral shifts starts with Lilien (1982). He found that the aggregate unemployment rate in post-war US data is strongly correlated with the variance of unemployment growth rates across sectors. Total unemployment is high when employment in various sectors or industries is growing at different rates. Higher volatility of sectoral shifts causes layoffs, and unemployment rises through search or through other labor market imperfections.[13]

Most sectoral shift theories have been presented in real terms, but the sectoral shift hypothesis does not rule out a transmission mechanism operating through the non-neutrality of money. Austrian trade cycle theories present alternative versions of sectoral shift hypotheses. Downturns arise when entrepreneurs shift out of risky, long-term investments, either because their time and risk preferences change, or because those investments prove unprofitable. Changes in monetary policy create sectoral shifts towards investment sectors, but those shifts will not always be validated by the demand side of the market.

One strand of the empirical literature looks for sectoral shocks of monetary expansions by examining the effects of money and inflation on relative price variability. A variety of tests find that both higher rates of price inflation and money growth are associated with a greater variability

---

[13] For another treatment of sectoral shift hypothesis, using stock market data, see Loungani *et al.* (1990). Brainard and Cutler (1993), however, find only partial support for sectoral shifts in stock market data.

of relative prices. When rates of money and price inflation are high, prices across sectors are more likely to be changing at different rates. The research in support of this view includes Vining and Elwertowski (1976), Parks (1978), Ashley (1981), Hercowitz (1981), Blejer (1983), Cukierman (1983), Blejer and Leiderman (1982), Fischer (1982), Danziger (1987), Domberger (1987), van Hoomissen (1988), Stockton (1988), Buck (1990), Kaul and Seyhun (1990), Lach and Tsiddon (1992), and Parsley (1996). Extant studies have examined Argentina, Germany, Israel, Mexico, the Netherlands, the UK, and the US, which accounts for the bulk of the studies. Golob (1993) provides a comprehensive overview of the relevant pieces; Marquez and Vining (1984) offer an earlier survey.

These articles establish a strong case for the non-neutrality of monetary shocks across sectors. If money growth causes prices to rise in some sectors more rapidly than other sectors, money is affecting relative supplies and demands.[14]

To date, little work has been done to identify the particular nature of the sectoral shifts caused by monetary non-neutrality. Several studies, however, do provide partial support for Austrian approaches. Ahmed (1987), Kretzmer (1989), and a variety of papers by Thorbecke find significant evidence for the non-neutrality of money across sectors. Kretzmer even finds an effect correlated with the durability of the goods produced in the various sectors.

Ahmed (1987) uses data on sectoral shifts to test theories of wage stickiness. Using Canadian data, he examines whether degrees of wage rigidity, or elasticities of indexation, can account for changes in unemployment. Ahmed proceeds by measuring the non-neutral sectoral shocks produced by inflation and by seeing whether those shocks are correlated with measures of wage stickiness or indexation. He concludes that the real effects of inflation do not follow from wage rigidities. Ahmed does not suggest an alternative, loanable funds channel for the non-neutrality of monetary shocks, but his empirical evidence does specify which nonneutral monetary effects have occurred in Canada. Hours worked are especially elastic with respect to nominal shocks in the sectors of agricultural implements, motor vehicles assembling, and veneer and plywood; the effects are weakest in soft drinks, slaughtering/meat, and pulp and paper (Ahmed 1987, pp. 40–1). The relevant coefficients are significant for a large number of the specified sectors.

---

[14] Other interpretations of the non-neutrality results, however, have been suggested. First, negative real shocks may be causing both high levels of price inflation and the dispersion of relative prices. Second, nominal demands might be increasing across all sectors in equal proportions, but some sectors may have higher menu costs than other sectors. In that case price dispersion will increase for as long as the inflation lasts (first prices in one sector will rise; in the next period prices in the other sector will catch up), but relative demands have not actually shifted. Neither of these alternative hypotheses supports the monetary scenario.

Ahmed's work only illustrates the non-neutrality of nominal shocks, and does not provide direct support for a capital market mechanism. We do not know whether the sectors encouraged by nominal shocks are riskier or more capital-intensive than other sectors. The study of Lang and Nakamura (1995), however, provides evidence that monetary policy influences the overall composition of risk. When monetary policy is loose, the ratio of risky loans to safe loans rises; the converse occurs when monetary policy is tight. They also find that the ratio of risky to safe loans Granger-causes both gross domestic product and inventory investment. Lang and Nakamura measure the riskiness of new loans (as a mark-up over the prime rate), rather than the riskiness of new projects, but their evidence nonetheless is consistent with a risk-based investment mechanism for business cycles.

A second test of monetary non-neutrality, run by Kretzmer (1989), specifies the distribution of monetary shocks across industries of differing durability. Kretzmer distinguishes between anticipated and unanticipated money, and considers the effects of unanticipated money on hours worked in thirty different industries. Unanticipated money has consistent lag effects on these sectors. The contemporaneous effect is positive but small, the effects are large and positive with a 1-year lag, the effects are small and positive with a 2-year lag, large and negative with a 3-year lag, and small and negative with a 4-year lag. Kretzmer's data fit a classic boom/bust cycle. The effects are weakest for the categories of agriculture, forestry, and fisheries, and relatively strong for machinery. Kretzmer (ibid., p. 289) notes that of the ten strongest elasticity effects, seven are associated with categories of durable manufacturing.

Kretzmer (ibid., pp. 293–5) adds durability of the industry's product as an explanatory variable in his regressions. Industrial sectors are assigned values to represent how long the associated final products are expected to last. When used to explain the variation in the distribution of peak hours effects across sectors, these durability variables are positive and significant at the 1 percent level (ibid., p. 293). The resulting regression explains almost half of the variation in the elasticities of hours worked with respect to unanticipated inflation.

Thorbecke and Coppock (1996) show how monetary policy affects differing economic sectors, although they do not rank these sectors on the basis of risk or covariance. They take innovations in the Federal Funds rate as an indication of monetary policy, and run Nonlinear Seemingly Unrelated Regression estimates of portfolio returns in a given sector. Most sectors experience declining returns when the Federal Funds rate rises; Thorbecke and Coppock examine firms in terms of size (deciles) and in terms of particular sectors.

Thorbecke (1995a, forthcoming) also uses stock market data to test which industries are most affected by monetary policy. He finds that highly cyclical, interest-sensitive sectors are positively affected most strongly by monetary expansions, and are negatively affected most strongly by contractions. Thorbecke (1995a, p. 10) offers the following summary of his results:

> The three most affected industries [lumber; clay, glass, and stone; and primary metals] and the sixth most affected industry [rubber] produce inputs to the construction or auto industries. The fourth most affected industry [transportation equipment] includes automobiles and aircraft. The fifth most affected industry [furniture], as Jones (1994) argued, is interest-sensitive. Capital goods industries [non-electrical machinery, metal products, electrical machinery, and instruments] take up places six, seven, eight, and ten. The bottom of the list is made up of industries producing nondurables or necessities such as food, textiles, utilities, tobacco, apparel, and leather ... the evidence indicates that a monetary contraction harms interest rate-sensitive industries and has little or no effect on industries producing necessities.[15]

In sum, the literature on sectoral shifts presents some of the most promising evidence in favor of Austrian approaches to business cycles. The empirical case for monetary non-neutrality across sectors is relatively strong, and we even see evidence that monetary shocks have greater real effects on industries that produce highly durable goods, and that monetary shocks influence the riskiness of investment. To examine monetary non-neutralities in more detail, the next two sections will examine data on securities market prices and data on investment.

HOW DOES INFLATION AFFECT STOCK RETURNS?

The consensus of the finance literature finds that both expected and unexpected price inflation tend to decrease stock returns (Bodie 1976; Nelson 1976b; Fama and Schwert 1977; Modigliani and Cohn 1979; Feldstein 1980; Fama 1981). These articles define inflation in terms of the percentage increase in some price index, typically the consumer price index. Expected and unexpected inflation are differentiated by procedures derived from Barro (1978).

The results of this literature contradict the postulate of long-run neutrality of nominal variables, especially since *expected* price inflation is correlated with declines in stock returns. While tax and accounting effects have been cited to explain the negative correlation (e.g., Feldstein 1980; Nelson 1976a), a fuller treatment of the problem, including fixed nominal debt liabilities, indicates that on the basis of direct distributional effects

---

[15] See also Thorbecke (1995a, p. 29).

alone, inflation should have neutral or even positive effects on share values (Pindyck 1984).

The negative relation between price inflation and stock market returns does not discriminate against the monetary scenario. The articles in question do not show that *increases in the money supply* (as opposed to price level increases) are associated with declines in stock returns. In fact, money supply increases tend to be associated with contemporaneous *increases* in stock returns, as the risk-based theory would predict.

The negative correlation between price inflation and stock returns arises largely from negative real shocks. Negative real shocks, such as oil price shocks, place upward pressure on the price level and lower stock returns. Marshall (1992, p. 1336) shows that the negative relationship between price inflation and stock returns arises from the negative real shock component of price inflation. Bernard (1986) uses cross-sectional data to support the claim that expected declines in future output, due to negative real shocks, are driving the decline in stock returns that follows an increase in the rate of price inflation. The inflation-associated decline in stock returns is strongest for highly cyclical stocks, precisely those stocks that would decline the most when a negative real shocks arrives. The tax and accounting distortion hypotheses do not generate that same prediction.[16]

Money supply measures, unlike the price inflation measures used in the articles discussed above, are not strongly associated with negative real shocks. Marshall (1992), the most comprehensive treatment of the issue, shows that stock returns do vary positively, albeit weakly, with detrended money growth. Marshall attributes this positive relationship to the portfolio effects occasioned by inflation, but does not consider Wicksell effect mechanisms or bank lending and credit channels. In any case Marshall's results lend support to Austrian and risk-based approaches.

Rozeff (1974), in his earlier study of the issue, supported Marshall's basic conclusion: increases in the rate of money growth are associated with increases in stock returns. The positive correlation applies to both expected and unexpected inflation. Rozeff finds that the stock market often can

---

[16] Researchers have found that the negative correlation between price inflation and stock returns disappears in a more fully specified model. Fama (1981) and Kaul (1987) claim that the negative correlation between inflation and the stock market arises from the negative correlation between the stock market and future expected output. Once measures of expected future output are included in the regression, the negative impact of inflation disappears. Under a hypothesis considered by Fama (1981), expectations of low future output lower money demand, leading to price inflation. Kaul (1987) postulates that the monetary authority will expand the money supply (i.e., increase price inflation) to try to stimulate the economy when output expectations are low. Geske and Roll (1983) produce evidence for the view that both expected inflation and stock market declines are driven by expectations about fiscal policy. The link between price inflation and declines in expected returns is in any case small. Variations in expected price inflation typically explain about 3 percent of the overall variation in returns; see Fama (1991, p. 1583).

anticipate forthcoming increases in the money supply and will increase in advance of monetary policy changes.

Adjusting for inflation variability and uncertainty eliminates the negative correlation between price inflation and low stock returns. Kaul and Seyhun (1990) rerun the standard tests on inflation and stock returns but insert a variable for the variability of relative prices. They also adjust for the variability of the rate of price inflation, which they find to be strongly correlated with the variability of relative prices.

After accounting for the variability of relative prices, the negative correlation between price inflation and stock market returns disappears. Most of the negative influence on stock returns is accounted for by relative price variability, rather than by price inflation *per se*. Since relative price variability and the variability of inflation are strongly correlated (ibid., p. 485), low stock returns are correlated with variable inflationary effects in a very broad sense. These results are consistent with the monetary scenario: money supply growth should raise stock returns, price inflation *per se* should not push down stock returns, and variable inflation should cause returns to fall.

How does inflation affect risk and volatility?

The monetary scenario implies that increases in the rate of money supply growth will tend to increase the aggregate risk of investment. This proposition receives only partial and ambiguous support from stock price data.

One body of literature, as exemplified by Schwert (1989), considers which factors are associated with changes in systematic market risk. Schwert analyzes the relationship between market volatility and a variety of economic indicators, including real and nominal macroeconomic volatility, output, financial leverage, and stock trading activity. Schwert concludes that no single measure, or combination of measures, explains changes in the risk premium over time.

Inflation and inflation volatility have a mixed record, at best, in predicting stock market volatility. Inflation volatility does have predictive power for monthly stock volatility from 1953 to 1987, but otherwise performs poorly in a data sample stretching back to 1857. Nor does stock return volatility generally help predict inflation volatility. Wartime effects, however, may interfere with the establishment of a proper correlation; most changes in inflation volatility come in wartime, yet stock prices tend to be relatively stable through those periods (ibid., p. 1127).

Stock market volatility does not directly measure the relevant notion of volatility suggested by the risk-based approach. Business cycles should be associated with increases in real volatility, not necessarily with volatility increases in purely financial terms. The two kinds of volatility do not necessarily move together. Riskier finance strategies, for instance, such as an increase in leverage, will increase the volatility of measured stock returns but will not necessarily affect the volatility of real output. Christie (1982) shows that purely financial effects through leverage account for a considerable degree of stock market volatility. A more complete measure of real volatility would include both equity and debt returns, but systematic, machine-readable data for the securities market as a whole have not generally been available.

The interest rate also influences stock market volatility, as studied by Christie (1982). High nominal rates of interest are associated with high levels of stock market volatility. Christie offers the hypothesis that high nominal rates are associated with a decline in equity values, therefore increasing relative leverage and equity volatility. Christie shows that financial leverage and interest rates, taken together, account for 16 percent of the time series variation in volatility, but for some sub-samples, account for as much as 48 percent of the variation in volatility. If high nominal rates are associated with lower real rates, due to Wicksell effects, Christie's results are consistent with the monetary scenario.[17]

A second body of literature examines how inflation affects different risk classes of investment. Boudoukh *et al.* (1994), for instance, find that the stock returns of non-cyclical industries tend to vary positively with expected price inflation, and that the returns of cyclical industries tend to vary negatively with expected price inflation. These results are directly contrary to the monetary scenario, although the study does not control for negative real shocks or inflationary volatility. These two factors played critical roles in interpreting the negative link between price inflation and stock returns (see above). Just as money supply growth, taken alone, increases rather than decreases expected stock returns, so might money supply growth, taken alone and isolated from negative real shocks, benefit rather than harm high-Beta stocks. The authors' result also does not adjust for the effects discovered by Sims (1980) and Litterman and Weiss (1985). The inflation 'penalty' on highly cyclical stocks might simply be reflecting the link between high nominal interest rates and declines in output growth. The Boudoukh *et al.* measure of inflation, changes in the CPI, is highly correlated with nominal interest rates. If high nominal interest rates are linked to output declines through some other mechanism, cyclical stocks will, by definition, respond more negatively to measured increases in expected price inflation.

Thorbecke (1995b) finds direct and strong evidence that expansionary monetary policy boosts highly cyclical sectors most strongly. The sectors most strongly affected include primary metals, transportation equipment,

---

[17] The higher nominal interest rate also may be signaling some forthcoming negative real shock, as suggested by Litterman and Weiss (1985), and as discussed above. The same real shock may contribute to stock market volatility.

and rubber and plastics. The sectors least affected include food and beverages, tobacco, and utilities (see also Thorbecke 1995a, 1997). While these results are encouraging for risk-based theories, they do not discriminate against competing points of view. *Any* theory that postulates a link between money and real output will predict that money affects highly cyclical sectors most strongly, if only because those sectors move most strongly with output. The risk-based theory does make a particular causal claim – real output varies *because* cyclicality rises, rather than because output moves for Keynesian reasons and cyclical sectors move with it. Econometrics, which is typically better at uncovering correlations than chains of causality, cannot easily evaluate this claim. Both the risk-based and Keynesian views predict that inflation will Granger-cause higher returns for highly cyclical stocks.

Arbitrage pricing theory

Research on arbitrage pricing theory supports the conclusion that inflation represents an independent, non-diversifiable source of risk for the stock market as a whole. Arbitrage pricing theory, unlike the capital asset pricing model, does not reduce undiversifiable risk to a one-dimensional magnitude, such as the covariance Beta. Rather, arbitrage pricing theory allows multiple, independent sources of risk to influence stock prices. Researchers have sought to ascertain which particular factors provide independent, non-diversifiable sources of risk and thus have explanatory power over stock returns.

A variety of studies have found priced risk factors, but Chen *et al.* (1986) provide perhaps the most influential treatment. They look for economic variables that are correlated with stock returns, and then test whether these same variables can explain cross-sectional variation in returns. They find that the two most powerful risk factors are the growth rate of industrial production and the return spread on long-term low-grade corporate bonds and long-term government bonds. Also significant, but less so, are the rate of unexpected inflation and the term structure of interest rates on government bonds.[18]

As in the literature on stock market returns and inflation, inflation refers to the rate of increase of price indices, rather than to money supply behavior. For this reason, arbitrage pricing theory models yield no direct implications for the risk-based theory, although they do discriminate against theories which predict no correlation between nominal variables and stock market returns.

---

[18] McElroy and Burmeister (1988) also find inflation to be a relevant factor in Arbitrage Pricing Theory.

DO MONETARY VARIABLES PREDICT INVESTMENT?

Business fixed investment accounts for only about 10 percent of US GDP, but investment is much more volatile over the business cycle than either consumption or government activity (Cummins, *et al.* 1994, p. 3). For developed countries, investment fluctuations tend to be at least three times as large as fluctuations in output, whether measured in terms of levels or first differences (Greenwald and Stiglitz 1988a, p. 219). For these reasons, many theories, especially of the Keynesian and Austrian varieties, have given investment a central role as a cyclical cause and propagation mechanism. It remains an open question, however, whether investment varies in the manner suggested by these theories. The empirical literature on investment has generated few unambiguous conclusions (Cummins, *et al.* 1994, p. 1).

Investment theory faces empirical conundrums. Econometricians do not have recourse to statistically exogenous variables when examining the macro-determinants of aggregate investment. In a general equilibrium model, any macro variable that 'explains' aggregate investment, or even the composition of investment, is itself endogenous to other relevant macro-economic variables. For this reason, interpretations of coefficient significance are open to question.[19]

In addition, relative prices do not have the explanatory power over investment that might be expected. Standard neoclassical approaches to investment are typically based on the 'user cost' of capital or on Tobin's Q, which represents the market value of capital over its replacement cost, a magnitude usually measured by book value. These variables, however, have not explained much of the variation in investment, whether at the aggregate time series level or with firm-specific data. Tests of Q theory, for instance, imply that changes in Q have very small effects on investment. The empirical results imply implausibly high estimates for the cost of adjusting the capital stock.[20]

Investment equations based on sales or profits, with *no* proxy for the net return to capital, typically outperform models based on substitution effects (see Clark 1979; Bernanke *et al.* 1988; Fazzari *et al.* 1988). Sales and profits, taken alone, typically bring relatively high degrees of explanatory power, and do not decline in statistical significance when measured net returns to capital are added to the equation.

The available data, at least at first glance, lend support to the crude 'accelerator' models of investment. In accelerator models, the economy

---

[19] Hall (1977, pp. 82–3) provides an excellent discussion of this issue.

[20] For an examination of Q theory, see, for instance, Clark (1979) and Chirinko (1993). In practice the replacement value of capital is measured by the book value of capital. Theory predicts the importance of marginal Q, but empirical studies typically measure only average Q.

starts with unemployed resources. An increase in the demand for consumer goods mobilizes a corresponding increase in the demand for capital goods. Alternatively, the data might support the risk-based scenario based on exogenous shocks to retained earnings and a subsequent expansion in risky investment. In that case the importance of sales and profits in investment equations supports models of credit rationing. In credit rationing models investment is constrained by cash flow and creditworthiness, rather than by a dearth of available opportunities. With credit rationing, we would expect changes in sales and profits, which proxy for liquidity, to outperform cost of capital measures in investment regressions.

Standard neoclassical treatments of investment would remain intact if we could establish that measures of Q or user cost provided sufficiently poor proxies for the real marginal return to capital, relative to sales or profit data. Even in such a case, however, the data still would not discriminate in favor of neoclassical theories as opposed to the accelerator view. We do not know whether cash flow is proxying for unmeasured changes in investment prospects, or whether cash flow itself has significant real effects on investment through funds availability.

Alternatively, some economists have sought to defend Q-based and neoclassical theories by a closer look at the evidence. Shapiro (1986), for instance, attributes the lack of correlation between investment returns and investment to an identification problem. Exogenous increases in productivity or the demand to invest will cause both investment and real interest rates to rise at the same time. On average, investment will appear to be uncorrelated with real interest rates, but at the margin, movements in real interest rates will still affect the quantity of investment. After correcting for the identification problem, Shapiro finds results supportive of neoclassical approaches. Cummins *et al.* (1994) use tax policy to isolate exogenous changes to the return to capital; in this context they also find evidence supporting a strong role for the traditional substitution effect on capital investment. Other tax studies, such as those contained in Feldstein (1987), also find evidence supporting the traditional substitution effect. These studies, by and large, attempt to sidestep the identification problem by treating changes in tax law as exogenous events. Bernanke (1983b) develops simulations in which well-defined substitution effects strongly influence investment demand.

The study by Taylor and Yücel (1996) examined how changes in real interest rates affect employment in Texas. They found that most Texas industries are insensitive to changes in real interest rates, but that construction, apparel, non-electrical machinery, and primary metals are sensitive to interest rate movements. Real interest rates have very little predictive power over aggregate employment in Texas, but they do influence its composition. Ceglowski (1989) found, for the United States as a whole, that construction and construction-related sectors are highly sensitive to real interest rate movements, and that transportation equipment, chemicals, textiles, rubber, and plastics are all moderately sensitive. Lonie *et al.* (1990), in their study of Great Britain in the 1980s, found significant real interest rate sensitivity for motors, shipping and transportation, textiles, metals, automobiles, chemicals, and textiles.

Money and investment

Several studies have attempted to measure whether monetary and financial variables have predictive power over aggregate investment. Wainhouse (1984), in his empirical study of the traditional Austrian theory, identified six periods as credit expansion periods in post-war US history; in each period he examined a variety of first differences in prices and quantities. He found that increases in credit were associated with increases in the production of investment goods in 102 out of the relevant 120 cases (ibid., p. 61). This result, however, does not discriminate against a variety of alternative business cycle theories, including Keynesianism. Wainhouse (ibid., p. 64) does provide additional evidence that the increase in investment is self-reversing in a longer time horizon, but the same result follows from any theory that incorporates mean reversion in macroeconomic variables. These results support both old and new Austrian approaches, but not decisively so.[21]

Additional results are provided by Gordon and Veitch (1986), who studied fixed investment in American business cycles from 1919 to 1983. They decomposed M1 into separate components for the monetary base and the multiplier. Both components prove to be significant predictors of investment; the monetary base and multiplier enter significantly into the equations for producer and consumer durables, for both the inter-war and post-war periods. For predicting residential and non-residential structures, the change in the money multiplier has moderate predictive power for both categories in the post-war period, and has predictive power for non-residential structures in the inter-war period. The significance of financial variables also is robust to the use of vector autoregression techniques (Gordon and Veitch 1986, pp. 303–5, 312).

Gordon and Veitch also examine disaggregated measures of investment across the four categories of Household, Business, Durables, and Structures. The resulting regressions indicate that financial variables have different effects on each category; overall, the link between financial factors and durables involves the coefficients of greatest statistical significance (ibid., p. 310).

---

[21] See the comments by Yeager (1986, p. 381).

HOW DO UNCERTAINTY AND VOLATILITY AFFECT INVESTMENT?

The volatility scenarios imply that an increase in real economic volatility should discourage long-term investment. To the extent that volatility can account for cyclical movements, the sensitivity of a particular firm's investment to a change in overall economic volatility should depend upon the riskiness, or Beta, of that firm, as suggested in Chapter 2. Firms with low Betas, by definition, will not go up in value much when the overall market goes up; firms with high Betas, in contrast, will find their risk correlated with the risk of the market. We therefore expect to find that the investment of risky, high-Beta firms varies more with measures of aggregate uncertainty.

Leahy and Whited (1995) tested propositions about investment and risk but did not find the expected results. They took a sample of 772 firms and split that sample by the median into high and low Beta sub-samples; they also classified firms by the variance of their returns, to see if variance would provide a better measure of risk than covariance. Variance was defined in terms of variance of daily return for each year in the sample, after adjusting for debt–equity ratios.[22]

The regressions yielded mixed results on how uncertainty affects investment. Variance of returns proved a significant component in explaining investment when measures of Tobin's Q were absent from the regression. Once measures of Q were added, however, the coefficient on variance became insignificant (ibid., pp. 12–13). Variance, if it has any effects on investment, must operate through expected returns. Increases in variance must affect Q before they can affect investment; in other words, an increase in variance may cause the stock market to fall immediately. Later, investment will decline. The coefficient on variance may appear insignificant, but variance may still have real effects through stock market values.

The analogous investment test with measures of covariance yields weaker results. The coefficients on covariance for predicting investment are not significant, whether or not Tobin's Q is included in the regression. When variance and covariance are included in the regression, without Q, variance has a negative and significant coefficient, but covariance has a positive and insignificant coefficient. The coefficient on variance remains negative and significant, under a variety of specifications, as long as Tobin's Q is absent.

Further tests show that variance of returns and Tobin's Q are highly correlated (ibid., p. 13). A 10 percent increase in variance, for instance, leads to a 5 percent decline in Q. Covariance and Q are much more weakly correlated. If variance and covariance are used in the same regression, the

---

[22] Adjusting for the debt-equity ratio is necessary. Otherwise, return variance, as measured, simply increases with the leverage of the firm.

negative correlation between variance and Q becomes stronger, whereas the sign on the covariance coefficient is positive and insignificant.

The superior predictive power of variance does not discriminate against the volatility scenarios. Imperfect diversifiability implies that variance may sometimes provide a better measure of risk than covariance, as discussed in Chapter 2. More importantly, variance will have independent negative effects on irreversible investments, even when entrepreneurs are risk- neutral. An increase in uncertainty about investment returns, for instance, will increase the returns to waiting and induce a decline in investment.

Leahy and Whited (ibid., pp. 14–15) also ran tests on uncertainty and investment by classifying firms on the basis of their industry capital–labor ratio. They found uncertainty has a more strongly negative relationship with investment when the capital–labor ratio was low, rather than high. Uncertainty has its greatest effects on investment in industries with *variable* capital–labor ratios, rather than in industries with high capital–labor ratios. Leahy and Whited (ibid., p. 15) interpret this result as suggesting that firms will choose variable capital to labor ratios if they find uncertainty very costly.

Other empirical studies of risk and investment also produce mixed results. Brainard *et al.* (1980) use a sample of 187 firms to measure the links between a Beta-derived measure of risk and Q. They find both positive and negative associations between risk and Q, and not all of the coefficients were significant. That is, when overall investment risk increases, relatively risky investments are not always penalized more than less risky investments (ibid., pp. 492–3). This result runs contrary to the contrac- tionary effects postulated by the volatility scenario.

The term structure of interest rates has been used to provide alternative measures of risk. Ferderer (1993) uses the size of the interest rate spread in the term structure to measure uncertainty. Unlike many other measures of uncertainty, this provides a forward-looking magnitude which attempts to capture the degree of uncertainty perceived at the time. Greater spreads in the term structure are taken to indicate higher levels of uncertainty. Ferderer finds that uncertainty affects aggregate investment, even after controlling for user cost and Q. This result supports theories of irreversible investment, in which the value of waiting increases when the spread of potential negative results increases (Bernanke's 'bad news' principle; see Bernanke 1983a).

Several criticisms have been leveled at Ferderer's work (see Leahy and Whited 1995, p. 4). First, the term structure spread is countercyclical and therefore may be picking up aggregate demand effects. Second, the measure directly captures interest rate uncertainty only, rather than uncer- tainty about quantities. Third, uncertainty may encourage precautionary saving and actually increase investment, rather than decreasing investment directly. Two other reservations may be added: increased uncertainty about interest rates may cause the term structure to narrow rather than widen if the desire to lock in rates outweighs the desire to remain liquid (see Woodward 1983). Furthermore, interest rate volatility does not necessarily provide an independent source of shocks. Interest rate volatility is not imposed exogenously on the economy, but presumably reflects some set of real shocks impinging on the loanable funds market.

Interest rate volatility, as measured by the interest rate spread, also has been used to explain the severity of the Great Depression. Ferderer and Zalewski (1994) show that the United States experienced unprecedented levels of interest rate volatility between 1931 and 1934. They isolate the *ex ante* risk premium implicit in the observed term structure and use that premium to explain declines in investment. Again, they find significant results, even after adjusting for monetary policy. Whether the term structure spread is measuring interest rate volatility, or proxying for some other negative real shock, however, remains unclear.

A further study, using cross-sectional data on growth, indicates a negative relationship between volatility of government policy and growth (Aizenman and Marion 1991). Using a variety of measures of policy uncertainty, these authors found that higher levels of policy volatility were associated with lower growth, especially for the fiscal measures of policy volatility. These authors attempt to explain these results by constructing a model where volatile and persistent policies discourage irreversible investment. Ramey and Ramey (1994) also find that policy volatility, measured in terms of fiscal shocks, is associated with lower growth. They do not find, however, that policy volatility discourages investment, or that investment share links volatility and growth.

Pindyck and Solimano (1993) find that the volatility of the marginal product of capital has negative effects on investment and growth. Unlike some of the literature discussed above, they derive this prediction explicitly from an irreversible investment model. Using cross-sectional data analysis, they find that countries with volatile investment conditions have lower rates of investment and growth. Most of this effect, however, comes from the developing countries in the sample, rather than the developed countries.

Monetary policy appears to provide an excellent predictor of the volatility of the marginal return to capital. Countries with very high rates of price inflation typically have more volatile investment conditions. Price inflation outperforms a variety of other measures of political or economic instability. The mean inflation rate also outperforms the variability of the inflation rate in predicting the volatility of marginal returns to capital (ibid.). These results may provide support for the potency of monetary policy over investment; at high rates of inflation rates of price increase provide good proxies for rates of money supply growth. Alternatively, the level of price inflation may be providing the best available proxy for other sources of real instability.

Further supportive results for the volatility scenario are presented by Mascaro and Meltzer (1983). They find that the increased variability of unanticipated money growth reduces the demand for real capital and increases the demand for safer, lower-yielding assets, such as money and short-term government debt. Mascaro and Meltzer use money demand analysis to generate this result. Monetary volatility also leads to an additional risk premium on interest rates, thereby moving the economy to a lower level of efficiency. These effects show up in US post-war data.[23]

Does interest rate volatility affect output?

The volatility of nominal interest rates appears to possess some explanatory power over output. Evans (1984) reran the well-known unanticipated money test of Barro (1978), but also included measures of nominal interest rate volatility. Whereas Barro decomposes money growth into anticipated and unanticipated components, Evans decomposes interest rate movements in similar fashion. Unlike the vector autoregression used by Litterman and Weiss (1985), Evans imposes a definite structural model on the data. He finds that increases in unanticipated nominal interest rate volatility are associated with output decreases, whereas anticipated nominal interest rate movements are not associated with movements in output (Evans 1984, p. 215).

Evans does not attempt to place his empirical results within a well-defined theoretical context, although he does suggest that interest rate volatility may affect output by increasing financial market risk and discouraging investment. Nominal interest rate movements also may be proxying for changes in monetary policy, credit conditions, real rates of interest, or real shocks.

The work of Evans has been subject to criticism and revision, but the critics have not challenged the basic conclusion that interest rate volatility has predictive power over output. Tatom (1985) argues that a properly specified model also yields significance for anticipated interest rate volatility, and attempts to demonstrate that interest rate volatility has its predominant influence through supply-side considerations.[24] Dutkowsky and Atesoglu (1990) confirm the basic results of Evans; they also argue that a proper specification of the model overturns Barro's results on money neutrality.

Recent empirical work by Poitras (1995) attempts to test a modified version of the traditional Austrian theory. Poitras interprets the Austrian

---

[23] Huizinga and Mishkin (1986, section V), however, question whether Mascaro and Meltzer do in fact show that the risk premium in interest rates results from inflation uncertainty.

[24] In this latter regard, Tatom is responding to Mascaro and Meltzer (1983), discussed further below, who find a predominant effect of volatility through money demand and the aggregate demand side.

model as a sectoral shock approach. The move from long-term investments to short-term investments will induce adjustment costs and set off an economic downturn. Poitras therefore differs from the traditional Austrian theory, which treats the move to long-term investments as inducing an economic boom.

Poitras takes changes in nominal interest rates as his measure of monetary shocks, specifically the absolute value of changes in the *long-term* nominal interest rate, his proxy measure for the relative cost of capital. He then tests whether such changes have predictive power over output. Poitras uses the estimation technique of Stock and Watson (1989), but extends the data set to 1991 and uses updated quarterly rather than monthly data. The results are mixed, but more negative than positive. Negative changes in the long rate do not have significant predictive power, but positive changes in the long rate correlate negatively with output. When the differenced 90-day T-Bill interest rate is included, however, even positive changes in the long rate lose their statistical significance. Poitras therefore finds evidence against theories relying on changes in long interest rates as a source of cyclical transmission. Whether monetary or real shocks are at work, the short rate appears to be a more potent predictor of macroeconomic variables.

ARE CAPITAL-INTENSIVE INVESTMENTS MORE CYCLICAL?

Both the traditional Austrian theories and their risk-based offshoots predict that economic fluctuations should strike particular industries with greater severity than other industries. Specifically, fluctuations should be strongest in capital-intensive sectors, sectors producing highly durable goods, and sectors with especially high term-lengths of investment. The risk-based approach also predicts that economic fluctuations will be strongest in relatively risky industries, but this prediction holds for most business cycle theories; supporting evidence would not discriminate in favor of a risk-based approach.

Although the greater cyclicality of capital-intensive sectors has long been considered a stylized fact of business cycle empirics, direct evidence on the matter is sparse. Researchers face the burden of specifying which sectors are more capital-intensive than others. One study, Kretzmer (1989), has already been discussed in the section on sectoral shifts. Kretzmer found that monetary shocks had greater positive influences on a sector, the greater the durability of the good produced by that sector.

The strongest evidence for the greater cyclicality of capital-intensive industries comes from Murphy *et al.* (1989). They examine a variety of measures of which sectors expand the most in a boom, and find systematic evidence for the pronounced pro-cyclicality of investment sectors. The stages of production furthest removed from ultimate consumption fluctuate the most in terms of price over the course of the business cycle. Crude materials, for instance, have the most strongly procyclical fluctuations in price. Finished goods have the least procyclical price fluctuations, and intermediate goods stand in between (ibid., pp. 276–7, Panel A).[25]

The cyclicality of sectoral prices relative to average wages in the private sector provides further supportive evidence. Once again, the sectors furthest removed from ultimate consumption show the greatest cyclicality of price fluctuation. Furthermore, in the production chain, the relative price of outputs to inputs is countercyclical (ibid., p. 278, Panel A; p. 280, Table 5).

Wainhouse (1984, p. 63), in his empirical study of the traditional Austrian theory, finds compatible results in his study of credit expansions. He identifies several periods as credit expansions and finds that the prices of producer goods further away from consumption increase more than the prices of producer goods close to consumption. Wainhouse computes fifty first differences in prices for the six identified periods of credit expansion. Of the resulting 300 cases, 213 conform to the price behavior explained above.

Ruth Mack (1956) provides statistical evidence and case study material for a single industry, shoe production. She considers shoe production as the relevant consumer good, and leather and hide production as the relevant higher-order capital goods. The higher-order goods definitely demonstrate greater cyclicality than shoes. Unlike in the traditional Austrian theory, however, the higher- and lower-order goods tend to move together, rather than in opposite directions.[26]

Drawing upon data for the United States, Greenwald and Stiglitz (1988a, pp. 219–23) find mixed results for the greater cyclicality of long-term investment. First, residential construction and inventory accumulation fluctuate the most of all investment classes. The former variable is consistent with Austrian stories but the latter provides closer support to Keynesian views. Second, the category of 'producers' durable equipment' typically fluctuates less than investment as a whole. Third, the category labeled 'business construction' fluctuates less than investment in producers' durable equipment. The latter two results are difficult to interpret, primarily because we cannot easily rank the risk or the capital-intensity of the relevant investment classes.

The greater cyclicality of capital-intensive industries, even if it can be strongly established, does not discriminate strongly in favor of traditional Austrian or risk-based views. Specifically, at least four other hypotheses

---

[25] Skousen (1990, pp. 292–3) presents some confirming results. Butos (1993) shows the greater cyclicality of higher-order goods during the 1980s and 1990s.

[26] For two other earlier studies, confirming the greater cyclicality of long-term investment sectors, see Mills (1946) and Means (1939).

might account for the greater cyclicality of capital-intensive or highly durable sectors.

First, and most traditionally, accelerator theories of investment imply that higher-order industries will be more cyclical than consumption goods and lower-order industries. In these models the demand for investment goods is some multiple of the demand for the related consumer goods. An increase in the demand for shoes, for instance, will lead to an even greater increase in the demand for shoe machinery, leather, etc. When applied at the economy-wide level, the accelerator mechanism requires an initial unemployment of resources. While accelerator mechanisms typically have been more popular with Keynesians than with economists of more standard neoclassical (or Austrian) persuasions, the data (as discussed above, also see Ramey 1989) do not unambiguously reject the accelerator theory.

Second, the stability of consumption may be driving the instability of investment. The data indicate that individuals smooth consumption over time; the consumption series is one of the most stable macroeconomic series (Carlino 1982; Christiano 1987a, 1987b; Campbell and Mankiw 1989). Following a change in income over the business cycle, individuals seek to maintain their previous level of consumption, either saving or dissaving as a result. Constantinides (1990) offers the hypothesis that individuals form persistent habits; they become accustomed to a particular level of consumption and are loath to accept a reduction in that level. If consumption remains relatively constant, regardless of variations in income, higher-order capital goods will have to bear much of the brunt of demand declines. Higher-order sectors will be more cyclical than consumption.

Third, the prices of higher-order capital goods will fluctuate more than the prices of finished products in some real business cycle models with increasing returns. Murphy et al. (1989) present such a model in their empirical investigation of the greater cyclicality of capital-intensive sectors, as discussed above.

Finally, higher-order capital goods may have stickier real and nominal prices than consumer goods or lower-order capital goods. As demands shift, sectors with stickier prices will experience greater quantity swings over time. Basu (1995) provides one account of why such differential price stickiness might arise. The greater cyclicality of higher-order industries therefore provides general support for theories that postulate an investment mechanism, but it does not discriminate decisively in favor of either the risk-based or the older Austrian view.

CONCLUDING REMARKS

This chapter has examined a variety of empirical tests of some relevance to both old and new Austrian approaches to business cycles. The results of this endeavor have been decidedly mixed. On the favorable side, we have seen a large number of results consistent with the monetary scenarios. We find relatively strong evidence for real interest rate effects of monetary policy, real effects of interest rate volatility, the non-neutrality of money, a bank lending channel for monetary policy, the importance of credit in business fluctuations, and the greater cyclicality of long-term investment goods.

None of these results, however, discriminates decisively in favor of risk-based (or traditional Austrian) theories as opposed to other potential business cycle mechanisms. Each postulated relationship could hold through some alternative theoretical mechanism. Verifying either old or new Austrian approaches – as opposed to merely establishing their plausibility – requires detailed knowledge about underlying structural economic relationships. Right now economists are not close to holding this kind of knowledge about macroeconomic mechanisms of any kind, much less about the relatively neglected Austrian approaches.

Risk-based approaches are amenable to potential falsification, have some empirical evidence in their favor, but cannot be judged as empirically superior to competing business cycle explanations. Nonetheless, the dual concepts of risk and investment provide a fruitful base for further research efforts in business cycle theory. The risk-based approaches outlined in this book are consistent with microeconomic theory, capture some relevant anecdotal intuitions, can account for many well-known features of business cycles, survive a battery of empirical tests, and possess some empirical evidence in their favor.

BIBLIOGRAPHY

Abrams, M. A. *Money and a Changing Civilization*, London: John Lane the Bodley Head Ltd, 1934.

Aftalion, Albert 'The Theory of Economic Cycles Based on the Capitalistic Techniques of Production,' *Review of Economics and Statistics*, October 1927, 9, 165–70.

Ahmed, Shaghil 'Wage Stickiness and the Non-Neutrality of Money: A Cross-Industry Analysis,' *Journal of Monetary Economics*, July 1987, 20(1), 25–50.

Aizenman, Joshua and Marion, Nancy *Policy Uncertainty, Persistence, and Growth*, National Bureau of Economic Research, Working Paper #3848, 1991, Cambridge: Massachusetts.

Altug, Sumru 'Time-to-Build, Delivery Lags, and the Equilibrium Pricing of Capital Goods,' *Journal of Money, Credit, and Banking*, August 1993, part I, 25(3), 301–19.

Amsler, Christine E. 'The Fisher Effect: Sometimes Inverted, Sometimes Not?,' *Southern Economic Journal*, January 1986, 52(3), 832–35.

Ashley, R. 'Inflation and the Distribution of Price Changes Across Markets: A Causal Analysis,' *Economic Inquiry*, October 1981, 14(4), 650–60.

Baldwin, Carliss Y. and Meyer, Richard F. 'Liquidity Preference Under Uncertainty: A Model of Dynamic Investment in Illiquid Opportunities.' *Journal of Financial Economics*, December 1979, 7 (4), 347–74.

Ball, Laurence 'Why Does High Inflation Raise Inflation Uncertainty?,' *Journal of Monetary Economics*, June 1992, 29(3), 371–88.

Barro, Robert J., 'Are Government Bonds Net Wealth?,' *Journal of Political Economy*, Nov–Dec 1974, 82, 6, 1095–117.

—— 'Reply to Perceived Wealth in Bonds and Social Security' and 'Barro and the Ricardian Equivalence Theorem,' *Journal of Political Economy*, April 1976b, 84, 2, 343–49.

—— 'Unanticipated Money, Output, and the Price Level in the United States,' *Journal of Political Economy*, August 1978, 86, 549–80.

—— 'A Capital Market in an Equilibrium Business Cycle Model,' *Econometrica*, September 1980, 48(6), 1393–417.

Barsky, Robert B. 'The Fisher Hypothesis and the Forecastability and Persistence of Inflation,' *Journal of Monetary Economics*, January 1987, 19(1), 3–24.

—— 'Why Don't the Prices of Stocks and Bonds Move Together?,' *American Economic Review*, December 1989, 79(5), 1132–45.

Basu, Susanto 'Intermediate Goods and Business Cycles: Implications for Productivity and Welfare,' *American Economic Review*, June 1995, 85(3), 512–31.

150

Bernanke, Benjamin S. 'Irreversibility, Uncertainty, and Cyclical Investment,' *Quarterly Journal of Investment*, February 1983a, 98(1), 85–106.

—— 'The Determinants of Investment: Another Look,' *American Economic Review*, May 1983b, 73(2), 71–5.

—— 'Alternative Explanations of the Money–Income Correlation,' in Karl Brunner and Alan Meltzer (eds). 'Real Business Cycles, Real Exchange Rates, and Actual Policies,' Carnegie-Rochester Series on Public Policy, 1986, 32, 49–99.

—— 'On the Predictive Power of Interest Rates and Interest Rate Spreads,' *New England Economic Review*, November/December 1990, 51–68.

—— 'Comments and Discussion,' [comment on Friedman and Kuttner], Brookings Papers on Economic Activity, 1993a (2), 267–71.

—— 'How Important is the Credit Channel in the Transmission of Monetary Policy? A Comment,' Carnegie-Rochester Conference Series on Public Policy, 1993b, 39, 47–52.

Bernanke, Ben S. and Blinder, Alan S. 'The Federal Funds Rate and the Channels of Monetary Transmission,' *American Economic Review*, September 1992, 82(4), 901–21.

Bernanke, Ben S., Bohn, Henning and Reiss, Peter C. 'Alternative Non-nested Specification Tests of Time-Series Investment Models,' *Journal of Econometrics*, March 1988, 37, 3, 293–326.

Bernard, Victor L. 'Unanticipated Inflation and the Value of the Firm,' *Journal of Financial Economics*, March 1986, 15(3), 283–321.

Bertola, Giuseppe and Caballero, Ricardo J. 'Irreversibility and Aggregate Investment,' *Review of Economic Studies*, April 1994, 61(2), 223–46.

Bizer, David S. and Sichel, Daniel E. 'Asymmetric Adjustment Costs, Capital Longevity, and Investment,' Working Paper Series, #119, *Board of Governors*, Washington, DC 1991.

Black, Fischer, 'Noise,' *Journal of Finance*, July 1986, 41(3), 529–43.

—— *Business Cycles and Equilibrium*, New York: Basil Blackwell, 1987.

—— *Exploring General Equilibrium*, Cambridge, Massachusetts: MIT Press, 1995.

Blanchard, Olivier J. and Summers, Lawrence H. 'Perspectives on High World Real Interest Rates,' Brookings Papers on Economic Activity, 1984 (2), 273–324.

Blaug, Mark *The Cambridge Revolution: Success or Failure?*, London: The Institute of Economic Affairs, 1974.

Blejer, Mario I. 'On the Anatomy of Inflation: The Variability of Relative Commodity Prices in Argentina,' *Journal of Money, Credit, and Banking*, November 1983, 15(4), 469–82.

Blejer, Mario I. and Leiderman, Leonardo 'Inflation and Relative-Price Variability in the Open Economy,' *European Economic Review*, July 1982, 18(3), 387–402.

Bodie, Zvi 'Common Stocks as a Hedge Against Inflation,' *Journal of Finance*, May 1976, 31(2), 459–70.

Boudoukh, Jacob and Richardson, Matthew 'Stock Returns and Inflation: A Long-Horizon Perspective,' *American Economic Review*, December 1993, 83(5), 1346–55.

Boudoukh, Jacob, Richardson, Matthew, and Whitelaw, Robert F. 'Industry Returns and the Fisher Effect,' *Journal of Finance*, December 1994, 49(5), 1595–615.

Brainard, S. Lael and Cutler, David M. 'Sectoral Shifts and Cyclical Unemployment Reconsidered,' *Quarterly Journal of Economics*, February 1993, 108(1), 219–43.

Brainard, William C., Shoven, John B. and Weiss, Laurence 'The Financial Valuation of the Return to Capital,' Brookings Papers on Economic Activity, 1980, 2, 453–502.

Bresciani-Turroni, C. 'The Theory of Saving II,' *Economica*, May 1936, 3(10), 162–81.

Bryant, John H. and Wallace, Neil 'The Inefficiency of Interest-Bearing National Debt,' *Journal of Political Economy*, April 1979, 87(2), 365–81.

—— 'Open-Market Operations in a Model of Regulated, Insured Intermediaries,' *Journal of Political Economy*, February 1980, 88(1), 146–73.

Buck, Andrew J. 'Inflation and Relative Price Change Variability: Some Evidence from Old Data,' *Journal of Macroeconomics*, Summer 1990, 12, 3, 415–26.

Burstein, Meyer Louis *Modern Monetary Theory*, London: Macmillan, 1986.

Butos, William N. 'The Recession and Austrian Business Cycle Theory: An Empirical Perspective,' *Critical Review*, 1993, 7(2–3), 277–306.

Cagan, Philip 'Why Do We Use Money in Open Market Operations?,' *Journal of Political Economy*, February 1958, 66(1), 34–46.

—— *The Channels of Monetary Effects on Interest Rates*, New York: National Bureau of Economic Research, 1972.

Campbell, John Y. and Mankiw, N. Gregory 'Consumption, Income, and Interest Rates: Reinterpreting the Times Series Evidence,' in *NBER Macroeconomics Annual 1989*, Cambridge: MIT Press, 1989, 185–216.

Carlino, Gerald A. 'Interest Rate Effects and Intertemporal Consumption,' *Journal of Monetary Economics*, March 1982, 9(2), 223–34.

Carlson, John A. 'Short Term Interest Rates as Predictors of Inflation: Comment,' *American Economic Review*, June 1975, 65(2), 469–75.

Carmichael, Jeffrey and Stebbing, Peter W. 'Fisher's Paradox and the Theory of Interest,' *American Economic Review*, September 1983, 73(4), 619–30.

Carter, Michael and Maddock, Rodney *Rational Expectations: Macroeconomics for the 1980s?*, London: Macmillan, 1984.

Cassel, Gustav *The Theory of Social Economy*, New York: Augustus M. Kelley, 1967 [1932].

Ceglowski, Janet 'Dollar Depreciation and U.S. Industry Performance.' *Journal of International Money and Finance*, June 1989, 8(2), 233–51.

Chen, Nai-Fu, Roll, Richard, and Ross, Stephen A. 'Economic Forces and the Stock Market,' *Journal of Business*, July 1986, 59(3), 383–403.

Chirinko, Robert S. 'Business Fixed Investment Spending: A Critical Survey of Modeling Strategies, Empirical Results, and Policy Implications,' *Journal of Economic Literature*, December 1993, 31(4), 1875–911.

Christiano, Lawrence J. 'Is Consumption Insufficiently Sensitive to Innovations in Income?,' *American Economic Review*, May 1987a, 77(2), 337–41.

—— 'Why is Consumption Less Volatile than Income?,' *Quarterly Review*, Federal Reserve Bank of Minneapolis, Fall 1987b, 11(4), 2–20.

Christiano, Lawrence J. and Eichenbaum, Martin 'Liquidity Effects and the Monetary Transmission Mechanism,' *American Economic Review*, May 1992a, 82(2), 346–53.

—— 'Identification and the Liquidity Effect of a Monetary Policy Shock,' in Alex Cukierman, Zvi Hercowitz, MA and Leonardo Leiderman (eds) *Political Economy, Growth, and Business Cycles*. Cambridge: MIT Press, 1992b, 335–70.

—— 'Liquidity Effects, Monetary Policy, and the Business Cycle,' *Journal of Money, Credit, and Banking*, November 1995, Part 1, 27(4), 1113–36.

Christiano, Lawrence J. and Todd, Richard M. 'Time to Plan and Aggregate Fluctuations,' *Quarterly Review*, Federal Reserve Bank of Minneapolis, Winter 1996, 20(1), 14–27.

Christie, Andrew A. 'The Stochastic Behavior of Common Stock Variances: Value,

Leverage and Interest Rate Effects,' *Journal of Financial Economics*, December 1982, 10(4), 407–32.

Clark, Peter K. 'Investment in the 1970s: Theory, Performance, and Prediction,' Brookings Papers on Economic Activity, 1979 (1), 73–113.

Cochrane, John H. 'The Return of the Liquidity Effect: A Study of the Short-Run Relation Between Money Growth and Interest Rates,' *Journal of Business and Economic Statistics*, January 1989, 7(1), 75–83.

Colonna, M. and Hagemann, H., (eds) *Money and Business Cycles: The Economics of F. A. Hayek*, Volume I, Aldershot: Edward Elgar, 1994.

Conard, Joseph *An Introduction to the Theory of Interest*, Berkeley, CA: University of California Press, 1959.

Constantinides, George M. 'Habit Formation: A Resolution of the Equity Premium Puzzle,' *Journal of Political Economy*, June 1990, 98, 3, 519–43.

Cook, Timothy 'Determinants of the Spread Between Treasury Bill Rates and Private Sector Money Market Rates,' *Journal of Economics and Business*, Spring/Summer 1981, 33(3), 177–87.

Cooley, Thomas F. and Leroy, Stephen F. 'Atheoretical Macroeconomics: A Critique,' *Journal of Monetary Economics*, November 1985, 16(3), 283–308.

Cooper, Russell and Ejarque, João *Financial Intermediation and Aggregate Fluctuations: A Quantitative Analysis*. Cambridge, Massachusetts: National Bureau of Economic Research Working Paper #4819, August 1994.

Cottrell, Allin 'Hayek's Early Cycle Theory Re-Examined,' *Cambridge Journal of Economics*, April 1994, 18(2), 197–212.

Cowen, Tyler 'Why Keynesianism Triumphed, Or Could So Many Keynesians Have Been Wrong?,' *Critical Review*, Summer/Fall 1989, 3, 518–30.

—— 'Can Keynesianism Explain the 1930s? Rejoinder to Smiley,' *Critical Review*, Winter 1991, 5, 115–20.

Cowen, Tyler and Kroszner, Randall *Explorations in the New Monetary Economics*, New York: Basil Blackwell, 1994a.

—— 'The Microfoundations of Keynes's Monetary Theory: A New Monetary Economics Perspective,' *Cambridge Journal of Economics*, August 1994b, 18, 379–90.

Craine, Roger 'Risky Business: The Allocation of Capital,' *Journal of Monetary Economics*, March 1989, 23(2), 201–18.

Cukierman, Alex 'The Effects of Uncertainty of Investment Under Risk Neutrality with Endogenous Information,' *Journal of Political Economy*, June 1980, 88(3), 462–75.

—— 'Relative Price Variability and Inflation: A Survey and Further Results,' Carnegie-Rochester Conference Series on Public Policy, 1983, 19, 103–57.

Cummins, Jason G., Hassett, Kevin A. and Hubbard. R. Glenn 'A Reconsideration of Investment Behavior Using Tax Reforms as Natural Experiments,' Brookings Papers on Economic Activity, 1994 (2), 1–74.

Danziger, Leif 'Inflation, Fixed Cost of Price Adjustment, and Measurement of Relative-Price Variability: Theory and Evidence,' *American Economic Review*, September 1987, 77(4), 704–13.

De Long, J. Bradford *'Liquidation' Cycles: Old-Fashioned Real Business Cycle Theory and the Great Depression*, Cambridge, Massachusetts: National Bureau of Economic Research, Working Paper #3546, 1990.

Deaton, Angus S. 'The Role of Consumption in Economic Fluctuations: Comment,' in Robert J. Gordon (ed.) *The American Business Cycle: Continuity and Change* Chicago: University of Chicago Press, 1986, 255–59.

Desai, M. 'Kaldor Between Hayek and Keynes, or: Did Nicky Kill Capital

Theory?,' in Edward J. Nell and Nicholas W. Semmler (eds) *Kaldor and Mainstream Economics: Confrontation or Convergence?* New York: St Martin's Press, 1991, 53–71.

Devine, James N. 'Capital Over-Investment and Crisis in a Labor-Scarce Economy,' *Eastern Economic Journal*, July–September 1987, 13(3), 271–80.

Dixit, Avinash K. and Pindyck, Robert S. *Investment Under Uncertainty*, Princeton, NJ: Princeton University Press, 1994.

Domberger, Simon 'Relative Price Variability and Inflation: A Disaggregated Analysis,' *Journal of Political Economy*, June 1987, 95, 547–66.

Dornbusch, Rudiger 'Expectations and Exchange Rate Dynamics,' *Journal of Political Economy*, December 1976, 84, 1161–79.

Dotsey, Michael and Ireland, Peter 'Liquidity Effects and Transaction Technologies,' *Journal of Money, Credit, and Banking*, November 1995, Part 2, 27, 4, 1441–57.

Durbin, E. F. M. *Purchasing Power and Trade Depression: A Critique of Under-Consumption Theories*, London: Jonathan Cape, 1933.

—— *The Problem of Credit Policy*, New York: John Wiley & Sons, Inc., 1935.

Dutkowsky, Donald H. and Atesoglu, H. Sonmez 'Interest Rate Volatility and Monetary Neutrality,' *Quarterly Review of Economics and Business*, Summer 1990, 30(2), 17–23.

Dwyer, Gerald P. 'Are Expectations of Inflation Rational? Or Is Variation of the Expected Real Interest Rate Unpredictable?,' *Journal of Monetary Economics*, July 1981, 8(1), 59–84.

Egger, John B. 'Shifting Triangles: A Modern Austrian Theory of the Business Cycle,' unpublished manuscript, 1984.

Eichenbaum, Martin 'Comment,' [on Kashyap and Stein 1994], in N. Gregory Mankiw (ed.) *Monetary Policy*, Chicago: University of Chicago Press, 1994, 256–9.

Evans, Martin D. D. 'Discovering the Link Between Inflation Rates and Inflation Uncertainty,' *Journal of Money, Credit, and Banking*, May 1991, 23(2), 169–84.

Evans, Martin D. D. and Lewis, Karen L. 'Do Expected Shifts in Inflation Affect Estimates of the Long-Run Fisher Equation?,' *Journal of Finance*, March 1995, 50(1), 225–53.

Evans, Paul 'The Effects on Output of Money Growth and Interest Rate Volatility in the United States,' *Journal of Political Economy*, April 1984, 92(2), 204–21.

Fama, Eugene F. 'Short-Term Interest Rates as Predictors of Inflation,' *American Economic Review*, June 1975, 65(3), 269–82.

—— 'Interest Rates and Inflation: The Message in the Entrails,' *Journal of Political Economy*, June 1977, 67(2), 487–96.

—— 'Banking in the Theory of Finance,' *Journal of Monetary Economics*, January 1980, 6(1), 39–57.

—— 'Stock Returns, Real Activity, Inflation, and Money,' *American Economic Review*, September 1981, 71(4), 545–65.

—— 'Financial Intermediation and Price Level Control,' *Journal of Monetary Economics*, July 1983, 12(1), 7–28.

—— 'What's Different About Banks?,' *Journal of Monetary Economics*, January 1985, 15(1), 29–39.

—— 'Efficient Capital Markets: II,' *Journal of Finance*, December 1991, 46(5), 1575–617.

Fama, Eugene F. and French, Kenneth R. 'Business Conditions and Expected Returns on Stocks and Bonds,' *Journal of Financial Economics*, November 1989, 25(1), 23–49.

—— 'The Cross-Section of Expected Stock Returns,' *Journal of Finance*, June 1992, 47, 427–65.

—— 'Common Risk Factors in the Returns on Stocks and Bonds,' *Journal of Financial Economics*, February 1993, 33(1), 3–56.

Fama, Eugene F. and Gibbons, Michael R. 'Inflation, Real Returns, and Capital Investment,' *Journal of Monetary Economics*, May 1982, 9(3), 297–323.

Fama, Eugene F. and Schwert, G. William 'Asset Returns and Inflation,' *Journal of Financial Economics*, November 1977, 5(2), 115–46.

Fazzari, Steven M., Hubbard, R. Glenn and Petersen, Bruce C. 'Financing Constraints and Corporate Investment,' Brookings Papers on Economic Activity, 1988 (1), 141–95.

Feldstein, Martin, 'Inflation, Income Taxes, and the Rate of Interest: A Theoretical Analysis,' *American Economic Review*, December 1976, 66(5), 809–20.

—— 'Inflation and the Stock Market,' *American Economic Review*, December 1980, 70(5), 839–47.

Feldstein, Martin (ed.) *The Effects of Taxation on Capital Accumulation*, Chicago: University of Chicago Press, 1987.

Ferderer, J. Peter 'The Impact of Uncertainty on Aggregate Investment Spending: An Empirical Analysis,' *Journal of Money, Credit, and Banking*, February 1993, 25(1), 30–48.

Ferderer, J. Peter and Zalewski, David A. 'Uncertainty as a Propagating Force in The Great Depression,' *Journal of Economic History*, December 1994, 54(4), 825–49.

Fetter, Frank A. *Capital, Interest, and Rent: Essays in the Theory of Distribution*, ed. Murray N. Rothbard, Kansas City, Kansas: Sheed, Andrews, and McMeel, 1977.

Fischer, Stanley 'Relative Price Variability and Inflation in the United States and Germany,' *European Economic Review*, May/June 1982, 18(1/2), 171–96.

Fisher, Irving *The Theory of Interest*, New York: A. M. Kelley, 1965 [1930].

Flood, Robert P. and Garber, Peter M. *Speculative Bubbles, Speculative Attacks, and Policy Switching*, Cambridge, Massachusetts: MIT Press, 1994.

Frankel, Jeffrey 'On the Mark: a Theory of Floating Exchange Rates Based on Real Interest Rate Differentials,' *American Economic Review*, September 1979, 69(4), 610–22.

French, Kenneth R, Schwert, G. William and Stambaugh, Robert F. 'Expected Stock Returns and Volatility,' *Journal of Financial Economics*, September 1987, 19(1), 3–29.

Fried, Joel and Howitt, Peter 'The Effects of Inflation on Real Interest Rates,' *American Economic Review*, December 1983, 73(5), 968–80.

Friedman, Benjamin M. 'Comments and Discussion,' [comment on Romer and Romer], Brookings Papers on Economic Activity, 1990 (1), 204–9.

Friedman, Benjamin M. and Kuttner, Kenneth N. 'Money, Income, Prices, and Interest Rates,' *American Economic Review*, June 1992, 82(3), 472–92.

—— 'Economic Activity and the Short-Term Credit Markets: An Analysis of Prices and Quantities,' Brookings Papers on Economic Activity, 1993a (2), 193–266.

—— 'Why Does the Paper-Bill Spread Predict Real Economic Activity?,' in James H. Stock and Mark W. Watson (eds) *Business Cycles, Indicators, and Forecasting*, Chicago: University of Chicago Press, 1993b, 213–49.

Friedman, Milton *The Optimum Quantity of Money and Other Essays*, Chicago: Aldine Publishing Company, 1969.

Frydman, Roman and Phelps, Edmund S. (eds) *Individual Forecasting and Aggre-*

gate Outcomes: 'Rational Expectations' Examined, Cambridge: Cambridge University Press, 1983.

Frydman, Roman and Rappaport, Peter 'Is the Distinction Between Anticipated and Unanticipated Money Growth Relevant in Explaining Aggregate Output?,' *American Economic Review*, September 1987, 77(4), 693–703.

Fuerst, Timothy S. 'Liquidity, Loanable Funds, and Real Activity,' *Journal of Monetary Economics*, February 1992, 29(1), 3–24.

—— 'Optimal Monetary Policy in a Cash-In-Advance Economy,' *Economic Inquiry*, October 1994a, 32(4), 582–96.

—— 'Monetary Policy and Financial Intermediation,' *Journal of Money, Credit, and Banking*, August 1994b, part 1, 26(3), 362–76.

Garbade, Kenneth and Wachtel, Paul 'Time Variation in the Relationship Between Inflation and Interest Rates,' *Journal of Monetary Economics*, November 1978, 18(4), 755–65.

Garber, Peter and Weisbrod, Steven *Banks in the Market for Liquidity*. National Bureau of Economic Research, Working Paper #3381, 1990, Cambridge, Massachusetts.

Garrison, Roger W. 'Austrian Macroeconomics: A Diagrammatical Exposition,' in Louis M. Spadaro (ed.) *New Directions in Austrian Economics*, Kansas City, Kansas: Sheed, Andrews, and McMeel, 1978, 167–204.

—— 'Comment: Waiting in Vienna,' in Mario J. Rizzo (ed.) *Time, Uncertainty, and Disequilibrium*, Lexington, Massachusetts: Lexington Books, 1979, 215–26.

—— 'Time and Money: The Universals of Macroeconomic Theorizing,' *Journal of Macroeconomics*, Spring 1984, 6(2), 197–213.

—— 'Intertemporal Coordination and the Invisible Hand: An Austrian Perspective on the Keynesian Vision,' *History of Political Economy*, Summer 1985, 17(2), 309–21.

—— 'Hayekian Trade Cycle Theory: A Reappraisal,' *Cato Journal*, Fall 1986, 6(2), 437–53.

—— 'The Austrian Theory of the Business Cycle in the Light of Modern Macroeconomics,' *The Review of Austrian Economics*, 1989, 3(3), 3–29.

—— 'New Classical and Old Austrian Economics: Equilibrium Business Cycle Theory in Perspective,' *The Review of Austrian Economics*, 1991, 5(1), 91–103.

—— 'Hayekian Triangles and Beyond,' in Jack Birner and Rudy van Zijp (eds) *Hayek, Co-ordination and Evolution*, London: Routledge, 1994, 109–25.

Gehr, Adam K. 'Risk and Return,' *Journal of Finance*, September 1979, 34(4), 1027–30.

Gertler, Mark 'Financial Structure and Aggregate Activity: An Overview,' *Journal of Money, Credit, and Banking*, August 1988, 20(3/2), 559–88.

—— 'Comments and Discussion,' [comment on Friedman and Kuttner], Brookings Papers on Economic Activity, 1993 (2), 271–7.

Gertler, Mark and Gilchrist, Simon 'The Role of Credit Market Imperfections in the Monetary Transmission Mechanism: Arguments and Evidence,' *Scandinavian Journal of Economics*, 1993, 95(1), 43–64.

—— 'Monetary Policy, Business Cycles, and the Behavior of Small Manufacturing Firms,' *Quarterly Journal of Economics*, May 1994, 109(2), 309–40.

Gertler, Mark and Grinols, Earl 'Monetary Randomness and Investment,' *Journal of Monetary Economics*, September 1982, 10(2), 239–58.

Geske, Robert and Roll, Richard 'The Fiscal and Monetary Linkage Between Stock Returns and Inflation,' *Journal of Finance*, March 1983, 33(1), 1–33.

Gilbert, J. C. 'Professor Hayek's Contribution to Trade Cycle Theory,' in *Economic*

Essays in Commemoration of the Dundee School of Economics 1931–55. Dundee: W. Culross & Son Ltd., Coupar Angus, 1955, 51–62.

Goldfeld, Stephen M. *Comments and Discussion,* [comment on Romer and Romer] Brookings Papers on Economic Activity, 1990 (1), 199–204.

Golob, John E. 'Inflation, Inflation Uncertainty, and Relative Price Variability: A Survey,' Working Paper RWP 93–15, Research Division, Federal Reserve Bank of Kansas City, 1993.

Gordon, Robert J. and Veitch, John M. 'Fixed Investment in the American Business Cycle, 1919–83,' in Robert J. Gordon (ed.) *The American Business Cycle: Continuity and Change,* Chicago: University of Chicago Press, 1986, 267–335.

Graham, Fred C. 'The Fisher Hypothesis: A Critique of Recent Results and Some New Evidence,' *Southern Economic Journal,* April 1988, 54(4), 961–8.

Gray, Jo Anna 'Wage Indexation: A Macroeconomic Approach,' *Journal of Monetary Economics,* April 1976, 2(2), 221–35.

Greenwald, Bruce C. and Stiglitz, Joseph E. 'Examining Alternative Macroeconomic Theories,' Brookings Papers on Economic Activity, 1988a (1), 207–60.

—— 'Money, Imperfect Information, and Economic Fluctuations,' in Meir Kohn and Sho-Chieh Tsiang (eds) *Finance Constraints, Expectations, and Macroeconomics,* Oxford: Clarendon Press, 1988b.

—— 'Macroeconomic Models with Equity and Credit Rationing,' National Bureau of Economic Research, Working Paper #3533, 1990 Cambridge: Massachusetts.

Greenwald, Bruce C., Stiglitz, Joseph E. and Weiss, Andrew 'Information Imperfections in the Capital Market and Macroeconomic Fluctuations,' *American Economic Review,* May 1984, 74(2), 194–9.

Grier, Kevin B. and Perry, Mark J. 'The Effect of Money Shocks on Interest Rates in the Presence of Conditional Heteroskedasticity,' *Journal of Finance,* September 1993, 48(4), 1445–55.

Grossman, Sanford J. and Stiglitz, Joseph E. 'On the Impossibility of Informationally Efficient Markets,' *American Economic Review,* June 1980, 70(3), 393–408.

Grossman, Sanford J. and Weiss, Laurence 'Heterogeneous Information and the Theory of the Business Cycle,' *Journal of Political Economy,* 1982, 90(4), 699–727.

—— 'A Transactions-Based Model of the Monetary Transmission Mechanism,' *American Economic Review,* December 1983, 73(5), 871–80.

Haberler, Gottfried *Prosperity and Depression: A Theoretical Analysis of Cyclical Movements,* Northampton: John Dickens & Co., 1964

—— 'Reflections on Hayek's Business Cycle Theory,' *Cato Journal,* Fall 1986, 6(2), 421–35.

Hall, Robert E. 'Investment, Interest Rates, and the Effects of Stabilization Policies,' Brookings Papers on Economic Activity, 1977 (1), 61–103.

—— 'Stochastic Implications of the Life Cycle–Permanent Income Hypothesis: Theory and Evidence,' *Journal of Political Economy,* December 1978, 86, 6, 971–87.

—— 'Monetary Trends in the United States and the United Kingdom: A Review from the Perspective of New Developments in Monetary Economics,' *Journal of Economic Literature,* December 1982, 20, 1552–6.

—— 'The Role of Consumption in Economic Fluctuations,' in Robert J. Gordon (ed.) *The American Business Cycle: Continuity and Change,* Chicago: University of Chicago Press, 1986, 237–54.

—— 'Intertemporal Substitution in Consumption,' *Journal of Political Economy,* April 1988, 96(2), 339–57.

Hamilton, James D. 'Uncovering Financial Market Expectations of Inflation,' *Journal of Political Economy,* December 1985, 93(6), 1224–41.

Hansen, Alvin H. *Business Cycles and National Income*, New York: W.W. Norton & Company, 1964.

Hansen, Alvin H. and Tout, Herbert 'Investment and Saving in Business Cycle Theory,' *Econometrica*, April 1933, 1, 119–47.

Harcourt, G. C. *Some Cambridge Controversies in the Theory of Capital*, Cambridge: Cambridge University Press, 1972.

Hasbrouck, Joel 'Stock Returns, Inflation, and Economic Activity: The Survey Evidence,' *Journal of Finance*, December 1984, 39(5), 1293–310.

Hawtrey, Ralph G. *Capital and Employment*, London: Longmans, Green and Co, 1952 [1937].

Hayek, Friedrich A. 'Money and Capital: A Reply,' *The Economic Journal*, June 1932, 17(166), 237–49.

—— *Profits, Interest, and Investment, and Other Essays in the Theory of Industrial Fluctuations*, London: Routledge & Sons, 1939.

—— 'The Ricardo Effect,' *Economica*, May 1942, 9(34), 127–52.

—— 'Time-Preference and Productivity: A Reconsideration,' *Economica*, February 1945, 12, 22–5.

—— *Monetary Theory and the Trade Cycle*, New York: Augustus M. Kelley, 1966 [1933].

—— *Prices and Production*, New York: Augustus M. Kelley, 2nd edition, 1967 [1935].

—— 'Three Elucidations of the Ricardo Effect,' *Journal of Political Economy*, March/April 1969, 77(2), 274–85.

—— *Monetary Nationalism and International Stability*, New York: Augustus M. Kelley, 1971 [1937].

The Pure Theory of Capital, Chicago: University of Chicago Press, 1975 [1941].

—— 'Intertemporal Price Equilibrium and Movements in the Value of Money,' in Roy McCloughery (ed.) *Money, Capital and Fluctuations: Early Essays*, London: Routledge & Kegan Paul, 1984, 71–117. The original version of this essay was published in German in 1928.

Hercowitz, Zvi 'Money and the Dispersion of Relative Prices,' *Journal of Political Economy*, April 1981, 89(2), 328–56.

—— 'The Real Interest Rate and Aggregate Supply,' *Journal of Monetary Economics*, September 1986, 18(2), 121–45.

Hicks, John R. *Value and Capital*, Oxford: Clarendon Press, 1939.

—— 'The Hayek Story,' in *Critical Essays in Monetary Theory*, Oxford: Clarendon Press, 1967, 203–15.

—— *Capital and Time: A Neo-Austrian Theory*, Oxford: Clarendon Press, 1973.

Hoover, Kevin D. 'Money, Prices and Finance in the New Monetary Economics,' *Oxford Economic Papers*, March 1988, 40(1), 150–67.

Hubbard, R. Glenn 'Investment Under Uncertainty: Keeping One's Options Open,' *Journal of Economic Literature*, December 1994, 32(4), 1816–31.

Huizinga, John and Mishkin, Frederic S. 'Inflation and Real Interest Rates on Assets with Different Risk Characteristics,' *Journal of Finance*, July 1984, 39(3), 699–712.

—— 'Monetary Policy Regime Shifts and the Unusual Behavior of Real Interest Rates,' Carnegie-Rochester Conference Series on Public Choice, 1986, 24, 231–74.

Hummel, Jeffrey Rogers 'Problems With Austrian Business Cycle Theory', Reason Papers, Winter 1979, 5, 41–53.

Hurn, A. S. and Wright, Robert E. 'Geology or Economics? Testing Models of Irreversible Investment using North Sea Oil Data,' *Economic Journal*, March 1994, 104(423), 363–71.

Ingersoll, Jonathan E., Jr. and Ross, Stephen A. 'Waiting to Invest: Investment and Uncertainty,' *Journal of Business*, January 1992, 65(1), 1–29.

Jaffee, Jeffrey F. and Mandelker, Gershon 'The "Fisher Effect" for Risky Assets: An Empirical Investigation,' *Journal of Finance*, May 1976, 31(2), 447–58.

Jones, D. 'Monetary Policy as Viewed by a Money Market Participant,' in David Colander and D. Daane (eds) *The Art of Monetary Policy*, Armonk, New York: M. E. Sharpe, 1994, 85–100.

Kaldor, Nicholas 'Professor Hayek and the Concertina-Effect,' *Economica*, November 1942, 36, 359–82.

Kashyap, Anil K. and Stein, Jeremy C. 'Monetary Policy and Bank Lending,' in N. Gregory Mankiw (ed.) *Monetary Policy*, Chicago: University of Chicago Press, 1994a, 221–56.

—— *The Impact of Monetary Policy on Bank Balance Sheets*, National Bureau of Economic Research Working Paper, #4821, August 1994b, Cambridge: Massachusetts.

Kashyap, Anil K., Stein, Jeremy C. and Wilcox, David W. 'Monetary Policy and Credit Conditions: Evidence from the Composition of External Finance,' *American Economic Review*, 1993, 83(3), 78–98.

Kaul, Gautam 'Stock Returns and Inflation: The Role of the Monetary Sector,' *Journal of Financial Economics*, June 1987, 18(2), 253–76.

Kaul, Gautam and Seyhun, H. Nejat 'Relative Price Variability Real Shocks, and the Stock Market,' *Journal of Finance*, June 1990, 45, 2, 479–96.

Keynes, John Maynard *General Theory of Employment, Interest and Money*, London: Macmillan, 1936.

Kimball, Miles S. 'Precautionary Saving in the Small and in the Large,' *Econometrica*, January 1990, 58(1), 53–73.

King, Robert G. 'Interest Rates, Aggregate Information, and Monetary Policy,' *Journal of Monetary Economics*, August 1983, 12(2), 199–234.

King, Robert G. 'The Role of Consumption in Economic Fluctuations: Comments,' in Robert J. Gordon (ed.) *In The American Business Cycle: Continuity and Change*, Chicago: University of Chicago Press, 1986, 259–63.

King, Robert G. and Plosser, Charles 'Money, Credit, and Prices in a Real Business Cycle,' *American Economic Review*, June 1984, 74(3), 363–79.

King, Stephen R. 'Monetary Transmission: Through Bank Loans or Bank Liabilities?,' *Journal of Money, Credit, and Banking*, August 1986, 18(3), 290–303.

Kirzner, Israel M. 'The Pure Time Preference Theory of Interest: An Attempt at Clarification,' in Jeffrey M. Hebener (ed.) *The Meaning of Ludwig von Mises: Contributions in Economics, Sociology, Epistemology, and Political Philosophy*, Boston: Kluwer, 1993.

Knight, Frank H. *Risk, Uncertainty, and Profit*, Chicago: University of Chicago Press, 1971 [1921].

Kohn, Meir 'A Loanable Funds Theory of Unemployment and Monetary Disequilibrium,' *American Economic Review*, December 1981, 91(5), 859–79.

Kydland, Finn and Prescott, Edward 'Time to Build and Aggregate Economic Fluctuations,' *Econometrica*, November 1982, 50(6), 1345–70.

Kretzmer, Peter E. 'The Cross-Industry Effects of Unanticipated Money in an Equilibrium Business Cycle Model,' *Journal of Monetary Economics*, March 1989, 23(2), 275–96.

Lach, S. and Tsiddon, D. 'The Behavior of Prices and Inflation: An Empirical Analysis of Disaggregated Price Data,' *Journal of Political Economy*, April 1992, 100(2), 349–89.

Lachmann, Ludwig M. 'A Reconsideration of the Austrian Theory of Industrial Fluctuations,' *Economica*, May 1940, 7(26), 179–96.

—— 'The Role of Expectations in Economics as a Social Science,' *Economica*, February 1943, 10(37), 12–23.

—— *Capital and its Structure*, Kansas City: Sheed, Andrews, and McMeel, 1978.

Laidler, David 'Hayek on Neutral Money and the Cycle,' in M. Colonna and H. Hagemann *Money and Business Cycles: The Economics of F. A. Hayek*, Volume I, Aldershot: Edward Elgar, 1994, 3–26.

Lang, William W. and Nakamura, Leonard I. ' "Flight to Quality" in Banking and Economic Activity,' *Journal of Monetary Economics*, December 1995, 36(1), 145–64.

Lastrapes, William D. and Selgin, George 'The Liquidity Effect: Identifying Short-Run Interest Rate Dynamics Using Long-Run Restrictions,' *Journal of Macroeconomics*, Summer 1995, 17(3), 387–404.

Lauterbach, Beni 'Consumption Volatility, Production Volatility, Spot-Rate Volatility, and the Returns on Treasury Bills and Bonds,' *Journal of Financial Economics*, September 1989, 24(1), 155–79.

Leahy, John V. and Whited, Toni M. *The Effect of Uncertainty on Investment: Some Stylized Facts*, National Bureau of Economic Research, Working Paper #4986, January 1995, Cambridge: Massachusetts.

Leeper, Eric M. and Gordon, David B. 'In Search of the Liquidity Effect,' *Journal of Monetary Economics*, June 1992, 29(3), 341–69.

Lilien, David M. 'Sectoral Shifts and Cyclical Unemployment,' *Journal of Political Economy*, August 1982, 90(4), 777–93.

Litterman, Robert B. and Weiss, Laurence 'Money, Real Interest Rates, and Output: A Reinterpretation of the US Postwar Data,' *Econometrica*, January 1985, 53(1), 129–56.

Long, John and Plosser, Charles 'Real Business Cycles,' *Journal of Political Economy*, February 1983, 91(1), 39–69.

Lonie, Alasdair A., Power, David M. and Sinclair, D. Donald 'The Discriminatory Impact of Interest Rate Changes,' *British Review of Economic Issues*, October 1990, 12(28), 79–106.

Loungani, Prakash, Rush, Mark and Tave, William 'Stock Market Dispersion and Unemployment,' *Journal of Monetary Economics*, June 1990, 25(3), 367–88.

Lucas, Robert E. Jr. 'Expectations and the Neutrality of Money,' *Journal of Economic Theory*, April 1972, 4(2), 103–24.

—— *Studies in Business Cycle Theory*, Cambridge, Massachusetts: The MIT Press, 1981.

—— *The Role of Overlapping Generations Models in Monetary Economics*, Carnegie-Rochester Conference Series on Public Policy, Spring 1983, 18, 9–44.

—— 'On Consequences and Criticisms of Monetary Targeting,' *Journal of Money, Credit, and Banking*, November 1985, 18(4), part 2, 570–97.

—— 'Liquidity and Interest Rates,' *Journal of Economic Theory*, April 1990, 50(2), 237–64.

McCallum, Bennett T. 'The Role of Overlapping Generations Models in Monetary Economics', Carnegie-Rochester Conference Series on Public Policy, Spring 1983, 18, 9–44.

—— 'On Consequences and Criticisms of Monetary Targeting,' *Journal of Money, Credit, and Banking*, November 1985, 17, part 2, 570–610.

—— 'On "Real and Sticky-Price" Theories of the Business Cycle,' *Journal of Money, Credit, and Banking*, November 1986, 17(4), 397–414.

McCormick, B. J. *Hayek and the Keynesian Avalanche*, New York: St Martin's Press, 1992.

McCulloch, J. Huston 'Misintermediation and Macroeconomic Fluctuations,' *Journal of Monetary Economics*, July 1981, 8(1), 103–15.

MacDonald, Robert and Siegel, Daniel 'The Value of Waiting to Invest,' *Quarterly Journal of Economics*, November 1986, 101(4), 707–27.

McElroy, Marjorie B. and Burmeister, Edwin 'Arbitrage Pricing Theory as a Restricted Nonlinear Multivariate Regression Model,' *Journal of Business and Economics Statistics*, January 1988, 6(1), 29–42.

Machlup, Fritz *The Stock Market, Credit, and Capital Formation*, London: William Hodge and Company, 1940.

Mack, Ruth P. *Consumption and Business Fluctuations: A Case Study of the Shoe, Leather, Hide Sequence*, New York: National Bureau of Economic Research, 1956.

Mankiw, N. Gregory and Miron, Jeffrey A. 'The Changing Behavior of the Term Structure of Interest Rates,' *Quarterly Journal of Economics*, May 1986, 101(2), 211–28.

Mankiw, N. Gregory and Summers, Lawrence 'Do Long-Term Rates Overreact to Short-Term Rates?,' and comments, *Brookings Papers on Economic Activity*, 1984 (1), 223–47.

Marget, Arthur William *The Loan Fund*, doctoral dissertation, Harvard University, 1926.

—— *The Theory of Prices: A Re-examination of the Central Problems of Monetary Theory*, vol. I, II, New York: Prentice-Hall, 1938, 1942.

Marquez, J. and Vining, D. 'Inflation and Relative Price Behavior: A Survey of the Literature,' in M. Balbon (ed.) *Economic Perspectives: An Annual Survey of Economics 3*, New York: Harwood Academic, 1984, 1–56.

Marshall, David A. 'Inflation and Asset Returns in a Monetary Economy,' *Journal of Finance*, September 1992, 47(4), 1315–42.

Mascaro, Angelo and Meltzer, Allan H. 'Long- and Short-Term Interest Rates in a Risky World,' *Journal of Monetary Economics*, November 1983, 12(4), 485–518.

Mayer, Thomas 'The Inflexibility of Monetary Policy,' *Review of Economics and Statistics*, November 1958, 60(4), 358–74.

—— 'Plant and Equipment Lead Times,' *Journal of Business*, April 1960, 33(2), 127–32.

Means, Gardiner C. (ed.) *The Structure of the American Economy, Part I: Basic Characteristics*, Washington, DC: Government Printing Office, 1939.

Meltzer, Allan *Keynes's Monetary Theory: A Different Interpretation*, New York: Basil Blackwell, 1988.

Melvin, Michael 'The Vanishing Liquidity Effect,' *Economic Inquiry*, April 1983, 21(2), 188–202.

Merrick, John J. Jr 'The Anticipated Real Interest Rate, Capital Utilization and the Cyclical Pattern of Real Wages,' *Journal of Monetary Economics*, January 1984, 13(1), 17–30.

Meulen, Henry *Free Banking: An Outline of a Policy of Individualism*, London: Macmillan, 1934.

Michael, Robert T. 'Variation Across Households in the Rate of Inflation,' *Journal of Money, Credit, and Banking*, February 1979, 11(1), 32–46.

Mills, Frederick C. *Price–Quantity Interactions in Business Cycles*, New York: National Bureau of Economic Research, 1946.

Mises, Ludwig von ' "Elastic Expectations" and the Austrian Theory of the Trade Cycle,' *Economica*, August 1943, 10(39), 251–2.

—— *Human Action: A Treatise of Economics*, third revised edition, Chicago: Contemporary Books, 1966.

—— *On the Manipulation of Money and Credit*, New York: Free Market Books, 1978.

Mishkin, Frederic S. 'Monetary Policy and Long-Term Interest Rates: An Efficient Markets Approach,' *Journal of Monetary Economics*, January 1981a, 7(1), 29–55.

—— 'The Real Interest Rate: An Empirical Investigation,' Carnegie-Rochester Conference Series on Public Policy, 1981b, 15, 151–200.

—— 'Does Anticipated Monetary Policy Matter? An Econometric Investigation,' *Journal of Political Economy*, February 1982, 90(1), 22–51.

—— 'Are Real Interest Rates Equal Across Countries?: An Empirical Investigation of Interest Parity Conditions,' *Journal of Finance*, December 1984a, 39(5), 1345–57.

—— 'The Real Interest Rate: A Multi-Country Empirical Study,' *Canadian Journal of Economics*, May 1984b, 17(2), 283–311.

—— 'What Does the Term Structure Tell Us About Future Inflation?,' *Journal of Monetary Economics*, January 1990, 25(1), 77–95.

—— 'Is the Fisher Effect For Real? A Reexamination of the Relationship Between Inflation and Interest Rates,' *Journal of Monetary Economics*, November 1992, 30(2), 195–215.

Modigliani, Franco 'General Discussion,' [Comment on Romer and Romer], Brookings Papers on Economic Activity, 1990 (1), 209–10.

Modigliani, Franco and Cohn, Richard A. 'Inflation and Security Returns,' *Financial Analysts Journal*, March/April 1979, 35(2), 3–23.

Moss, Laurence S. and Vaughn, Karen I. 'Hayek's Ricardo Effect: A Second Look,' *History of Political Economy*, 1986, 18(4), 545–65.

Mundell, Robert 'Inflation and Real Interest,' *Journal of Political Economy*, June 1963, 71(3), 280–3.

Murphy, Kevin M., Shleifer, Andrei and Vishny, Robert W. 'Building Blocks of Market Clearing Business Cycle Models,' *NBER Macroeconomics Annual*, Cambridge: MIT Press, 1989, 247–87.

Muth, John F. 'Rational Expectations and the Theory of Price Movements,' *Econometrica*, July 1961, 29(3), 315–35.

Myers, Stewart C. 'The Capital Structure Puzzle,' *Journal of Finance*, July 1984, 39(3), 575–92.

Myers, Stewart C. and Majluf, Nicholas S. 'Corporate Financing and Investment Decisions When Firms Have Information That Investors Do Not Have,' *Journal of Financial Economics*, June 1984, 13, 187–221.

Neisser, Hans 'Monetary Expansion and the Structure of Production,' *Social Research*, 1(4), November 1934, 434–57.

Nelson, Charles R. 'Inflation and Capital Budgeting,' *Journal of Finance*, June 1976a, 31(3), 923–31.

—— 'Inflation and Rates of Return on Common Stocks,' *Journal of Finance*, May 1976b, 31(2), 471–87.

Nelson, Charles R. and Schwert, G. William 'Short-Term Rates as Predictors of Inflation: On Testing the Hypothesis That the Real Rate of Interest is Constant,' *American Economic Review*, June 1977, 67(3), 478–86.

Nickell, S. J. *The Investment Decisions of Firms*, Cambridge: Cambridge University Press, 1978.

O'Driscoll, Gerald P. Jr. *Economics as a Coordination Problem: The Contributions of Friedrich A. Hayek*, Kansas City: Sheed, Andrews, and McMeel, 1977.

—— 'Frank A. Fetter and "Austrian" Business Cycle Theory,' *History of Political Economy*, Winter 1980, 12(4) 542–57.

O'Driscoll, Gerald P. Jr. and Rizzo, Mario J. *The Economics of Time and Ignorance*, New York: Basil Blackwell, 1985.

Oliner, Stephen D. and Rudebusch, Glenn D. 'Is There a Bank Lending Channel for Monetary Policy?,' *Economic Review*, Federal Reserve Bank of San Francisco, 1995 (2), 3–20.

Orosel, Gerhard O. 'A Reformulation of the Austrian Theory of Capital and Its Application to the Debate on Reswitching and Related Paradoxa,' *Zeitschrift für Nationalökonomie*, 1979, 39(1–2), 1–31.

Parks, Richard W. 'Inflation and Relative Price Variability,' *Journal of Political conomy*, February 1978, 86(1), 79–95.

Parsley, David C. 'Inflation and Relative Price Variability in the Short and Long Run: New Evidence from the United States,' *Journal of Money, Credit, and Banking*, August 1996, 28(3), Part 1, 323–41.

Patel, Jayendu and Zeckhauser, Richard 'Shared Price Trends: Evidence from US Cities and OECD Countries,' *Journal of Business and Economic Statistics*, April 1990, 8(2), 179–89.

Pellengahr, Ingo 'Austrians vs. Austrians I: A Subjectivist View of Interest,' in Matte Faber (ed.) *Studies in Austrian Capital Theory, Investment, and Time*, Berlin: Springer-Verlag, 1986a, 60–77.

—— 'Austrians vs. Austrians II: Functionalist vs. Essentialist Theories of Interest,' in Matte Faber (ed.) *Studies in Austrian Capital Theory, Investment and Time*, Berlin, Springer-Verlag, 1986b, 78–95.

Pesaran, M. Hashem *The Limits to Rational Expectations*, New York: Basil Blackwell, 1987.

Phillips, C. A., McManus, T. F. and Nelson, R. W. *Banking and the Business Cycle*, New York: The Macmillan Company, 1938.

Pindyck, Robert S. 'Risk, Inflation, and the Stock Market,' *American Economic Review*, June 1984, 74(3), 335–51.

Pindyck, Robert S. and Solimano, Andrés 'Economic Instability and Aggregate Investment,' *NBER Macroeconomics Annual*, Cambridge: The MIT Press, 1993, 259–303.

Poitras, Marc 'The Hayek Model: Output Effects of Long-Term Monetary Shocks,' in *Money and Economic Activity: An Empirical Investigation*, PhD dissertation, Virginia, George Mason University, 1995.

Presley, John R. *Robertsonian Economics: An Examination of the Work of Sir D. H. Robertson on Industrial Fluctuation*, New York: Holmes and Meier Publishers, Inc., 1979.

Ramey, Garey and Ramey, Valerie A. *Cross-Country Evidence on the Link Between Volatility and Growth*, National Bureau of Economic Research, Working Paper #4959, 1994, Cambridge: Massachusetts.

Ramey, Valerie 'Inventories as Factors of Production and Economic Fluctuations,' *American Economic Review*, June 1989, 79(3), 338–54.

—— 'How Important is the Credit Channel in the Transmission of Monetary Policy?,' Carnegie-Rochester Series on Public Policy, December 1993, 39, 1–45.

Redman, Deborah A. *A Reader's Guide to Rational Expectations: A Survey and Comprehensive Annotated Bibliography*, Aldershot: Edward Elgar, 1992.

Robbins, Lionel *The Great Depression*, New York: Macmillan, 1934.

Roll, Richard and Ross, Stephen A. 'On the Cross-Sectional Relation Between Expected Returns and Betas,' *Journal of Finance*, March 1994, 64(1), 101–21.

Romer, Christina D. and Romer, David H. 'Does Monetary Policy Matter? A New

Test in the Spirit of Friedman and Schwartz,' *NBER Macroeconomics Annual 1989*, Cambridge: MIT Press, 1989, 121–70.

—— 'New Evidence on the Monetary Transmission Mechanism,' Brookings Papers on Economic Activity, 1990 (1), 149–98.

Rose, Andrew K. 'Is the Real Interest Rate Stable?,' *Journal of Finance*, December 1988, 43(5), 1095–112.

Rotemberg, Julio J. 'A Monetary Equilibrium Model with Transactions Costs,' *Journal of Political Economy*, February 1984, 92(1), 41–58.

Rothbard, Murray N. *America's Great Depression*, 3rd edition, Kansas City: Sheed and Ward, 1975.

Rouwenhorst, K. Geert 'Time to Build and Aggregate Fluctuations: A Reconsideration,' *Journal of Monetary Economics*, April 1991, 27(2), 241–54.

Rozeff, Michael S. 'Money and Stock Prices: Market Efficiency and the Lag in Effect of Monetary Policy,' *Journal of Financial Economics*, September 1974, 1(3), 245–302.

Rudebusch, Glenn D. 'Federal Reserve Interest Rate Targeting, Rational Expectations, and the Term Structure,' *Journal of Monetary Economics*, April 1995, 35(2), 245–74.

Samuelson, Paul A. 'Risk and Uncertainty: A Fallacy of Large Numbers,' in Joseph E. Stiglitz (ed.) *The Collected Papers of Paul A. Samuelson*, Cambridge, Massachusetts: The M.I.T. Press, 1966, 153–58.

Scheide, Joachim 'New Classical and Austrian Business Cycle Theory: Is There a Difference?,' *Weltwirtschaftliches Archiv*, 1986, 122(3), 575–98.

Scheinkman, Jose A. and Woodford, Michael 'Self-Organized Criticality and Economic Fluctuations,' *American Economic Review*, May 1994, 84(2), 417–21.

Schwert, G. William 'Why Does Stock Market Volatility Change Over Time?,' *Journal of Finance*, December 1989, 44(5), 1115–53.

Selgin, George *The Theory of Free Banking*, Totowa, New Jersey: Rowman and Littlefield, 1988.

Selgin, George and White, Lawrence H. 'The Evolution of a Free Banking System,' *Economic Inquiry*, July 1987, 25, 439–58.

Shapiro, Matthew, D. 'Investment, Output, and the Cost of Capital,' Brookings Papers on Economic Activity, 1986, 1, 111–52.

Shapiro, Carl and Stiglitz, Joseph E. 'Equilibrium Unemployment as a Worker Discipline Device,' *American Economic Review*, June 1984, 74, 433–44.

Sherman, H. J. *The Business Cycle: Growth and Crisis Under Capitalism*, Princeton. NJ: Princeton University Press, 1991.

Sheshinski, Eytan and Weiss, Yoram 'Inflation and the Costs of Price Adjustment,' *Review of Economic Studies*, June 1977, 44(2), 287–303.

Shiller, Robert J. 'Can the Fed Control Real Interest Rates?,' in Stanley Fischer (ed.) *Rational Expectations and Economic Policy*, Chicago: University of Chicago Press, 1983, 117–56.

Shleifer, Andrei 'Implementation Cycles,' *Journal of Political Economy*, December 1986, 94, 1163–90.

Shleifer, Andrei, Murphy, Kevin and Vishny, Robert 'Industrialization and The Big Push,' *Journal of Political Economy*, October 1989, 97(5), 1003–26.

Siegel, Jeremy J. 'The Real Rate of Interest from 1800–1990: A Study of the US and the UK,' *Journal of Monetary Economics*, April 1992, 29(2), 227–52.

Sims, Christopher A. 'Macroeconomics and Reality,' *Econometrica*, January 1980, 48(1), 1–48.

Skousen, Mark *The Structure of Production*, New York: New York University Press, 1990.

Small, David H. 'Unanticipated Money Growth and Unemployment in the United States: Comment,' *American Economic Review*, December 1979, 69(5), 996–1003.

Smith, Bruce D. 'Money and Inflation in Colonial Massachusetts,' *Quarterly Review*, Federal Reserve Bank of Minneapolis, Winter 1984, 1–14.

—— 'The Relationship Between Money and Prices: Some Historical Evidence Reconsidered,' *Quarterly Review*, Federal Reserve Bank of Minneapolis, Summer 1988, 18–32.

Sraffa, Piero 'Dr Hayek on Money and Capital,' *The Economic Journal*, March 1932, 42(165), 42–53.

—— *Production of Commodities by Means of Commodities*, Cambridge: Cambridge University Press, 1960.

Stadler, George W. 'Business Cycle Models with Endogenous Technology,' *American Economic Review*, September 1990, 80(4), 763–78.

Stiglitz, Joseph E. 'Capital Markets and Economic Fluctuations in Capitalist Economies,' *European Economic Review*, April 1992, 36(2/3), 269–306.

Stiglitz, Joseph E. and Weiss, Andrew 'Credit Rationing in Markets with Imperfect Information,' *American Economic Review*, June 1981, 71, 393–410.

Stock, James H. and Watson, Mark W. 'Interpreting the Evidence of Money–Income Causality,' *Journal of Econometrics*, January 1989, 40(1), 161–81.

Stockton, David J. 'Relative Price Dispersion, Aggregate Price Movement, and the Natural Rate of Unemployment,' *Economic Inquiry*, January 1988, 26(1), 1–22.

Summers, Lawrence H. 'The Nonadjustment of Nominal Interest Rates: A Study of the Fisher Effect,' in James Tobin (ed.) *Macroeconomics, Prices, and Quantities*, Washington, DC: Brookings Institution, 1983.

—— 'Investment Incentives and the Discounting of Depreciation Allowances,' in Martin Feldstein (ed.) *The Effects of Taxation on Capital Accumulation*, Chicago: University of Chicago Press, 1987, 295–304.

Svensson, Lars E. O. 'Money and Asset Prices in a Cash-In-Advance Economy,' *Journal of Political Economy*, October 1985, 93, 919–44.

Sweeney, Richard J. *Wealth Effects and Monetary Theory*, New York: Basil Blackwell, 1988.

Tatom, John A. 'Interest Rate Variability and Economic Performance: Further Evidence,' *Journal of Political Economy*, October 1985, 93(5), 1008–18.

Taylor, Lori L. and Yücel, Mine K. 'The Interest Rate Sensitivity of Texas Industry,' *Economic Review*, Federal Reserve Bank of Dalls, 1996, Second Quarter, 27–34.

Temin, Peter *Did Monetary Forces Cause the Great Depression?*, New York: Norton, 1976.

Thalenhorst, Jobst and Wenig, Alois 'F. A. Hayek's "Prices and Production" Reanalyzed,' *Jahrbücher für Nationalökonomie und Statistik*, 1984, 199(3), 213–36.

Thorbecke, Willem 'Stock Market Returns and Monetary Policy,' *Journal of Finance*, June 1997, 52, 2, 635–54.

—— 'The Distributional Effects of Disinflationary Monetary Policy,' Virginia, George Mason University, 1995a.

—— 'Monetary Policy, Industry Cash Flows, and the Burden of Disinflationary Policy,' Virginia, Jerome Levy Institute, and George Mason University, 1995b, Fairfax: Virginia.

Thorbecke, Willem and Coppock, Lee 'Monetary Policy, Stock Returns, and the Role of Credit in the Transmission of Monetary Policy,' *Southern Economic Journal*, April 1996, 62(4), 989–1001.

Tobin, James 'A General Equilibrium Approach to Monetary Theory,' *Journal of Money, Credit, and Banking*, February 1969, 1(1), 15–29.

Trautwein, Hans-Michael 'Hayek's Double Failure in Business Cycle Theory: A

Note,' in M. Colonna, and H. Hagemann, (eds) *Money and Business Cycles: The Economics of F. A. Hayek*, Volume I, Aldershot: Edward Elgar, 1994, 74–81.

Tsiang, S. C. 'Liquidity Preference and Loanable Funds Theories, Multiplier and Velocity Analysis: A Synthesis,' *American Economic Review*, September 1956, 46(4), 539–64.

Tullock, Gordon 'Why the Austrians are Wrong About Depressions,' *Review of Austrian Economics*, 1988, 2, 73–8.

US Dept of Commerce, Bureau of Economic Analysis *Fixed Reproducible Tangible Wealth in the United States, 1925–85*, 1987, Washington DC, GPO.

Van Hoomissen, T. 'Price Dispersion and Inflation: Evidence from Israel,' *Journal of Political Economy*, December 1988, 96(6), 1303–14.

Vining, Daniel R. and Elwertowski, Thomas C. 'The Relationship Between Relative Prices and the General Price Level,' *American Economic Review*, September 1976, 66(4), 699–708.

Wainhouse, Charles E. 'Empirical Evidence for Hayek's Theory of Economic Fluctuations,' in Barry N. Siegel (ed.) *Money in Crisis*, Cambridge, Massachusetts: Ballinger Publishing Company, 1984, 37–71.

Wallace, Neil. 'A Modigliani–Miller Theorem for Open-Market Operations,' *American Economic Review*, June 1981, 71(3), 267–74.

Warburton, Clark *Depression, Inflation, and Monetary Policy: Selected Papers 1945–53*, Baltimore: Johns Hopkins University Press, 1966.

White, Lawrence H. *Free Banking in Britain*, New York: Cambridge University Press, 1984a.

—— 'Competitive Payments Systems and the Unit of Account,' *American Economic Review*, September 1984b, 74: 699–712.

—— 'Accounting for Non-Interest-Bearing Currency,' *Journal of Money, Credit, and Banking*, November 1987, 19(4), 448–56.

—— 'What Kinds of Monetary Institutions Would a Free Market Deliver?,' *Cato Journal*, Fall 1989, 9(2), 367–91.

Wicksell, Knut *Interest and Prices*, London: Macmillan, 1936 [1898].

Wien-Claudi, Franz *Austrian Theories of Capital, Interest, and the Trade-Cycle*, London: George Allen & Unwin, 1936.

Wilcox, James A. 'Why Were Real Interest Rates So Low in the 1970s?,' *American Economic Review*, March 1983, 73(1), 44–53.

Wilson, Tom 'Capital Theory and the Trade Cycle,' *Review of Economic Studies*, 1940, 7, 169–79.

Wood, J. Stuart 'Some Refinements in Austrian Trade-Cycle Theory,' *Managerial and Decision Economics*, 5(3) 1984, 141–9.

Woodward, Susan 'The Liquidity Premium and the Solidity Premium,' *American Economic Review*, June 1983, 73(3), 348–61.

Yeager, Leland B. 'Towards Understanding Some Paradoxes in Capital Theory,' *Economic Inquiry*, September 1976, 14(3), 313–46.

—— 'The Significance of Monetary Disequilibrium,' *Cato Journal*, Fall 1986, 6(2), 369–400.

Zijp, Rudy van *Austrian and New Classical Business Cycle Theories: A Comparative Study Through the Method of Rational Reconstruction*, Aldershot: Edward Elgar, 1993.

INDEX

accelerator models of investment 140–1, 148

adjustment: costs 7; frictions of 98–100

Aftalion, Albert 26

aggregate risk 19–21, 38

Ahmed, Shaghil 132–3

Aizenman, Joshua 144

Altug, Sumru 74

Amsler, Christine E. 118n

'animal spirits' 25, 39

arbitrage 65; pricing theory 138

ARCH techniques 118

Ashley, R. 132

Atesoglu, H. Sonmez 145

Austrian Claim 11–12, 76–81, 90–1

Austrian school of economics 1, 10–12; business cycle theory 13; capital theory 35; critique of 80–1; expectational assumptions behind traditional theory 77–80; traditional claim 76–81, 101–2; traditional claim compared with risk-based theory 102–5

Baldwin, Carliss Y. 26

Ball, Laurence 83n

banking, 100 percent reserve 58–9

banks: central 4, 53–4, 66, 71, 119; credit rationing 47–52; 'lending channel' 67, 123–31; role of lending in cycle 126–9

Barro, Robert J. 68, 70, 80, 134, 145

Barsky, Robert B. 118n

Basu, Susanto 148

Bernanke, Ben S.: (1983) 143; (1983b) 140; (1986) 127n, 129n; (1990) 130; (1993a) 130; (1993b) 128; and Blinder

(1992) 46, 124, 125–7; et al (1988) 139

Bernard, Victor L. 135

Bizer, David S. 3

Black, Fischer 1, 2–3, 6, 33n, 66

Blanchard, Olivier J. 121

Blejer, Mario I. 132

Blinder, Alan S. 46, 124, 125–7

Bodie, Zvi 134

boom: comovement 29–33; initial 45; investment 16, 24; size of 43

boom/bust cycle 4, 10, 32, 123, 133

Boudoukh, Jacob 137

Brainard, S. Lael 131n

Brainard, William 143

Bresciani-Turroni, C. 105

Bryant, John H. 69n

Buck, A. 132

Burmeister, Edwin 138n

Burstein, Meyer 70, 71n

business cycles: and growth rate changes 42–3; immediate contractions 36–40; monetary transmission 60–4; real and monetary theories of 1; risk-return trade-offs 1, 30–2; theories 116

bust(s) 4; and cluster of errors 34–6; boom/bust cycle 4, 10, 32; changes in growth rate and 43; size of 43

Butos, William N. 121, 147n

Cagan, Philip 71–2, 74n

Cambridge debates 108–14

Campbell, John Y. 89, 148

Canadian economy 32n

capital: asset pricing model 22; average durability 3 (Table 1.1); durability